®

Bi/Polar®

Foundations of Productivity

J. W. Thomas, Ed.D.

and

T. J. Thomas, Ph.D.

The Institute of Foundational Training and Development
Austin, Texas

About the Cover

By assigning a color to each of the six strengths possessed by everyone, a unique combination color is produced to represent each of the eight patterns of core strengths. This unique combination color is produced by combining only the colors of the three lead strengths within each pattern. However, the expression of a particular flavor of a personality by emphasizing a specific combination of three lead strengths does not mask the fact that we all have all six strengths operating within us at the core of our being.

This entire book was printed on recycled paper.

The word "Bi/Polar" and the tree with three double-lobed leaves are registered trademarks owned by The Institute of Foundational Training and Development.

Printed in the United States of America.
Third printing, July, 1993.

Library of Congress Catalog Card No. 91-143775
ISBN 0-9637450-0-X

To

Alison Gayle Thomas

Contents

III: Understanding Other People

IV: Strengthening Your Relationships

List of Illustrations

Preface

This book is a revised edition of the 1985 book on Bi/Polar called *Bi/Polar: Understanding People Through Strengths*. It contains all the material in that book plus additional insights into the nature of people and the growth process. In addition, the terminology used to explain Bi/Polar has been updated to current usage.

The senior author (J. W. Thomas) is the inventor of the Bi/Polar System. It evolved out of his experiences beginning in 1955 as a management psychologist. Previous books on Bi/Polar were the results of his writing efforts based on his experiences.

The junior author (T. J. Thomas) is J. W.'s son. We have been working together for over a decade in conducting seminars, writing, and consulting. This book is the result primarily of the content of the previous book written by J. W. and updated and revised by T. J.

Parts of the book are written from the first person perspective. These parts all are written by J. W.

Both of us want to thank the many people who have contributed insights and confirmations to the Bi/Polar System over the years and those many clients who have used Bi/Polar to our mutual benefit. In particular, we want to thank Richard A. (Robby) Robinson, Jr. for his continued support, discussions, business, and friendship.

We wish to thank four people who helped to push this new book along to its current publication. Diane Hunter spent many hours inputting the content of the original text into a word processor for use by T. J. in editing. Lori White masterminded the final formatting in the computer. Joanna Hill of Santa Fe, New Mexico designed both the cover and the look and feel of the text. Ron Nielsen of Bookcrafters took our final master pages and turned them into the printed book.

J.W.T.
Richardson, Texas

T.J.T.
Austin,Texas

October, 1990

How to Use this Book

To get the most meaning and usefulness from this book, it should be used along with attending the seminar called *Bi/Polar: Foundations of Productivity.* This seminar was developed and refined by the same people who developed this book.

These seminars are sponsored by organizations who wish to have them conducted for organization members or employees. There are two ways in which these seminars can be conducted in an organization. First, the organization can contract with the Institute of Foundational Training and Development to provide both seminar materials and an experienced seminar leader to facilitate the program. Second, organizations which are licensed to do so by the IFTD may have their own employees trained by the IFTD to conduct the seminar in "train-the-trainer" courses and then conduct the seminar internally with materials purchased directly from the IFTD.

This book is written primarily for participants in that seminar so that, while they are participating or before they participate in this experience, they can gain a better intellectual understanding of what Bi/Polar is all about and how they can use it to become a healthier, more productive human being.

If you are unable to attend the seminar, this book can be used as a stand-alone introduction to Bi/Polar without the accompanying experience of the seminar. You can benefit from reading this book without attending the seminar. However, you are encouraged to attend this seminar because that is where the concepts really come alive and come home to you in your everyday life.

In addition to the seminar, we have developed a training game entitled *Foundations*. This game can be played with any number of people, and instructions included in the game teach a facilitator how to successfully conduct the game in about an hour and a half. *Foundations* is an excellent way for an organization to quickly discover for themselves the power of positive change that Bi/Polar has to offer.

To order or find out more about *Foundations* or to receive more information on how your organization can utilize the seminar *Bi/Polar: Foundations of Productivity*, please call the Institute of Foundational Training and Development at 1-800/899-5115 or 512/327-2656. Or write the Institute at P.O. Box 160220, Austin, Texas 78716-0220.

Introduction

What is a Foundation?

After many years of trying to understand exactly what it is we do, we have finally hit upon an expression of it that speaks to us and that we hope speaks to you, the reader.

A short history of Bi/Polar would have to include the fact that we have been conducting seminars and publishing books around one central theme since 1966. That central theme is called the Bi/Polar Concept and is explained in detail later in this Introduction.

All of what we do is psychologically oriented. However, we knew all along that what we had to offer was very different from what easily came to be perceived as "similar stuff" (e.g. Jungian psychology and the Myers-Briggs Type Indicator, Performax and the DISC system, etc.). The thing that makes us different is the fact that what we teach is so fundamental that we call it "foundational" to all that a person does.

This means that we reach within. We touch the core of the individual and help the individual truly understand why they do the things they do and why they do them the way they do.

We are also very different from such teachings as are contained in the work of B. F. Skinner. Dr. Skinner believes that all that can be observed and that is important to report on is behavior. And what affects behavior most of all is the environment. Although we recognize that the environment can have important influences on who we are (see Chapter 4), our emphasis is just the opposite. We look within the individual to see what exists within — regardless of the influence from the outside.

Some friends in Canada use the analogy of an iceberg in talking about the fact that we deal with "self skills" — the 90% of the iceberg that is below the water and that you can't see. Most other training and development activities deal with the 10% of the skills that you can learn and acquire — "work skills" and "technical skills". But what is the "foundation" of those "work and technical skills"? We might as well ask what it is that holds up the 10% of the iceberg that we can see.

What is it that we admire about a beautiful tree? Imagine those huge and aged redwoods from northern California. They grow several hundred feet high and can be as much as 50 feet around. But what is it that makes that beautiful trunk and branches and leaves possible? The roots — the foundation of any tree. But again, the foundation is hard to see — and even harder to tell how big. But the importance is immediate — without an extensive root system to anchor the tree to the ground and to provide life-giving substance to the trunk and the branches, the tree would not exist.

How many people these days have become dependent upon personal computers? Millions — the present authors included. And the two most popular personal computers are the ones sold by IBM (and the many clones) and the Apple Macintosh.

What makes a computer work? In any computer, you must have the right software — for accounting, data base management, word processing. If you don't have the right software, the computer is nothing better than a paperweight. And even if you have the best word processing program in the world, it still won't work on an IBM PC unless you have a software program called DOS — Disk Operating System. (In an Apple Macintosh, it is called the Finder.)

DOS is the foundation of the IBM PC. Without DOS, you can't get the computer to do the most basic things. DOS allows the computer to work, and it provides the capability of the application programs (word processing, data base management, etc.) to operate. Without DOS, all is lost.

Bi/Polar is a Personal Operating System. Bi/Polar helps people to understand their personal foundation. It allows people to find that inner core — to know why they do the things they do. To understand how and why they are the same as and different from other people. To know how to relate to others. To understand what is innate and natural — and what requires effort and concentration to do.

In terms of training, development, and educational activities, Bi/Polar shows a person how to make the most of other training experiences. If a person attends a program in management development, he or she will be able to personalize that experience to who he or she is by understanding Bi/Polar. No longer will training, development, and education treat everyone the same nor expect everyone to benefit in the same ways from the same experiences.

What is Productivity?

Productivity has been a buzzword in the business world and in training and development circles for a number of years. Thus, we need to define what we mean by productivity.

Productivity has two very specific meanings to us. The first has to do with personal productivity, and the second has to do with organizational productivity.

From a standpoint of personal productivity, an individual is productive first of all from a standpoint of how well he or she achieves their potential. This can be in terms of realizing who that person was meant to be, how to live a satisfying life, and how to develop healthy relationships with others. In a work setting, an individual is productive according to how well he or she achieves goals or completes projects that benefit the organization. This includes a primary emphasis on how well that individual relates to and communicates with those with whom he or she works.

From the standpoint of organizational productivity, an individual helps an organization to meet its stated goals. If an organization exists to accomplish certain goals, then how well those goals are achieved is a measure of how productive that organization is. There are many factors which affect how productive an organization is — the market, economic conditions, demand for the organization's product, the availability of materials, laws, and many others. What we focus on is that sometimes overlooked (but always of paramount importance) issue of how well the people in an organization are working together.

Sometimes, other factors work against the production of people who work together well (such as when demand for the product drops), so that their personal productivity becomes a moot issue for the organization. However, in many cases, an organization can have every other factor working in its favor, but the people in that organization simply do not produce because of a lack of interpersonal communication, recognition of their respective abilities and strengths, or a knowledge of where the organization is headed.

This situation is where Bi/Polar helps an organization become productive. Bi/Polar helps people communicate with one another, recognize one another's strengths, focus on common goals, help one another, and, in general, work to helping the organization achieve its goals.

Personal productivity and organizational productivity — the foundation of Bi/Polar helps people to achieve both.

The Seminar

The seminar experience that accompanies this book (also called *Bi/ Polar: Foundations of Productivity*) is foundational. It creates a foundation of understanding that allows the individual to make personal choices that result in personal growth and increased productivity.

The seminar rests on the solid bedrock of a fundamental concept — an idea regarding the nature of The Creative Process Itself. This idea is referred to as the "Bi/Polar Concept". It has been the undergirding and pervasive concept of the seminar since its inception in 1966. It is the strong anchor point of the entire Bi/Polar System.

The Bi/Polar Concept is a ridiculously simple idea, yet, at the same time, contains one of the most profound truths about life and existence. At first blush, the simplicity of the concept may cause one to miss the deep meaning that is within it. The depth of the idea is usually revealed over time as one has the opportunity to apply it to different situations and reflect upon its fundamental truth.

A simple statement of the Bi/Polar Concept is that creativity and productivity are the result of a process in which two opposite strengths are interacting together and contributing equally to the process. This is in contrast with the view that two opposites are in conflict and one is more valuable than the other. An example may help to clarify these two positions: Consider the two strengths Thinking and Risking (action). A common human tendency is to regard these two opposite strengths as being in conflict with one another and one more important and valuable than the other. Some people regard Thinking as more valuable, others regard Risking as more valuable. The Bi/Polar Concept establishes a different view of these two strengths — Thinking and Risking are regarded as complementary and as having equal intrinsic value in their creative interaction. Even more explicitly, in Bi/Polar, Thinking and Risking are conceived as two complementary strengths working together as equal partners to produce individual and organizational productivity.

The Bi/Polar Concept is the fundamental underlying concept in each of the four essential areas of understanding that form the foundation for personal and organizational development. These four areas are:

1. Understanding and appreciating oneself,
2. Understanding and experiencing the growth process,

3. Understanding and appreciating other people,
4. Understanding and strengthening one's relationships.

In the seminar, all four of these areas are firmly grounded in the bedrock of the Bi/Polar Concept. The first part of the seminar focuses on understanding and appreciating oneself.

Understanding and Appreciating Oneself
In the seminar, we use the Bi/Polar System to help us understand and appreciate who we are at the core. The system itself has evolved out of working with normal, healthy people rather than people who are in the need of therapy. Its approach is positive — it enables people to understand themselves in terms of their strengths rather than weaknesses — what is creative and good about them rather than what is wrong with them. The seminar does deal with normal human tendencies that get us into trouble and cause us problems, but this comes later in the seminar when we deal with how we express our core strengths.

High productivity and robust self-development requires that we be ourselves — be natural — and express our own unique blend of core strengths. In turn, our ability to be ourselves depends upon, first, our understanding of who we really are at the core, and, second, the extent to which we have positive, accepting feelings towards ourselves.

A rational and reality-based understanding of ourselves helps us to know when we are "being ourselves" or being a "phony". Awareness of who we really are gives us practical and concrete guidance as we seek to find those situations in which we feel "at home". It helps us to identify the work situation that "fits" us — where we can be the most productive and make our greatest contribution. The increased self-understanding developed in this first part of the seminar helps us to "be ourselves" more fully in the real world.

Our feelings of self-worth are also important in determining our ability to "be ourselves". If we have low self-esteem and tend to view ourselves in a negative way, it makes it difficult for us to "be ourselves". If we feel that we are somehow "bad" or "inferior" or "not acceptable", we tend to hide who we really are and try to be something different from our natural self. The Bi/Polar System and its undergirding philosophies provides a logical way of looking at ourselves in terms of our strengths.

It gives us a rational basis for understanding ourselves as "good" at the core and equally acceptable to everyone else regardless of what others may think. This approach tends to yield a positive, accepting attitude both towards ourselves and other people.

In the first part of the seminar, we help participants build a solid foundation of self-understanding that is based on strengths and develop a healthy, reality-based attitude of self-affirmation. In the next part, we consider the growth process through which we grow and become a stronger and more productive individual.

Understanding and Experiencing the Growth Process

In building our foundation for personal development, it is essential that we understand the growth process — how it really works. We use the Bi/Polar Concept as the central tool to deepen our understanding of what is actually going on in the process of growth.

In addition to understanding the growth process itself, it is equally important that we understand how we, as individuals, relate to this process. In the Bi/Polar approach, we assume that every person participates naturally in the growth process. We also assume that we can get out of the process either through the influence of a negative environment or through making wrong personal choices ourselves. Our task in this part of the seminar is to understand those forces that tend to take us out of the growth process and to identify the personal choices we must make to stay in it.

In the first part of the seminar, we say that "being ourselves" is essential for self-development. We say this in spite of the realization that in being ourselves we will experience problems with the world.

Now, in this part, we introduce an equally important requirement for growth — we must solve the problems created by our being ourselves. We solve these problems by emphasizing the strengths that are polar opposites to those that we normally emphasize when we are being ourselves. When we make this shift of emphasis we usually feel awkward and uncomfortable and can even feel as if we are not being ourselves.

I'll give you an example. When I am being myself, I naturally express more independence than I do dependence (independence and dependence is a pair of equally valuable strengths in the Bi/Polar System). As a result of my natural emphasis on independence, I tend to become "too independent" and this can cause problems, particularly in my relationships. I must solve these problems by consciously becoming more dependent. When I emphasize my dependent strength I feel awkward and uncomfortable, but it is required if I am to grow and become a more productive and mature individual.

Understanding the growth process and knowing what we must do to experience personal growth in our own lives is an essential part of our foundation for personal development.

Understanding and Appreciating Other People
In the first two parts of the seminar, we are guided to look within — discovering who we really are as a unique, one-of-a-kind individual and understanding what we must do, as individuals, to grow and become a more productive person. Now we are ready to direct our attention outward — toward other people and our relationships with them.

The third part of the seminar deals with understanding and appreciating others. Here we use the Bi/Polar System in much the same way as we used it to understand and appreciate ourselves. The difference is that we focus on the other person rather than ourselves.

The Bi/Polar System helps us to understand other people as they really are — how they are put together at the core of their being. We come to understand that we are all the same in that we have the same human strengths, but we are different in that we tend to favor different strengths. Understanding the strengths that a particular person tends to favor goes a long way in helping us to understand that individual as a person.

Becoming aware of other people's favored strengths not only helps us to understand them in terms of their strengths, but it also helps us to understand why they think and behave in the way they do — sometimes in ways much different from our own. It helps us to understand their natural tendencies and gives us a better appreciation of the problems and growth challenges they tend to experience.

The understanding and appreciation we develop for other people in this part of the seminar coupled with our own self-understanding and appreciation lays the groundwork for the attitudes and behaviors that are essential for developing strong and productive relationships with other people. The last part of the seminar deals directly with how we go about strengthening our relationships and improving our communication with others.

Understanding and Strengthening One's Relationships

Other approaches to understanding the dynamics of human relationships tend to shy away from "attitudes" and focus on "behaviors". We regard this as a mistake. In the Bi/Polar approach, we consider "attitude" and "behavior" as equally important in determining the quality of our relationships.

There are two essential ingredients in a creative relationship between two people. One has to do with our attitude and the other has to do with our behavior. The required attitude is that of an "Attitude of Equality". The required behavior is that of an "Appropriate Blend of Assertive and Reserved Behavior".

We communicate an "Attitude of Equality" to other people when we. . . .

1. value the other person equally with ourselves.
2. look straight across — neither "up to" or "down on" the

other person.
3. are concerned with our own welfare and equally concerned
   with the welfare of the other person.
4. have self-respect as well as respect for the other person.
5. take equal responsibility for making the relationship work.
6. focus as much attention on the other person as we do
   ourselves.

To the extent that we deviate from an "Attitude of Equality", we lose the potential creativeness of the relationship. Two common attitudes that are destructive to our relationships are (1) an "Attitude of Superiority" and (2) an "Attitude of Inferiority". We tend to communicate an "Attitude of Superiority" when we consistently focus more on ourselves than the other person — when we are more concerned with our own wants, needs and desires more than we are the other person's. We tend to communicate an "Attitude of Inferiority" when we consistently focus more on the other person than we do ourselves when we are more concerned with the other person's wants, needs and desires than we are our own.

During this part of the seminar, we help participants become aware of the attitude they tend to communicate in their relationships and give them guidance in how to develop and communicate an "Attitude of Equality".

"Being Assertive" and "Being Reserved" are the two opposite kinds of behavior that are appropriately blended in a creative relationship. The appropriate blend of these two behaviors is determined by the core characteristics of the two people involved and the particular situation in which they find themselves. While the "Attitude of Equality" remains constant regardless of the situation or the differing characteristics of the two people, the "Appropriate Blend of Behavior" is a dynamic changing blend that is continually modified and adjusted to fit the situation.

Both understanding ourselves and understanding the other person is critical for determining the appropriate behavior in a relationship with a particular person. It is here that we draw heavily on the understandings of ourselves and others that we developed in the earlier part of the program.

In fact, the seminar itself has a building aspect about it. First, we deepen our understanding and appreciation of ourselves, next we develop an understanding of the growth process and how we can experience growth more fully in our own lives, and finally we develop a deeper understanding and appreciation of the unique individuality of every other person. These understandings are then used to help us understand what is going on in our relationships and what we need to do to strengthen them.

Many people who have attended the seminar report that the most practical value of the seminar experience has been in helping them to understand and strengthen their relationships. On the other hand, many have felt that the insights they develop into themselves and other people have been the most rewarding personally.

The Bi/Polar Concept

"The test of a first-rate intelligence is the ability to hold two opposed ideas in the mind at the same time and still retain the ability to function."

F. Scott Fitzgerald

The Bi/Polar Concept is the most fundamental and pervasive concept in the Bi/Polar System. The whole system hangs on this one simple idea: that creativity and effectiveness come from the blending of two opposite and polar strengths.

The first step in my own awareness of the concept came from the recognition of two distinct types of company presidents — both successful, yet very different. In fact, in many ways they were exact opposites. One type tended to be dynamic, enthusiastic, and action-oriented. They seemed to have a natural propensity toward risk-taking. The other type tended to be stable, analytical, and well-organized. Contrasted with the risk-taking presidents, they seemed to have a propensity toward thoughtful analysis. I discovered that either type could be successful as a chief executive officer of a company, but invariably both types developed foreseeable problems stemming from their natural bent towards either dynamic action or thoughtful analysis.

Companies that had dynamic, self-confident, action-oriented presidents tended to develop problems associated with quick decisions, lack of sufficient planning, lack of organization, and a need for stability, efficiency, and control. The activity and movement resulting from their dynamic, risk-taking strengths were an essential part of the company's growth — but only a part. The other part needed to come from opposite and balancing strengths — the stable thinking strengths.

Some of the action-oriented presidents had an appreciation for the value of the thinking strengths and found effective ways to bring more thoughtful analysis to their decision making. The presidents who did this tended to build strong and growing companies. Their companies maintained their basic orientation towards action and dynamism but became stronger and more successful by blending in more rational analysis and thoughtful planning.

In those instances where the dynamic president failed to make these thinking strengths a greater force in the management of the company, things became progressively worse. The organization seemed to go into a spiral of decay. Rather than solving problems by using more of their thinking strengths, they tried to solve them by becoming even more active and taking even greater risks. As a result, more and more bad decisions were made — operational problems compounded and caused even greater inefficiencies — financial problems loomed larger and larger and threatened the existence of the company. At some point in this decay process one of two things usually happened — the company either declared bankruptcy or was taken over by a stronger and more stable company.

The stable, thought-oriented presidents were, in many ways, opposite from the dynamic entrepreneurs — and they developed opposite kinds of problems. Their natural leaning toward thinking and planning brought stability, structure, and efficiency to their organizations. These are valuable and essential strengths in any strong and growing organization; however, they are only a part of its creative growth. The other part comes from dynamic, action-oriented strengths — the very strengths that characterized the more dynamic presidents.

Organizations led by these conservative, thinking-oriented leaders tended to develop a need for stronger expressions of the dynamic strengths. The companies' growth was inhibited because of a lack of decision, lack of action, and a need for more dynamism. In some instances, the thought-oriented presidents recognized the values of the dynamic, action-oriented strengths and found effective ways to make these strengths a stronger part of their organizations. When they did this, they created stronger and more dynamically growing companies. Their organizations remained stable and well organized, but the introduction of more dynamism made them more active, aggressive, and profitable.

In those instances where the dynamic strengths were not brought in, the organizations tended to become stagnant and die on the vine. They entered their own spiral of decay characterized by indecisiveness, weak commitments, and boring inactivity. Management tried to solve these problems by doing even more thinking, rather than getting into action and taking more risks. As the decay process progressed, these companies either gradually withered away or were taken over by more aggressive and dynamic companies.

These experiences put me on the track of the Bi/Polar Concept. It made sense to me that growth would just naturally come from strengths — not weaknesses. So my focus was on strengths from the very beginning. My challenge was to identify the strengths that produce growth and to understand how these strengths relate to each other. In trying to meet this challenge, I gradually formulated the six hypotheses presented below. Taken together, they constitute the essential features of the Bi/Polar Concept.

First Hypothesis

Each polar strength is non-productive by itself.
Although each polar strength is positive in its fundamental nature, it must blend with its polar opposite in order to produce growth. Productivity comes from a blend and interaction of two polar strengths, not from one alone.

Second Hypothesis

Each of the two strengths involved in the process is wholly positive — neither is negative.
The two polar strengths in each pair are inherently positive in themselves. A polar strength should never be regarded as a "weakness" or a "negative". It is always a strength that makes its own positive contribution to the creative growth process. The strength may be expressed at an inappropriate time, but this does not make it a negative in itself. The negative comes from an inappropriate use of the strength — not from the strength itself.

Third Hypothesis

The two polar strengths in each pair contribute equally to the process.
The two strengths are inherently equal. Although they are opposites and contribute different values, their contributions are of equal worth and value to the whole. It is important to recognize that we are

referring to the inherent value of the two strengths to the total process — not an immediate need of a particular situation. A particular situation may require more of one of the strengths to stimulate growth, but this immediate need for an emphasis on one of the strengths does not make that strength inherently more valuable to the process itself — the opposite polar strength may need to be emphasized at a later time.

Fourth Hypothesis

The expression of one strength creates a need for
the expression of the other.
As one strength is used, a consequent need for the expression of its polar opposite strength builds in the individual. The need for this expression builds over time. This need is alleviated only with the expression of the opposite strength.

Fifth Hypothesis

The two polar strengths support and feed each other.
Although the two polar strengths are direct opposites and may sometimes appear to be in conflict (such as thought and action), they actually support and feed one another. In the growth process, they have a reciprocal relationship — each gives to and takes from the other.

The key to this understanding was the insight that each polar strength could be divided into two component parts — one part being the activity of the strength and the other part being the result or product of that activity. This insight laid the foundation for understanding how the polar strengths actually relate to each other in the creative growth process. The relationship may be described in the following way.

Each polar strength produces a product (fruit) that, in turn, becomes the raw material used by its polar opposite in the production of its own fruit. In other words, each polar strength is dependent upon the activity of its polar opposite to provide the raw material it needs to produce its own fruit. An example may be useful in clarifying this concept. The two opposite strengths that identified the two opposite types of presidents discussed earlier can be used to represent two polar strengths — thought and action. The thinking strengths of the thought-oriented presidents produced well-thought-out strategies and plans to follow. The risking strengths of the action-oriented presidents produced the drive and courage to get into action and do things. In the creative growth of a company, these two polar strengths work together and feed each other in this way: The thinking strength provides the strategies for creative action, and the risking strength provides new data and information for developing even better strategies. Each feeds the other and both become more productive in the process.

Sixth Hypothesis

Growth is a process in which two opposite and polar strengths interact with one another.

This hypothesis points to the inherent duality of the fundamental forces that power the growth process. Growth and creativity are conceived as being expressed in pairs of strengths not single strengths or even tri-polar strengths, but always Bi/Polar strengths. The two strengths in each pair are "polar" to each other in much the same way as the north and south poles are at opposite ends of the earth — they are "opposites", yet both are essential parts of a common reality. The same is true of the two polar strengths — they are "opposites", yet both are essential parts of one process.

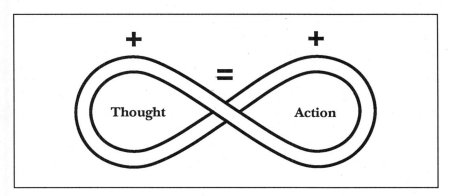

Figure 1

The infinity symbol drawn in Figure 1 may be used to review and illustrate each of the five hypotheses undergirding the Bi/Polar Concept. The two loops in the symbol may be used to represent the two polar strengths in a pair. (In this drawing we are using a basic pair that is well understood — thought and action — but one needs to keep in mind that there are many other pairs of polar strengths.)

By tracing the outline of the symbol back and forth, we can illustrate the first hypothesis that (1) growth is a process in which thought and action interact with each other. By placing an "equals" sign between the two loops, we can indicate that (2) thought and action have equal value in the process. By placing a "plus" sign above each of the two loops, we signify that (3) both strengths are inherently positive. We can show that (4) either thought or action is nonproductive by itself by blocking out one of the loops. Finally, we can indicate how (5) thought and action feed and support each other by tracing the outline of the symbol back and forth.

I do not want to convey the impression that these six hypotheses came all at once in one fell swoop. Actually, they evolved gradually over a period of years. This is especially true of the insight described under the fifth hypothesis. The idea that each polar strength could be subdivided into its activity and what is produced by this activity occurred at least ten years after my first awareness of the Bi/Polar Concept.

In summary, the Bi/Polar Concept may be simply stated in this way: Creativity and growth come from a blending of two opposite and polar strengths. Each of these two strengths makes its own positive contribution to the process, and they are equal partners in the creative whole formed by their interaction.

It would be difficult to over-emphasize the fundamental importance of this simple idea in the development of the Bi/Polar System.

Summary

In this Introduction, we have attempted to give the reader a handle on what Bi/Polar is about, how the book is structured, and what benefits you and your organization can expect from attending the seminar. The remainder of the book is devoted to the substance of what Bi/Polar is all about and how you can use it to your own benefit.

I.

Discovering Your Strengths

1.

The Bi/Polar Theory of Personality

This chapter presents the philosophical and theoretical foundations of the Bi/Polar approach. It is divided into two sections. The first, entitled Basic Assumptions, develops the philosophical base on which the system is built; the second, Four Personality Forces, presents the Bi/Polar theory regarding the nature of the human personality and how it is formed.

Basic Assumptions

Any effort to establish a sound theoretical base for a psychological system eventually leads to fundamental questions regarding the source of life and the human being's relationship to this source. Such questions as these arise: What is the nature of the primordial force that creates all existence? What is the relationship between this force and human beings? What does this relationship say about the basic nature of human beings? What follows is an attempt to answer these questions.

In Bi/Polar philosophy, a fundamental assumption is that there is one primordial force out of which all existence and meaning comes into being. It is conceived as a "unified" and "bi-polar" force — a unity in that it is "one" with nothing existing outside it and "bi-polar" in that it manifests itself in pairs of polar forces.

This primordial force is conceived as creative in its most fundamental nature — its creativity coming from a balanced interaction of the polar forces that constitute its being. These polar forces are viewed as positive strengths interacting in pairs — each making its own particular contribution to the creative whole. In essence, this primordial force is seen as a wholly positive Bi/Polar force.

A second fundamental assumption is that human beings (along with all entities in the world) are created and sustained by this one primordial force. We have our being and live our lives as a part of the creative process powered by this unified primordial force. All that we are and will ever be comes from the creative interaction of these primordial Bi/Polar forces.

What do these assumptions about the source of our existence and our relationship to it have to do with Bi/Polar? Well, they provide the foundation for our psychological system. These assumptions establish a particular view regarding the basic nature of human beings, and this view becomes the cornerstone of the Bi/Polar System. Specifically, it means that the Bi/Polar approach is based on the assumption that human nature is grounded in strengths — not weaknesses! We are naturally creative at the core, and our task is to find ways to release this creative potential. This makes Bi/Polar a positive psychology that sees strengths rather than weaknesses — what is right about a person rather than what is wrong.

I do not want to create the impression that Bi/Polar is a "Pollyanna" psychology — one that refuses to look at the reality of the problems and pains we all experience. The Bi/Polar approach recognizes and affirms the reality of destructive forces in the world but views the creative forces as more fundamental. The negative, destructive force comes from our inappropriate use of a strength, not from the strength itself. The position I am trying to establish is that our natural strengths come from the creative force in the universe and these strengths are the essence of our being, while the problems, pains, and frustrations we experience are more peripheral. Describing these negatives as peripheral does not in any way lessen their importance in our lives nor deny their reality, but it does establish their relationship to our creative core. Another way to describe this relationship is to say that whenever we have a problem or a pain, we can be confident that we have a positive strength within that is more fundamental and has the power to overcome and solve the problem.

Four Personality Forces

Personality refers to the total person — who we are as a result of all the influences that contribute to our development. The Bi/Polar System is based upon a theory regarding these influences and the role they play in forming our personality.

Bi/Polar theory postulates that human beings are created by the Bi/Polar interaction of the two basic forces within the unified primordial force that creates the universe. These two basic polar forces are (1) a stabilizing force that creates structure and (2) a dynamic force that creates change. In the creation of an individual personality, these two basic forces are expressed through four distinct and identifiable personality forces — two that give stability to the personality and two that produce personality change. The stabilizing force is expressed in our personality through the genetic structures underlying (1) our pattern of core strengths and (2) our innate capacities. The dynamic force is expressed through the changes produced by the forces in (3) our environment and (4) our personal choices (see Figure 2).

Our pattern of core strengths and our innate capacities are governed by the laws of heredity and genetics. This makes them stable and enduring forces in our own personality. Despite a changing environment and our flexibility to make personal choices, these forces retain their indelible imprint on our personality. Because these forces and their underlying structures within us are genetically based, certain of our personality characteristics tend to remain the same.

Four Personality Forces

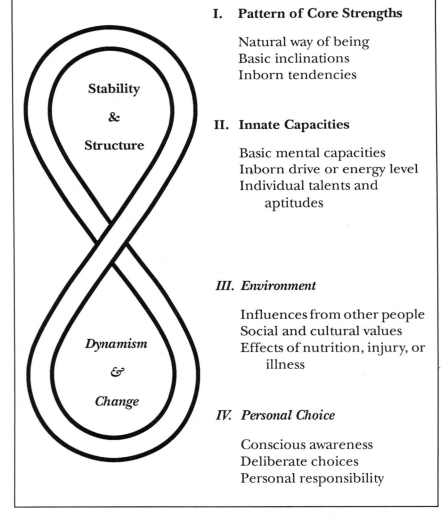

I. Pattern of Core Strengths

Natural way of being
Basic inclinations
Inborn tendencies

II. Innate Capacities

Basic mental capacities
Inborn drive or energy level
Individual talents and
       aptitudes

III. Environment

Influences from other people
Social and cultural values
Effects of nutrition, injury, or
       illness

IV. Personal Choice

Conscious awareness
Deliberate choices
Personal responsibility

Stability
&
Structure

Dynamism
&
Change

Figure 2

The two forces that allow for change in our personality are our environment and our personal choices. Different environments can produce different attitudes. For example, if a young person of high intelligence (which is a hereditary trait) is deprived of early reward-ing educational experience, he or she will be less likely to develop an interest in learning and reading than if exposed to a rich educational environment. The level of intelligence or capacity for learning remains constant in any one individual (innate capacity), but the attitude towards learning can be drastically different (through expo-sure to different environments). The other dynamic force — personal choice or free will — reflects our ability to control our own lives by conscious choice. For example, a person can overcome bad experiences in school and develop a healthy attitude toward learning simply by wanting to learn and consciously working toward that goal.

In Bi/Polar, all four forces are regarded as inherently equal in their importance to the effect on human personality. However, in the life of an actual person, the influence of each force is unequal. Any of the forces may be the dominant influence in a particular person's life. For example, some people are more greatly affected by significant personal experiences (environment), while others may be guided most by significant personal talents (innate capacities). Also, the relative influence of these forces may be different at different times in any one person's life. At times, personal choice may be the significant force that shapes the personality. At other times, environment may be the heaviest contributor. The main point is that all of the forces are having some influence at all times, and any one may have the dominant influence on a particular person. In our attempt to understand ourselves and other people, we cannot afford to depreciate or disregard any of the four fundamental forces.

So, what of the question often asked of psychologists, "Are people basically the same or are we all unique?" The answer to this question is Bi/Polar — meaning that there is an element of truth in both possible answers. But that the answer closest to the truth incorporates both. What this means is that people are basically the same *and* they are unique.

Another question often asked is, "Do we remain basically the same during our lives or do we change?" Again, the answer lies in the truth of the paradox — we stay the same *and* we change. Any attempt to resolve the paradox in favor of one side or the other takes you farther from the truth.

Pattern of Core Strengths

At conception, an individual is created with a particular pattern of core strengths — Bi/Polar strengths coming from the primordial creative force in the universe. Although all individuals have a common humanity in that they participate in the same strengths, they are different in that they participate in these strengths in different ways.

This cluster of strengths at the core of every individual is a part of the creative process — it makes every person a participant in the creativeness of the universe. It is that person's "foundation of productivity". Our core is made up entirely of strengths — there is nothing weak, evil, or destructive within our core. The Bi/Polar philosophy provides no basis on which to judge the value of one cluster compared to another. Since we have no standard by which we can judge one as better than another, the clusters are regarded as equally important and valuable — one is not better than another. There are no misfits or inferior people at the core.

In an effort to understand this personality core, Bi/Polar uses a system of three pairs of interrelated Bi/Polar strengths. The three pairs are identified as a basic pair (thinking/risking) and two additional pairs that come out of the basic pair — a thinking pair (practical/theoretical) and a risking pair (dependent/independent). All these core strengths are positive in their basic nature and contribute to the creative process at work in the world. They have equal value to one another, and all are required in the creation process.

In Bi/Polar philosophy, it is postulated that each person has a lead strength and a supporting strength in each of the three pairs. When a lead strength is identified in each pair, it yields a particular pattern of core strengths. This procedure results in eight possible combinations of three lead strengths or eight distinctive patterns of core strengths. These are the personal "foundations of productivity" from which we operate as individuals.

The eight patterns of core strengths are the basic tools used in the Bi/Polar system for understanding the personality core. A good understanding of each pattern and an appreciation for its distinctiveness is critical for any effective use of the Bi/Polar approach. Since much of the development work in Bi/Polar has focused on the pattern of core strengths, much of what the system has to offer comes from its contribution to understanding this force as a part of our personality.

The pattern of core strengths discussed above refers to a configuration of relative strengths within a person. No attempt is made to measure its magnitude compared to any outside standard. People do differ, however, in how much strength they have compared with one another. The term "innate capacities" is used to point to this additional way in which we differ.

Innate Capacities
Through the years, many psychologists have attempted to identify and measure individual differences. Much progress has been made — particularly in measuring various kinds of mental abilities. Bi/Polar, as a psychological system, has made practically no contribution to this area of investigation. However, the Bi/Polar philosophy affirms the validity of individual differences in innate capacities and recognizes the importance of understanding them them in any attempt to truly understand an individual as a unique person.

The critical point to recognize is that we are referring to two separate and distinct forces when we use the terms pattern of core strengths and innate capacities. Our pattern of core strengths is a particular configuration of relative strengths within and says nothing about how much strength we have compared with other people. On the other hand, our innate capacities are a measure of how much strength we have compared with other people and say nothing about our own internal pattern of these strengths.

Environment

External environment is a third important force that interacts with the other three to produce an authentic human being. The emphasis that has been placed on this force, particularly by social scientists, has tended to exaggerate the importance of the environment and depreciate the importance of the other three forces. Many people, including many psychologists, tend to believe that environment is consistently the most influential force in determining our personality. The Bi/Polar philosophy rejects this view and maintains that all four of the personality forces discussed here have equal status — none is consistently more important than any other. Environment may be the dominant force at a particular time in a person's life, and it may be the most influential overall force in a particular person's life, but the same can be said of any of the other three forces as well!

A great number of professionally competent people have made valuable contributions to our understanding of the effects of environment on the formation of the human personality. Those of us who use the Bi/Polar concepts do not seek to depreciate the contributions made by those who emphasize the importance of environment — we use their concepts and insights with deep gratitude and a keen appreciation for their value. All the Bi/Polar philosophy calls for is that all four of the personality forces be given equal consideration when trying to understand a particular person.

Environmental forces influence people in some important ways. They are a major force in conceptual and emotional learning. Our value system, our attitudes, our prejudices, and our knowledge of the world comes largely from people around us. However, the influence of our environment is limited. The same can be said for the other three personality forces as well — each is limited by the other forces. In the case of environment, it is limited by the stabilizing forces within the genetic structures underlying our internal pattern of core strengths or innate capacities. The effects of environment are also limited by our power to make personal choices regarding how we respond to our environment.

Just as in the case of innate capacities, Bi/Polar does not focus on the effects of the environment in the formation of personality. Many professionals focus on the environment force, and much can be learned from their work. The emphasis in Bi/Polar is on the first and last forces — pattern of core strengths and personal choice.

Personal Choice
The fourth personality force is referred to as personal choice — our power to make conscious choices in how we think and how we behave. These choices make a difference in who we become as unique personalities.

Our personal freedom to make conscious choices is the last of the four forces to come into being. In the beginning, an individual is created as a particular pattern of core strengths with particular amounts of innate capacities — laws of genetics and inheritance are in operation here. Immediately after conception, the environment surrounding the individual begins to have its influence on how and to what extent the basic pattern and innate capacities are expressed. This influence begins in the womb, is dramatically expanded at birth, and continues throughout the lifetime of the individual. As the strengths within the individual interact and feed each other, eventually conscious awareness comes into being. Our power to make personal choices is born at the instant personal consciousness becomes a reality. Conscious awareness creates our freedom to choose.

We don't choose personal freedom — it is thrust upon us. It comes to us through the unconscious creative interaction of the strengths within us. Although we are not accountable for the existence of our personal freedom, we are accountable for its use once it is there. How we choose to think and act makes a difference, both in our own lives and the lives of those we touch.

As is true with the other three personality forces, our personal freedom is limited. Not only is our personal freedom limited in some important and obvious ways by the environment, but also by the stable forces expressed through the genetic structures underlying our pattern of core strengths and our innate capacities. Our pattern and our innate capacities are stable features of our personality and, as such, keep their biological structures regardless of how we choose to think and behave. Through conscious choice, we can influence how our basic pattern and our innate capacities are expressed, but this does not involve a change in our natural way of being or our innate capacities.

A constant objective in the development of the Bi/Polar system has been to identify what people can and cannot do about their own personal growth. Much of what Bi/Polar has to offer comes through its concepts of how we may use our power of personal choice to consciously express our strengths in creative ways — ways that are in harmony with the creative process at work in the world.

2.

Patterns of Core Strengths

The Bi/Polar Concept provides a conceptual system that allows us to describe the core of one's personality in terms of positive strengths — with no negatives. The Bi/Polar theory of personality gives us a framework within which we can place this personality core and understand how it relates to the other three forces that influence the formation of the human personality.

As mentioned earlier, Bi/Polar focuses on two of the personality forces that produce a complete person — our pattern of core strengths and our freedom to make personal choices. This chapter deals with one of these forces — our pattern of core strengths. The presentation reviews the basic nature of the pattern of core strengths, identifies the polar strengths that constitute it, describes how these polar strengths relate to one another, shows how eight distinctive patterns are formed, describes the personality characteristics produced by each of these patterns, and, finally, discusses how we may go about discovering our own core pattern.

Nature of Our Pattern of Core Strengths

A pattern of core strengths is a structured and dynamic cluster of interacting polar strengths at the core of every personality. It is an ever-present force helping to shape each individual's unique personality. In the Bi/Polar system, we make the a priori assumption that this core pattern does, in fact, exist within every person. Additionally, we make the following five assumptions regarding its basic nature.

First, the pattern of core strengths is wholly positive — made up entirely of strengths. It is composed of interacting polar strengths that come from the primordial creative force that forms all existence. Whatever may be considered as negative, bad, weak, or destructive about a person is not in this core pattern of strengths. To the extent that these negatives exist, they are found in some of the other forces that shape the personality but not in the core.

Second, it has a unique structure that remains constant throughout one's lifetime. This core pattern is genetically based. Its unique structure is established at conception and maintains the same structure as long as the individual lives. It is the constant thread of self-identify that runs through all the changes and variability that every person experiences throughout a lifetime. The pattern of core strengths is the personal foundation from which a person experiences life to the fullest.

Third, it is dynamic and continuously active. The polar strengths in the core pattern are active as long as the individual lives. Its expression may be blocked or distorted by environmental forces and personal choices made by an individual, but it is always there as a constant force seeking to express itself. Our pattern of core strengths may be regarded as the force that gives the "flavor" to our personality — it is basic and permeates our every thought and action. It is what gives form and structure to our natural way of being.

Fourth, it has the same potential to influence a person's thinking and behavior as do the other three personality forces. Our pattern of core strengths is always influencing our thoughts and actions to some extent, but its actual influence at any particular time is a variable. It varies with different individuals, and it varies at different times within the same individual. With some people, the pattern of core strengths may be the dominant force that has shaped their personality. With others, it may have had the least influence. Within a particular person, the influence will vary depending upon the particular situation and the personal choices made by that person.

Fifth, the pattern of core strengths is a way of understanding that paradox about people — that we are all the same and yet we are all unique. We all share in the same strengths at the core of our beings, but we experience and use them in our own unique ways.

Three Pairs of Core Strengths

The pattern of core strengths is composed of three pairs of polar strengths. The basic pair is thinking and risking. Two additional pairs are obtained by identifying two opposite kinds of thinking and two opposite kinds of risking. The two opposite thinking strengths are practical thinking and theoretical thinking. The two opposite risking strengths are dependent risking and independent risking. (See Figure 3.)

Although the three pairs of strengths are interrelated in this way, they are expressed as independent variables in one's pattern of core strengths.* What this means is, if you know your lead strength in one of the pairs, this does not in any way predict what your lead strength may be in another pair.

The Basic Pair — Thinking/Risking

Let's first consider the two basic strengths — thinking and risking. We all know about these two strengths because we experience them every day: we think, and we feel; we plan, and we do; we analyze a problem, and we do something about it; we try to understand, and we get involved. We see other people expressing the same two strengths: they study, and they make decisions; they try to figure things out, and

---

*The independence of these three pairs of strengths was first demonstrated in research presented in the *Manual for the Bi/Polar Inventory of Strengths*, 1978. These results were confirmed later in research reported by T. J. Thomas in his Ph.D. dissertation entitled *Self-Other Agreement as Manifested by Differential Responses on Self-Report and Other Report Forms of Personality Inventories*, The University of Texas at Austin, 1982.

Three Pairs of Core Strengths

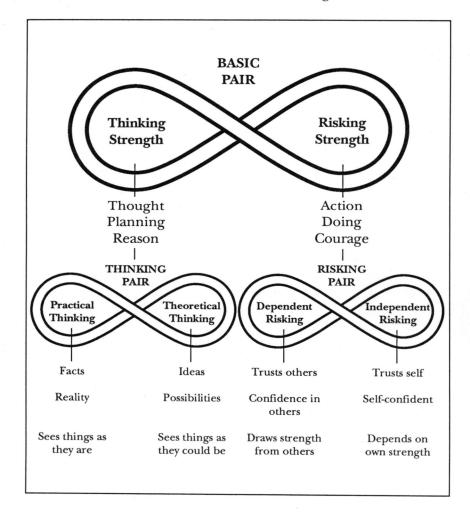

Figure 3

they take chances; they think about what to do, and they move into action. Every person has both of these strengths — a thinking strength and a risking strength.

In my first attempt to classify the two basic strengths, I used reason and emotion as the two defining terms, with reason pointing toward the thinking, rational, stable side and emotion pointing toward the risking, action, dynamic side. It didn't take long, however, for me to discover that I had made a bad choice in using the word emotion. I was viewing both sides as positive strengths but I had chosen a word for the dynamic side that, to many people, was more negative than positive. I remember one executive reacting in this way, "What do you mean emotion is a strength? That's what we want to get rid of or, at least, control. Emotions are what cause most of our problems around here". It was obvious that I needed to find a more suitable word for the dynamic side — one that would more clearly identify that side as a strength, not a weakness or a negative.

As I was seeking a more positive word to take the place of emotion, I happened to be reading Paul Tillich's book, *The Courage to Be*. In reading his analysis of courage, it became apparent to me that he was writing about the same strength that I was trying to identify with the word emotion. The difference was that Tillich was using much better terminology. The word courage really captured the meaning I was after much better than did the word emotion. So I immediately started to use the word courage to describe the strength on the emotional side. This switch was very helpful. Not only did it deepen my own grasp of a strength I was trying to understand, but it gave me a term that was universally admired and regarded as desirable. Although the word courage is still used as one of the descriptive terms for the strength on the dynamic side, risking has become the more commonly used term.

Our thinking strength is a stabilizing strength. It enables us to understand where we are and see where we are going. Through our thinking strength, we can plan, reason, and figure things out on a logical, analytical basis. It enables us to evaluate, weigh, and judge. It gives us the ability to visualize goals and develop strategies to reach them. Our thought processes give stability and structure to our lives. It is our cognitive side.

Our risking strength is a dynamic strength. It is our emotional, feeling, affective side. It is an active, moving, doing kind of strength — sometimes associated with the heart or the "gut". It provides us with the courage to risk, to expose, to move out, to take a change, to initiate, to be involved, to cause things to happen, in spite of the risk.

Both thinking and risking are happening in our lives at all times. However, they do so unevenly. Sometimes our thinking strength is most active; at other times, the reverse is true — our risking is more active than our thinking. As I sit at my desk writing this book, the focus is on my thinking: I am thinking more than I am risking. This does not mean that my risking strength is inactive. I am still using my risking strength, but it is in a subordinate role supporting my thinking. When I submit the finished manuscript to a publisher and do so in spite of the risk of having it rejected, I will be calling mostly on my risking strength. Certainly, both strengths are constantly active, but one or the other is always in the foreground.

We think and we risk, and we continually shift emphasis from one to the other. In addition, each of us feels more at home and comfortable expressing one of them than we do the other. In other words, we naturally "favor" either thinking or risking. It is much like being right-handed or left-handed — we are naturally inclined one way or the other out of our basic nature.

One of the assumptions of Bi/Polar is that every person is naturally out of balance in each of the three pairs of core strengths. That is, every person naturally leads with one of the strengths in each pair. Identifying our lead strengths in each pair results in a particular combination of three lead strengths. This combination of three lead strengths is what determines one's pattern of core strengths.

Some of us lead with thinking. Others of us lead with risking. My own lead strength is in thinking. Yours may be either thinking or risking. These two strengths have equal value in human life, and which way one happens to lean is neither good nor bad. Bi/Polar holds the position that if you have a lead strength in thinking — fine! Be an active thinker and use your risking as a supporting strength to make your thinking more productive and creative. If you have a lead strength in risking — fine! Be an active risker and use your thinking as a supporting strength to make your risking more productive and creative. The Bi/Polar System provides no basis on which to judge one strength as inherently more important and valuable than the other. It is true that one or the other may need to be emphasized at different times and in different situations, but we are talking about the need for an expression of a particular strength in a particular situation, not an evaluation of the intrinsic value of the strength itself.

If thinking is your lead strength, you are likely to be more stable than dynamic, more of a "head-person" than a "heart-person". You like to reason things out and look before you leap. You are cautious and deliberate in your decision making. You tend to be emotionally reserved and usually keep a tight rein on your feelings. You are probably better at organizing and planning than you are at putting the plan into action.

On the other hand, if risking is your lead strength, you are likely to feel and behave quite differently. You are a dynamic, moving kind of person — more oriented toward action than thought. You readily take chances and leave yourself vulnerable. You get involved and express your feelings. You trust your feelings and aggressively seek interaction with other people. You tend to decide quickly and move into action without much delay.

If you lean more toward thinking, your decisions are likely to be based mostly on rational analysis. If you lean more the other way — toward the risking side — you tend to make your decisions more on intuitive feel. These two ways of making decisions are equally valuable. One way is not inherently better than the other.

We feel most comfortable and are most effective when we lead with our naturally dominant strength. Those who have a major strength in thinking naturally lead with rational analysis and use their intuitive feel as a supporting and energizing strength. Those who have a major strength in risking naturally lead with their intuitive feel and use thinking as a supporting and stabilizing strength.

A person who leads in thinking tends to learn best when given an opportunity to think about it first and then get involved. Now, that is just not so with those who lead in risking. They learn best through immediate personal involvement. "Thinkers" tend to say, "Let me think about it first — then I will be prepared to experience it". "Riskers" do the opposite — they say, "Let me experience it first — then I want to think about my experience and see what it means".

We observe this happening with those who attend our seminars on Bi/Polar. Sometimes we furnish the participants with this book before they attend and ask them to read it before the seminar begins. During the seminar, we ask, "Who has read the book?" We find that most all of those who lead in thinking have read the book, but hardly any of those who lead in risking have even bothered to open it. The "riskers" want to experience the seminar first, then read about it. The "thinkers" want to read about it before they attend the seminar.

Two different approaches to life have been presented. These approaches are based upon the proposition that every person has a natural lead strength in either thinking or risking. Those who lead in thinking approach life mostly on an intellectual basis — things have to make sense. They make their decisions primarily through rational analysis and learn best by thinking about things. On the other hand, those who lead in risking approach life mostly on a feeling basis — things have to feel right. They make their decisions primarily on intuitive feel and learn most efficiently through experience — by actually doing it.

Thinking and risking are the two basic strengths that blend together in a creative life. They seem to be opposites in many ways, and sometimes we experience them pulling us in different directions. At times, the blending of those two strengths appears to be a paradox: How can a person be both stable and dynamic at the same time? How are we going to be emotionally involved and objective at the same time? What does it look like when we blend reason with emotion? How do these two strengths actually relate to each other?

Bi/Polar's answer to these questions is that they relate as Bi/Polar strengths — each one feeding on the fruit of the other and becoming creative in the process. Expressed from a personal point of view, we could say that we use our thinking strength to make our risking more creative and effective, and we use our risking strength to make our thinking more creative and productive.

The Thinking Pair — Practical Thinking/Theoretical Thinking
Now let's consider the two thinking strengths — practical thinking and theoretical thinking. These two thinking strengths are polar to each other, and, when blended together, produce our total reasoning, thinking abilities.

Every person has both kinds of thinking. We see how things are, and we see how things could be. We deal with facts and we deal with ideas. We identify problems and see possible solutions. We live with reality and dream about a better tomorrow. Life would not be human without these two strengths.

Although we think in both ways all the time, one or the other is always in the foreground. Sometimes the emphasis is on practical problems: How am I going to get enough money to pay my bills? At other times, the emphasis is on our imagination. What a delight it would be to be lounging on the beach at Hawaii! When one kind of thinking is in the foreground, the other recedes into the background, but the one in the background is still active, even if we are not conscious of it.

Both types of thinking are always active. But we find ourselves shifting emphasis from one to the other. Sometimes situations demand that we shift; other times we deliberately choose to shift. This ability to make the shift by personal choice is part of our basic freedom as human beings.

We all have both kinds of thinking ability, and we are are continually shifting emphasis from one to the other. In addition, we are naturally better at one type of thinking than we are at the other. We are naturally out of balance in our thinking. Some lean toward the practical; others lean toward the theoretical. I happen to favor the theoretical. It has always been so with me as far back as I can remember. As a child, I tended to be a daydreamer. It was a problem for me to shift my attention to the practical problem at hand. I preferred to read and live in my own thoughts. I still have this tendency as an adult. I delight in coming up with new ideas and find it an effort to keep up with the practical things that I must do.

Every person naturally leans one way or the other — toward the practical or the theoretical. Which way we happen to lean says something important about our basic nature, but it says nothing about our value as a person. These two kinds of thinking have equal value in creative thinking, and by nature we all are bound to lean one way or the other. This being the case, there is no good reason why we should "look up at" or "down on" another person because of their tendency to favor either of the two types of thinking.

In the early development of the Bi/Polar System, I used the words "concrete" (for practical thinking) and "abstract" (for theoretical thinking) as identifying terms for the two types of thinking. The term "abstract" gave us problems, however. Many people tended to associate the word "abstract" with "abstract painting" and, therefore, couldn't identify with that strength. We finally settled down on the word "theoretical" in the early 70s, and it has served its purpose well since that time.

If you have a lead strength in practical thinking, you are likely to be realistic and down to earth. You probably prefer to deal with facts rather than ideas. You are more concerned with the problem at hand than you are the overall concept. You like to collect facts and see how things really work. You look for the practical way. Usually you are more skillful in applying an idea than you are dealing with the idea itself. When you describe a situation, you prefer to use specifics rather than general terms.

If theoretical thinking is your lead strength, you tend to be philosophical and idealistic. You think more in terms of generalities than specifics. You look for the general principle. Frequently, you are imaginative. You tend to imagine possibilities and alternatives. You like to theorize and think about the overall concept. You enjoy talking about ideas and continually ask the question "Why?"

Creative thinking is a blended interaction of these two types of thinking — a Bi/Polar interaction in which each type of thinking is producing its own particular product by feeding on the products of the other. Specifically, practical thinking activity produces an awareness of the facts. These facts become the raw material used by theoretical thinking to produce new concepts and ideas. In turn, the concepts produced by theoretical thinking become the tools used by practical thinking to produce an even greater awareness of the facts. It is a back and forth, give and take, feeding interaction.

The Risking Pair — Dependent Risking/Independent Risking
Now let's look at the two risking strengths: dependent risking and independent risking. These two poles of risking have equal status, and, when blended together, they make our risking creative.

I first became aware of the nature of creative risking while reading Tillich's book *The Courage to Be.* In Tillich's presentation, he identified two kinds of courage: the "courage to be oneself" and the "courage to be a part". The Bi/Polar Concept was taking form in my mind at that time, and immediately I made the connection. Here were two types of courage that were opposites, and each had a positive value. The revelation to me was the idea that being dependent (Tillich's "courage to be a part") could be regarded as a strength. I had been taught that it was a weakness — being dependent was a sign of a weak person. The value system that I had learned was one in which independence was the real strength and a quality to be admired. Its opposite — dependence — was something to be ashamed of and gotten rid of as you grew stronger. The very idea that dependence could be regarded as a strength was a shock to me.

This negative view of the word dependence seems to be a commonly held attitude in our society. Because of this, during the development of the Bi/Polar System, I was very hesitant in using the term. For a long time, I used the term "courage to be in relationship" when talking about dependence. This worked fairly well and approached the meaning of dependence, but still did not go directly to the polar meaning that I thought was needed. Finally, in the middle 70s, I decided to "bite the bullet" and use the word dependence as the key word for this strength. We began using it in all our printed matter at that time and have used it ever since. It has worked. Using the word dependence enables us to face the issue directly and describe the basic meaning of this strength more accurately.

Dependent risking is an others-oriented strength. It enables us to establish a relationship, to depend upon others, and to draw strength from them. Through this strength, we develop confidence in others and learn to trust them. We use this strength when we delegate to others. It enables us to become a part of a community and receive emotional support and approval from other people. Through being dependent, we are encouraged by others and actually participate in their strength. It is our avenue to the world and all the values that wait for us out there. It is called a risking strength because we run a risk when we express it. When we lay ourselves open in an act of dependence, we become vulnerable. Our defenses are down, and we're at the mercy of the world. People can take advantage of us, and we can be hurt.

In contrast, independent risking is a self-oriented strength. It gives us the strength to depend upon ourselves and follow our own convictions. It enables us to stand on our own two feet and make our own decisions. As we express independence, we develop self-confidence and become aware of ourselves — we know who we are. Through its expression, we experience personal freedom and create personal power. It gives us a sense of self-worth and significance. It is called a risking strength because we run a risk when we express it. When we separate out as a distinct individual, we run the risk of losing our relationships. We may lose the support and approval of others. We may find ourselves cut off from the community and alone.

All of us have the courage to risk both dependence and independence. It is a natural part of being human. Both are continuously active as we live our lives. However, we are continually shifting emphasis back and forth from one to the other. Sometimes we express our independence strongly, and our dependence recedes into the background. At other times, we emphasize our dependence by actively seeking the support and approval of others. When we do this, our independence recedes into the background.

Sometimes we make extreme shifts from one to the other. This dramatic shift from extreme independence to extreme dependence is characteristic of teen-agers. One minute they are extremely independent; the next minute, they are extremely dependent. This is how they learn to express independence and dependence in a blended way. As they mature, the extreme shifts from one to the other are replaced by a blend of both strengths. As they develop a healthy and unique personality, their own natural inclination toward either independence or dependence continues to give a distinct flavor to their personality, but they also have greater flexibility and skill in shifting to their supporting strength when needed.

Not only do we shift emphasis from one type of courage to the other as the need arises, but we are naturally stronger in one than the other. One is easier for us to express than the other. I find it easier and more natural to express independence. You may find it easier and more comfortable to express dependence. Which way we happen to lean says something important about our natural way of being but says nothing about how much courage we have. It takes just as much courage to express dependence as it does independence. The only difference is that we risk losing different things when we express them.

If you are naturally stronger in dependent risking, you are likely to enjoy working with a group. People know you for your cooperation and your willingness to consider the views of others. Relationships with others are very important to you. You find it easy to depend on others. You seek other people's opinions and rely on what they say. Their support and approval mean a great deal to you. You are people oriented and you experience a great deal of warmth toward others. You are accepting, understanding and tolerant of others. You are supportive in your relationships.

If independence is your lead strength, you tend to feel quite a lot of self-confidence and self-sufficiency. You like to work on your own and tend to keep your own counsel. You are inclined to follow your own convictions and value your independence. You frequently feel competitive with others and tend to have quite a lot of ambition. It is easier for you to depend on yourself than to depend on others. You tend to be territorial.

Creative risking is a process that works in the same way as creative thinking. It is a blended interaction of the two types of risking—each one feeding on the fruit of the other. Expressions of independence feed on the support and approval of others — the fruit of dependence. Expressed in another way, the support of others encourages us to be more independent. On the other hand, expressions of dependence feed on our self-confidence the fruit of independence. In other words, we feel enough self-confidence to go ahead and risk dependence on others: even if they let us down, we can still stand on our own strengths.

Eight Patterns of Core Strengths

When the lead strength in each of the three pairs of core strengths is identified, the result is a particular combination of three lead strengths. This combination of three lead strengths determines the pattern of core strengths. Since there are eight possible combinations of three lead strengths, we have eight core patterns to use, each one giving its own distinctive flavor to a particular personality.

Listed below are the eight possible combinations of three lead strengths with the pattern number that has arbitrarily been assigned to each combination:

Three Lead Strengths	Pattern Number
Thinking/Practical/Dependent	I
Thinking/Practical/Independent	II
Thinking/Theoretical/Dependent	III
Thinking/Theoretical/Independent	IV
Risking/Dependent/Practical	V
Risking/Dependent/Theoretical	VI
Risking/Independent/Practical	VII
Risking/Independent/Theoretical	VIII

All eight patterns are displayed in Figure 4. Each pattern drawing has a thinking axis and a risking axis drawn as dashed lines perpendicular to each other. The two thinking strengths are at the ends of the thinking axis. The two risking strengths are at the ends of the risking axis. These two perpendicular axes divide the circle into four quadrants, allowing us to draw in different size loops to show which is the lead strength in each of the two pairs of practical/theoretical and independence/dependence. The larger loop in each pair indicates the lead strength in that pair. In addition, the axis with the larger loops indicates the lead strength in the basic thinking/risking pair of strengths.

Patterns of Core Strengths

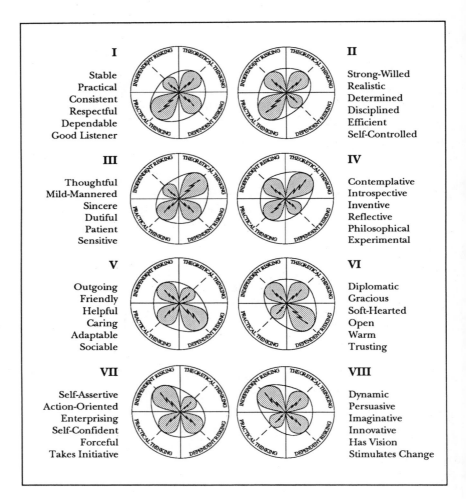

I

Stable
Practical
Consistent
Respectful
Dependable
Good Listener

II

Strong-Willed
Realistic
Determined
Disciplined
Efficient
Self-Controlled

III

Thoughtful
Mild-Mannered
Sincere
Dutiful
Patient
Sensitive

IV

Contemplative
Introspective
Inventive
Reflective
Philosophical
Experimental

V

Outgoing
Friendly
Helpful
Caring
Adaptable
Sociable

VI

Diplomatic
Gracious
Soft-Hearted
Open
Warm
Trusting

VII

Self-Assertive
Action-Oriented
Enterprising
Self-Confident
Forceful
Takes Initiative

VIII

Dynamic
Persuasive
Imaginative
Innovative
Has Vision
Stimulates Change

Figure 4

Patterns, I, II, III, and IV all have a lead strength in thinking and a supporting strength in risking. This is shown by drawing the two loops along the thinking axis so they take in a larger space than the two loops along the risking axis. On the other hand, Patterns V, VI, VII, and VIII have risking as the lead strength. This is shown by drawing the loops on the risking axis so they are larger than those on the thinking axis.

Practical thinking is the lead strength in Patterns I, II, V, and VII. This is shown by drawing the practical loops in these patterns larger than the theoretical loops. In Patterns III, IV, VI, and VIII, theoretical thinking is the lead strength. In these patterns the theoretical loops are larger than the practical loops.

Patterns II, IV, VII, and VIII have a lead strength in independent risking. The independent loops are larger than the dependent loops in those patterns. Patterns I, III, V, and VI have a lead strength in dependent risking. In these patterns, the dependent loops are drawn larger than the independent.

Notice that in each of the eight pattern drawings the two intermediate sized loops are drawn equal. This should not be interpreted to mean that we think those two strengths are actually equal. Rather, it should be interpreted to mean that we have not made any judgment about their relative strength. Either could be stronger than the other, and it wouldn't make any difference in the basic understanding of the pattern itself.

Our next task is to describe how each of these eight patterns of core strengths is expressed in the life of a particular person. One of the most basic tenets of Bi/Polar is that each pattern creates a constant force — a foundation — that produces distinctive personality characteristics. The rest of this section is devoted to describing the personality strengths and characteristics that tend to be produced by each pattern.

As a first step, let's divide the eight patterns into two groups of four. The first four core patterns (Patterns I, II, III, and IV) tend to produce thinkers — intellectual, rational, reasoning people. On the other hand, the last four patterns (V, VI, VII, and VIII) tend to produce doers — dynamic, moving, action-oriented people. Keep in mind that, as the lead strength is emphasized in the pattern description, it automatically de-emphasizes the supporting strength. The point I want to make is that when a descriptive word pointing to the lead strength is used, we need to keep in mind that the supporting strength is there and active also. In other words, thinkers are also doers, and doers are also thinkers. It is simply a matter of which is the dominant strength.

As a second step, let's consider the eight patterns in pairs.

Patterns I and II produce many similar personality characteristics. Both patterns lead in basic thinking and practical thinking. The combination of these two lead strengths tends to produce a rational, realistic, fact-oriented person. Those who have one of these patterns of core strengths tend to be practical people who see things as they are. They concentrate on the present and deal with the realities of a situation. They put things in order and bring stability to an organized effort. Patterns I and II tend to produce realistic people.

The next pair — Patterns III and IV — also has thinking as a lead strength. However, these patterns are different from Patterns I and II in that they have their dominant strength on the theoretical side. This combination tends to produce people who delight in dealing with ideas and concepts. They usually enjoy going to school and are naturally geared to doing well in scholastic pursuits. They like to gather knowledge and tend to have a philosophical bent. Patterns III and IV tend to produce idealistic people.

The third pair — Patterns V and VI — has other people as their main focus in life. Those who have these patterns tend to be warm and outgoing people. They enjoy being with other people and thrive on recognition and compliments. Frequently, people who have these core patterns are highly effective in sales, particularly in sales situations that require a soft-sell. Patterns V and VI tend to produce people who are active, dynamic, and assertive in their efforts to establish warm and close relationships.

The last pair — Patterns VII and VIII — has a good deal in common. People who have these patterns of strengths are usually very aware of their own strengths and have a clear idea of what they are trying to accomplish. They are goal oriented. They usually feel a good deal of self-confidence and are self-assertive in their relationships. They are self-starters and experience a high drive to accomplish. Those who have Patterns VII and VIII are dynamic, enthusiastic, action-oriented people. They take the initiative and provide out-front leadership. They want to score.

Has anything negative or depreciating been said about any of the patterns? I hope not. I have certainly not intended to. Each pattern has its own unique blend of strengths to contribute to the creative process. Since we are dealing only with different patterns of equally valuable strengths, we have no basis to judge one pattern as better or more important than any other pattern. Certain kinds of strengths and certain patterns are needed to do the best job in particular situations. But this has nothing to do with the intrinsic value of the pattern itself. All people have every right to feel good about their own natural patterns of strengths, whatever they may be. This value system of Bi/Polar truly means that all people are created equal (equal in worth as individual persons).

Now that we have considered the patterns in pairs, let's consider each one separately. In our earlier discussion, Patterns I and II were discussed as being very similar: Both lead in basic thinking, and both have their greatest strength in practical thinking. Now let's look at how they are different. They are different in that Pattern I leads in dependent risking, and Pattern II leads in independent risking. This makes quite a lot of difference in how people with these patterns tend to feel and behave.

When I am dealing with management people, I use the term kindly administrator to describe, in a general way, the characteristics of people who have Pattern I core strengths. On the other hand, I use the term control manager to point toward the style of management usually displayed by those who have Pattern II strengths. Those who have Pattern I strengths tend to run a family type of operation — where everyone is cared for as a person and there is an emphasis on human values. In contrast, those having Pattern II strengths tend to place more value on efficiency and productivity. They tend to pay more attention to production and less attention to the people involved. Those who have Pattern I strengths tend to run a "loose ship", and, conversely, those who have Pattern II strengths tend to run a "tight ship". Either approach, "loose" or "tight", can be creative, productive, and enjoyable — it all depends on the need of the situation.

Those who have Pattern I strengths are dependable, loyal, and consistent. They are conservative, accepting people and are usually good listeners. Their stability, warmth, and practicality make the world a comfortable place in which to live. My wife Jane has the Pattern I combination of strengths, and for that I am grateful. For several years, she ran the administration of the Bi/Polar office and did it in such an understanding way that our Bi/Polar seminar leaders came to appreciate her a great deal. She handled problems with the seminar leaders that would drive me to distraction. I am still amazed at how calmly and effectively she did it. When she got on the telephone, things just seemed to settle down and problems got solved. I didn't know I was getting this added bonus 44 years ago when we were married.

Those who have Pattern I strengths tend to experience a persistent need for more self-confidence. I have interviewed hundreds of people who have this pattern. I think it is a safe guess to say that 90 percent of them tell me that they feel a need for more self-confidence. Although we all feel a need for more self-confidence at times, those who have this pattern feel this need more deeply and consistently. Another need they have is to think in more positive ways, particularly about themselves. They tend to underrate themselves, especially in groups. Because of this tendency to think negatively of themselves, they sometimes feel depressed.

Those who have Pattern II strengths are realistic and independent. They are usually reserved and private people. They initiate stability, while those who have Pattern I strengths tend to maintain it. People with Pattern II strengths are usually strong on self-discipline. They tend to feel self-sufficient and normally experience a good deal of self-confidence. They are stimulated by a tough challenge and derive a great deal of enjoyment out of personal accomplishment. Efficiency is their middle name.

People who have Pattern II strengths usually express a need for better communication with others. They tend to hold a tight rein on their feelings and not share them with other people. This interferes with their ability to communicate on a personal level. Another thing that interferes with their relationships is their tendency to think negatively of others. They are very good in spotting the shortcomings of other people — and are usually right, too! Such ability can have great value; however, if left unchecked, it can certainly interfere with good relationships and openness in communication. Pattern II's usually want to relate to others in a more warm and accepting way but have to consciously work at it.

The term "warm" is not used to describe the people who have Pattern II strengths. However, this does not mean that people with this pattern can't be warm people. They can be genuinely warm toward others as they grow in maturity and learn to express their relationship strengths in their own way. I worked with a company president from 1973 to 1985 who is an outstanding example of this fact. He has clear Pattern II strengths. He knows and affirms this and so does almost everyone else who knows him well.

But he is one of the warmest people that I know, and others in the company attested to this out of their own personal relationship with him. His Pattern II strengths show through clearly, but he is still a very warm person and really cares for people. The maturity this points toward was manifested in his exceptional effectiveness as the chief executive officer of his company. Under his leadership, the company became a very people-oriented company and increased its profits ten-fold during the time I worked with him.

Let's turn our attention to those people who have core Patterns III and IV. People having these patterns are similar in that they are thinkers and stronger on the theoretical side. They are different in that those having Pattern III strengths lean toward dependent risking, and those having Pattern IV strengths lean toward independence. This disparity in risking orientation makes a big difference in how these people feel and behave. It also makes a difference in what they can do the best.

Those who have Pattern III strengths are theoretical and cooperative. They have a natural ability to understand other people's ideas and concepts. They usually have a good ability to understand proven theories and relate them to one another. Beyond this, they are usually effective in communicating these concepts to other people. Their people-centeredness frequently expresses itself in student-centered teaching. Those having this pattern frequently find teaching to be an appropriate vocation.

Those who have either Pattern III or IV core strengths tend to be technical people; however, they express their technical abilities in very different ways. Frequently, people having Pattern III strengths are very effective in heading up research and development operations. They tend to be thorough, careful, academic, and oriented toward research. They usually have a good ability to compare one theory to another. On the other hand, those having Pattern IV strengths usually express their technical ability through intuitive insight in the development of new ideas. Those who have Pattern III strengths usually prefer to work as members of a group, and those having the Pattern IV strengths usually prefer working alone.

People having Pattern III core strengths tend to feel a persistent need for more self-confidence. In this way, they are very similar to those having Pattern I strengths. They are forever selling themselves short and underrating their own importance. They tend to think about themselves this way: "What I have to say doesn't amount to much, so I will just keep quiet and not say anything". Most always, those having this pattern feel a painful need to develop more self-confidence.

A friend of mine has the Pattern III combination of strengths. He is a retired professor of Christian Education at Perkins School of Theology at Southern Methodist University. He has all of the right credentials — a Phi Beta Kappa and a Ph.D. from a respected eastern university. I first became acquainted with him in 1970 when the Bi/Polar concepts were introduced to the faculty at Perkins.

In the years I have known him, he has consistently displayed the characteristics of people who have Pattern III strengths. He is philosophical, articulate, scholarly, cultured, thin-skinned, gentle, considerate, dutiful, and terribly conscientious. Not only does he show these strengths clearly, but he affirms the needs that people with this pattern usually experience. He tends to think negatively of himself and experiences a painful need to be more assertive in his relationships. I have observed a great deal of growth in him in these areas during the years I have known him, but he reports that his point of pain is still at the same place.

Those who have Pattern IV strengths are creators of new ideas and approaches. They react differently than those who have Pattern III strengths. Rather than read about other people's theories, they have a strong inclination to develop their own ideas. People having Pattern IV strengths stay more within themselves, while those having Pattern III strengths tend to reach out more to other people.

People having Pattern IV strengths have leaps of insight that sometimes are "brand new". This frequently causes a problem. Although their intuitive insight may be accurate, it may take a long time to fill in the gap between where they have leaped to and where the other people are.

To compound the problem, those having this pattern have great difficulty in documenting how they arrived at their intuitive insight. They don't arrive at their insights in a linear, step-by-step thinking process. They do it with a quantum leap, then they have to go back and fill in the logical steps. I am not saying by this that their intuitive insight is always right. What I want to say is that their insights are usually in the ball park. If their intuitive insights are shaped and sharpened by reality, they frequently evolve into very useful ideas.

I feel I know the Pattern IV combination very well — it is my own core pattern. I have experienced all the strengths and the problems attributed to this pattern. I delight in dealing with ideas and particularly enjoy coming up with a new insight. I thoroughly enjoy philosophy and thinking about abstract ideas. It is well nigh impossible for me to describe the great feeling I have when a new idea comes to me. To me, the experience of having a new idea is the closest I ever come to complete happiness. When it happens, I have a strong sense of well-being. I really feel good.

Perhaps an example would communicate better. In 1973, I was working with two faculty members at Southern Methodist University on a new revision for our seminar workbook and had agreed to meet with them one evening in their office on the campus. The insight came while I was making the drive from my home in Richardson to the SMU campus in Dallas.

The insight itself had to do with how two polar strengths relate to each other. It was already clear to me that the two strengths in a Bi/Polar pair were both positive strengths and both became stronger in growth. What I didn't have was an understanding of how they related to each other in order to bring that about. Before the insight came, I was not at all clear about what I was looking for. The best I can describe it is to say that I was uneasy. I felt confused and unsure. I was agitated and worried. Just before the insight came, I felt a good deal of depression. The whole Bi/Polar System just seemed to fall apart at my feet. Then, all of a sudden, the insight came. It was real simple:

Polar strengths feed each other! With it came a tremendously good feeling. It was a mountaintop experience for me.

I was still a few minutes away from the campus when the idea hit me. I can remember precisely where I was when it happened — about 100 yards from the Mockingbird Lane exit on Central Expressway, going toward downtown Dallas. I floated on over to the meeting eager to share my insight with my colleagues.

They were both there, and we started to work on the new workbook immediately. I was able to contain myself for awhile, but not for long. Finally, I couldn't hold it any longer. I blurted out my idea and demonstrated it with the infinity symbol displayed in Figure 1. I traced this figure, showing how I conceived each strength producing a fruit that feeds the other. I shall never forget their response. They nodded their heads, said, "Uh huh," and started talking about something else. I was disappointed that they didn't share my excitement, but, as I recall, my own enthusiasm and confidence in the insight was not dampened in the least. I believe this is characteristic of those of us who have Pattern IV strengths — what others think of our ideas is not nearly as important as our own mental clarity and internal conviction.

People who have Pattern IV strengths experience many of the same needs as those having Pattern II strengths, especially in their relationships. One of their most painful needs is for better communication with others, particularly on an emotional level. Those who have core Pattern IV frequently feel uncomfortable in social situations. They usually want to talk about ideas (especially their own) and are frustrated with small talk. They hardly know what to say in a light conversation. It takes quite a lot of learning for them just to enjoy other people. They tend to see relationships with others as a means to an end — not an end in itself.

Becoming aware of the problems that are normal for people having Pattern IV strengths has helped me deal with my own problems. People with my pattern usually have difficulty communicating their intuitive insights. Usually, they emphasize the theory and fail to communicate on a practical level. This has been a frustrating problem for me, particularly in the early days when the Bi/Polar concepts were taking form. In those days, when I conducted seminars, I was sure of my insights, but about all I would do was to continually repeat the concepts in abstract terms. This resulted in rather dry and boring theoretical lectures that were highly ineffective.

Recognizing that it was my problem helped me start looking for a solution. The solution was simple: I needed to communicate the concepts by giving examples. I found I was much less frustrated and communicated much more effectively when I shifted to the practical and gave examples, rather than just repeating the concept in another abstract form.

I have always had a problem in understanding what is going on between me and another person emotionally. I recognize that I have a tendency to be sort of reserved and stand-offish. It is very difficult for me to express my dependence on others. Even to admit I am dependent on others has been a chore for me. The Bi/Polar System has helped me realize that dependence is really a strength. This realization has enabled me to admit and express my dependent feelings more fully. In turn, it has made me a warmer person in my relationships. Now I enjoy people much more and get a real emotional lift from my relationships. This is a new and delightful experience for me. I believe this positive emotional support from others has enabled me to express my natural strengths even more strongly.

Now it is time to look at the people who have Patterns V and VI as their natural combination of lead strengths. They are the warm people of the world. This isn't to say that those of us who have other core patterns aren't warm, but it does say that people who have these patterns place a premium on warm relationships with others and have a natural talent for developing them. People who have these two patterns are similar in that they both are outgoing and take the initiative in establishing a relationship. Both are usually effective in "soft-sell" situations. They are different in that the people who have Pattern V strengths lean toward practicality, and those who have Pattern VI strengths tend to be more romantic and lean toward idealism.

Although all of us want and need recognition from others, it is especially important to the people who have these two patterns. They almost demand to be told how you feel about them. Again, we all like praise; however, for those who have Pattern V and VI strengths, praise and compliments can't come too often.

They are very social people and usually have highly developed social skills. They feel comfortable with others. They are very accepting and sympathetic, and enjoy relationships for their own sake. In social situations, I frequently find myself following along in their warm wake.

Those having Pattern V strengths are outgoing and practical. They are usually effective in jobs requiring skill in coordinating the activities of others. They are very aware of what is going on inside people and are especially sensitive to their feelings. This base of awareness gives them a great deal of skill in communication, particularly on an emotional level. They know how others are feeling and what it takes to please them. Frequently, they are good counselors. They feel comfortable dealing with feelings and are usually effective in getting others to share their feelings with them. The practicality inherent in those with Pattern V strengths is frequently used to help others find practical solutions to their relationship problems.

In business, many of those who have Pattern V strengths go into personnel work, which gives them many opportunities to help people in practical ways. A job in training and development seems to fit their natural strengths very well, usually making them effective as training specialists.

The people who have Pattern VI core strengths are naturally assertive and intuitive about people. They are emotionally expressive and frequently have a flair for dramatics. A number of professional entertainers have the Pattern VI combination of strengths. One of their great strengths is an intuitive feel for an audience. From this, they have a powerful ability to move their audience emotionally.

Many of those who have Pattern VI strengths find that the public relations business fits their natural talents very well. They usually have a good facility with words and ideas, and enjoy being involved with lots of people.

I recently counseled with a public relations man. He is warm, talkative, outgoing, witty, and a very comfortable person to be with. Sure enough, the *Bi/Polar Inventories of Core Strengths* showed him to have Pattern VI strengths. His problem was not difficult to uncover. For the past nine years, he had been working for a man who constantly belittled him, thus robbing him of his self-confidence. He was in the right field but working for the wrong man. He has now changed jobs and gone to another public relations firm. If his new employer recognizes his talents and encourages him, my bet is that he will be an outstanding success in his new job.

People who have Pattern V and VI strengths experience very similar needs. One of their most frequent pains is that they let the demands of others rule their lives. Many of them say their greatest need is for more self-confidence. Most of them wish they could be more self-assertive and stand up for their own rights more effectively.

Now let's consider Pattern VII and VIII individually. We have referred to those who have Patterns V and VI strengths as the "soft-sell" people. In contrast, those having core Patterns VII and VIII are "hard-sell" people. They take an independent stance and strongly assert their own views and opinions. People who have these two patterns are similar in that they are both independent riskers and have a good deal of self-confidence. They are different in that those having Pattern VII strengths lean toward facts and reality, whereas those with Pattern VIII strengths lean toward ideas and visions of possibility.

People having Pattern VII core strengths are self-assertive and enterprising. They are clearly the Horatio Alger, bring-yourself-up-by-the bootstraps kind of people. This pattern represents the strength of our American hero — the true pioneer, the practical, self-reliant, enterprising hero of the American dream. They are characterized by Yankee practicality and feet-on-the-ground realism. They feel comfortable being "out-front" leaders. They want other people to interact with them and follow their leadership. Those having Pattern VII strengths are "high-drive" people who have an intense desire to accomplish. They usually feel a great deal of self-confidence and willingly take calculated risks.

Those that have core Pattern VII have a natural intuitive feel for people and situations. They tend to "fly by the seat of their pants". They are very competitive and are stimulated by a tough challenge. A friend of mine who has Pattern VII strengths put it this way, "I don't like to lose worth a damn!"

People having Pattern VII strengths frequently start their own businesses from scratch. Their high drive and willingness to take risks tends to make them hard driving and successful salespeople. The companies they head up are usually aggressive, dynamic, and exciting. Their companies grow fast and expand rapidly. The mature ones recognize their own tendencies toward dynamism and change, and, as a result, eventually bring in someone with strong stabilizing strengths (usually a person with Pattern II strengths) to give balance to the organization. Although a person with Pattern VII strengths is usually the president during a company's beginning and rapid growth period, frequently a person with the Pattern II combination of strengths becomes the president of a large, well-established company. Of course, a person with any of the patterns, through maturity and self-discipline, can function effectively as a president of a business organization. However, the strengths usually required to function effectively as a chief executive officer in a business enterprise seems to fit the natural lead strengths of those who have Pattern VII and Pattern II strengths more closely.

When I first started giving seminars, I used the label "promoter" to describe the person that has Pattern VIII core strengths. Although the term promoter is very descriptive and to me very accurate, it has given me some problems.

About 15 years ago, I had an interesting experience using the term "promoter". I was presenting a Bi/Polar seminar to a group of Methodist executives in the Dallas area. Three in the group turned out to have Pattern VIII core strengths. I used "promoter" as a basic term to describe the people having this pattern. After my presentation, one of the participants came up to me and said, somewhat facetiously, "Say, Doc, would it be all right with you if we would call those with Pattern VIII strengths pioneers rather than promoters?" He was reacting to the "con-man" connotation in the term promoter. I was in sympathy with his problem. In fact, in response to his comment, I decided not to use the term any more in my presentation. I replaced it with pioneer.

Well, I tried that for a year or so, and it just did not have the flavor and accuracy of promoter. So I came back to promoter, and now I frequently use it as a label for those having this pattern. It is such a good word and so descriptive of that pattern that I think it's worth risking the negative connotations we might be communicating. However, I am careful to explain the pattern in terms of strengths and do all I can to get rid of any negative meanings the term promoter may suggest.

Those having core Pattern VIII strengths tend to be dynamic and persuasive. They are people of vision who take the risks required to make a vision become real. People with Pattern VIII see the potential and have the courage to "bet the farm". They have the ability, through independence and imagination, to put promotional deals together. They get things going — they push, initiate, and sell a dream. They cause people to get excited and emotionally involved by seeing the potential. They are dynamic, personable, strong-impact people. In fact, people having core Pattern VIII tend to be the most dynamic people of all.

A few years ago, I was retained as a psychological consultant by a small college. The president of the college had Pattern VIII core strengths. When he became president, about a year prior to my arrival, he found a college that was in dire straits. The former president had resigned; the faculty was in a state of confusion and uncertainty; the college was in desperate need of financial support; and the board was giving serious thought to closing the school. It needed strong leadership if it were to survive.

In hindsight, the board made a wise decision. They hired a person with Pattern VIII strengths — a strong promoter — as president. Then they gave him free rein to exert his dynamic and inspiring leadership. By the time I arrived on the scene, he had already made considerable progress in turning gloom into hope. The administrative staff and faculty were beginning to share the president's confidence. They were starting to see and share his vision of what the college could become. The president was clearly the central force that turned the bankrupt college into what it is today: a dynamic institution that has hope for the future. He did many things to bring this about, and there were many people who joined his team in a common effort to do the job. He "bet the farm", and he won!

What are the points of pain for those who have Patterns VII and VIII? One of the problems most of them recognize clearly is their tendency to talk too much and not listen enough. Another common problem they share is impatience. Sometimes this impatience is expressed by pushing others to decide quickly. They frequently get themselves into trouble by jumping to conclusions and moving too fast — deciding before they have had time to make a good judgment.

Another common problem is that they want to do it themselves; they find it difficult to step back and rely on other people. Many of those with whom I have worked in business find the most difficult thing they have to learn is delegating to another person — letting go and effectively getting the other person to assume responsibility.

The people who have core Patterns VII and VIII tend to experience different needs in their thinking. Those who have Pattern VII strengths tend to feel a need for a better grasp of abstract concepts. Those with Pattern VIII strengths feel a need for a better grasp of reality.

It may give a better understanding of the eight core patterns if a well-known personality could be identified for each one. Of course, this will be a guessing game since I don't know these people personally, but it may be instructive if we could find a former President of the United States that would fit each of the eight patterns. I could not, with confidence, say that they actually have the core pattern I select, but I can say that they tend to show the personality characteristics normally produced by that pattern.

As a representative for Pattern I, I would select Eisenhower. The kinds of strengths he showed as Commander-in-Chief for the Allied Forces during World War II strongly suggest that he had the core strengths of Pattern I: skill at organization, stability, planning, coordination of diverse groups, sound and realistic thinking, warm and understanding leadership. Then, as President, people respected his conservative, stable leadership and expressed their warmth toward him with the endearing term of "Ike".

Truman seems to fit Pattern II, although he expressed many of the characteristics of people who have Pattern VII strengths. One of the reasons I think he had core Pattern II is his extensive reading. As I recall from his autobiography, he read all the books in the Independence, Kansas library before he finished high school. This indicates that he leans more toward thinking than action. Many of his qualities — his objectivity, ability to make hard decisions independently, toughness, reality orientation, and ability to cut through to the core of a problem point toward Truman having the core strengths of Pattern II.

I believe Richard Nixon would represent Pattern II also. Some people may feel that Nixon expressed his strengths in a destructive way. However, this has nothing to do with his basic pattern. How we express our strengths is a separate issue from our basic pattern of strengths.

Woodrow Wilson's natural strengths seem to fit Pattern III. His university background before he became President is also suggestive of this pattern. His idealism, as manifested by his involvement in the League of Nations, points toward the Pattern III combination of strengths.

I believe Jack Kennedy had the core strengths of a Pattern IV. His independence, idealism, and ability to deal skillfully with concepts and words point toward this pattern. Such historical figures as Leonardo Da Vinci, Thoreau, Charles Darwin, Copernicus, and Albert Einstein all display the major characteristics produced by the Pattern IV blend of core strengths.

Jimmy Carter shows many of the characteristics of people who have the core strengths of Pattern V. He appears to communicate extremely well, particularly on an emotional level. He shows a good deal of "warmth" and seems to live mostly in a world of people. He is also a very practical politician.

One of our seminar leaders made a study of "Teddy" Roosevelt and concluded that he was a Pattern VI. Will Rogers and Mark Twain are also excellent examples of Pattern VI.

We have many good examples of those who have Pattern VII characteristics. Lyndon B. Johnson fits Pattern VII very well. His style of leadership, particularly when he was a major figure in Congress, points clearly toward Pattern VII. Other examples are General George Patton (an excellent example), Charles DeGaulle, and Amelia Earhart.

Franklin D. Roosevelt appears to fit Pattern VIII. His persuasiveness and idealism suggest this pattern. His energy, self-confidence, vision of the New Deal, and fireside chats all point toward the characteristics of those who have Pattern VIII strengths. Others who appear to have had Pattern VIII core strengths are Martin Luther King ("I have a dream"), Saint Paul, and Adolf Hitler (remember that how people express their strengths is a separate issue from the pattern itself).

Identifying Your Own Core Pattern

Your core pattern of strengths is identified by discovering your natural lead strength in each of the three Bi/Polar pairs. This core pattern determines your natural way of being and suggests how you can make your greatest contribution to the creative process. Although you have a natural pattern of strengths that "flavors" everything you do, you also have the ability to emphasize any of your supporting strengths and actually express any of the eight basic patterns. Your ability to emphasize any of your core strengths gives you the flexibility to respond differently to different situations and thus adapt effectively to your environment. Being flexible in expressing your strengths is an essential part of being a creative and effective human being.

Your natural flexibility in expressing your strengths tends to mask your core pattern, at least to the outside world. If you have developed a good deal of flexibility in expressing your supporting strengths, it will probably be more difficult for you to identify your natural core pattern. This does not mean that you don't have a core pattern. It just means that you will need to spend more time and effort in discovering what it is.

Most of us have been taught a value system that places more value on some core strengths than on others. If you have been taught a value system in which one of your lead strengths is depreciated, it will tend to cause you to block this strength and not show it to the outside world. It can influence you to hide your natural way and even make you want to be something other than what you really are at the core. Having a value system that depreciates one of your natural lead strengths can make it hard for you to accept and affirm your natural core pattern.

Sometimes the demands of our environment have required that we exercise our supporting strengths so much that our natural lead strengths have been neglected. For example, your work situation may have required you to consistently exercise one of your support-ing strengths, and, as a result, you have not had the opportunity to fully experience and develop skill in expressing your natural lead strength. Consistently emphasizing one of your supporting strengths over a long period will not make it into a natural lead strength for you, but it may make it more difficult for you to identify your natural core pattern.

One of the most effective ways to discover your core pattern is to "try on" each of the eight patterns to see how they fit. You can do this by reading a description of the personality characteristics each pattern tends to produce. These descriptions may be found at the end of this chapter. The one that feels most "natural" or "comfort-able" is a good indicator of your core pattern.

When trying to identify one's lead strength in each of the three Bi/Polar pairs, most people find they are confident about their lead strength in one and perhaps two of the pairs. Their lead strength in one of the pairs is frequently less obvious and sometimes very difficult for them to identify. This usually means they see themselves in two patterns and can't decide which of the two is actually their core pattern. Since these patterns have two lead strengths in common, they are closely related and produce many similar personality char-acteristics.

Each of the eight patterns has two lead strengths in common with three other patterns. These three closely related patterns are referred to as flex-patterns. You will usually find that you display many of the characteristics described in your three flex-patterns. You can express each of your flex-patterns by emphasizing one of your supporting strengths. You may find you can express one of your three flex-patterns rather easily and effectively, but find it somewhat more difficult to express the other two. You may also find that expressing one of your flex-patterns is especially difficult. The three flex-patterns for each core pattern are identified in the descriptions of the eight patterns found at the end of this chapter.

Each pattern has an opposite pattern — the pattern that has opposite lead strengths in all three pairs. Here are the four combinations of opposite patterns: I and VIII, II and VI, III and VII, and IV and V. Sometimes you can confirm the selection of your core pattern by reading the description of your opposite pattern and feeling that it doesn't fit you at all.

Although you may be able to identify your own core pattern by thinking subjectively about yourself within the context of the Bi/Polar concepts, a more scientific and reliable way to identify your pattern is through the *Bi/Polar Inventories of Core Strengths*. This is a professionally-validated psychological instrument designed specifically to reveal a person's Bi/Polar pattern of core strengths. It is a part of the materials for the *Bi/Polar: Foundations of Productivity* seminar.

The Bi/Polar Inventories of Core Strengths

Development of the *Bi/Polar Inventories of Core Strengths* began with the birth of the Bi/Polar Concept in the early 1960s. From the very beginning, some type of paper-and-pencil inventory has been used to help people discover their personal leanings in the three pairs of Bi/Polar strengths. Through the years, many different words and phrases have been used to describe the Bi/Polar strengths, and a variety of inventory designs have been tried.

The *Bi/Polar Inventories of Core Strengths* now being used are the result of 28 years of experience and extensive research. In 1977, Dr. Clyde Mayo, an industrial psychologist in Houston, Texas spearheaded a research effort that produced the inventory now in use. Dr. Mayo and I published a manual at that time that gives a complete description of the inventory and the research that made it a professionally validated instrument.

In 1982, Dr. T. J. Thomas performed additional research that included even more sophisticated mathematical analyses on an even larger sample. The results of his study confirmed the original validity and reliability measurements obtained by Mayo and provided research information that has enabled us to make it an even more effective instrument. Since that time, many other research studies using the *Bi/Polar Analysis of Core Strengths* have been completed.

In its present design, the *Bi/Polar Inventories of Core Strengths* are made into a packet that includes six separate copies of the same inventory. One is for the person to fill out on him/herself, and the other five are for other people to fill out on how they see that person. All six of these inventories are then mailed directly to the offices of the Institute of Foundational Training and Development. The data from these six inventories are then computer-analyzed, and the results identify the person's core pattern. The computer produces a printout of the *Bi/Polar Analysis of Core Strengths*, and this final *Analysis* is then disseminated to the individual.

One of the unusual features of this approach is the use of a self-report combined with the reports of five other people. Obtaining the person's self-image plus how they are seen by others is extremely valuable in a number of ways.

First, it provides a wider data base for the conclusions. The combined result of how people view themselves and how they are viewed by others is probably more accurate than either view by itself.

Second, the results tend to be more convincing. Frequently, a person's own self-image agrees very closely with the view of others. When this happens, it invariably gives the person an added measure of confidence about his or her pattern.

Third, it is highly interesting to most people to see how other people view them. Many times, people have used this information to deepen their understanding of their relationships with other people.

The *Bi/Polar Inventories of Core Strengths* are now being used in the *Bi/Polar: Foundations of Productivity* seminar that is designed to accompany this book.

Eight Patterns of Core Strengths

Pattern I

Lead Strengths	Thinking	Practical Thinking	Dependent Risking
Supporting Strengths	Risking	Theoretical Thinking	Independent Risking
Flex-Patterns	V	III	II

Personality Characteristics	Stable, quiet, dependable, accepting, steady, loyal, orderly, respectful, consistent, conforming, methodical, attentive, cautious, economical, receptive, practical, hesitant, systematic **A good listener — a "down-to-earth" person.**
Relationship Strengths	Focus attention on the practical situation. Makes others feel secure and comfortable Waits for other person to make the first move. Follows the leadership of others. Avoids confrontation and conflict. Keeps thoughts and feelings to self.
Vocational Strengths	Maintain established routines. Watches over details. Provides a warm and accepting work environment. Keeps things running smoothly. Loyal and dependable team player.
Wants Others To . . .	Take the initiative in a respectful way. Ask for their help. Give them encouragement. Show them appreciation. Invite them to go along.

Pattern II

Lead Strengths	Thinking	Practical Thinking	Independent Risking
Supporting Strengths	Risking	Theoretical Thinking	Dependent Risking
Flex-Patterns	VII	IV	I
Personality Characteristics	Rational, determined, logical, firm, analytical, disciplined, objective, conservative, deliberate, prudent, self-reliant, self-controlled, strong-willed, calm, tenacious, discerning, industrious, realistic **Shows sound judgment — uses common sense.**		
Relationship Strengths	Focus attention on objective reality. Provides stable leadership. Brings rationality to emotional situations. Keeps own counsel. Holds feelings inside. Avoids "small talk".		
Vocational Strengths	Analyzes problems. Takes initiative to solve problems. Brings order out of chaos. Brings efficiency to operations. Keeps tight control.		
Wants Others To . . .	Listen to them. Show them respect. Give them space — don't crowd. Stay rational and objective. Give them the facts — preferably in writing.		

Pattern III

Lead Strengths	Thinking	Theoretical Thinking	Dependent Risking
Supporting Strengths	Risking	Practical Thinking	Independent Risking
Flex-Patterns	VI	I	IV

Personality Characteristics	Thoughtful, mild-mannered, polite, gentle, sincere, faithful, knowledgeable, dutiful, learned, patient, academic, tolerant, scholarly, benevolent, sensitive, studious, shy, courteous **A moral philosopher—interested in fundamental principles.**
Relationship Strengths	Focus attention on the relationship. Gives support in a quiet way. Careful not to hurt feelings. Understanding and affirming. Seeks to be cooperative and agreeable. Goes along with the group.
Vocational Strengths	Organizes and communicates knowledge. Writes textbooks and historical works. Teaches and nurtures. Keeps cultural values alive. Sensitive and supportive adviser.
Wants Others To . . .	Take the initiative in a quiet way. Give them a chance to respond. Listen to their thoughts and ideas. Take the lead in making decisions. Include them in the action.

Pattern IV

Lead Strengths	Thinking	Theoretical Thinking	Independent Risking
Supporting Strengths	Risking	Practical Thinking	Dependent Risking
Flex-Patterns	VIII	II	III
Personality Characteristics	Contemplative, intense, reflective, persistent, introspective, self-sufficient, philosophical, individualistic, insightful, inventive, earnest, experimental, perceptive, serious, ingenious **An intuitive thinker — concentrates deeply on one thing at a time.**		
Relationship Strengths	Focus of attention on own thoughts. Follows ideas rather than people. Works out problems alone. Reserved and private. Selective in choosing friendships. Reticent in social situations.		
Vocational Strengths	Has original ideas. Creates new products. Takes initiative to explore and invent. Catalyst for change. "Cut and try" inventor.		
Wants Others To . . .	Be thoughtful and reserved. Ask for their thoughts and ideas. Give them time to think. Respect their privacy. Let them make their own decisions.		

Pattern V

Lead Strengths	Risking	Practical Thinking	Dependent Risking
Supporting Strengths	Thinking	Theoretical Thinking	Independent Risking
Flex-Patterns	I	VI	VII

Personality Characteristics	Outgoing, giving, friendly, helpful, sociable, flexible, cordial, gregarious, fashionable, cooperative, generous, accommodating, caring, adaptable, empathetic, big-hearted, supportive, likeable **Facilitates communication — easy to talk to.**
Relationship Strengths	Focus of attention on other person. Seeks to please others. Wants to interact and be involved. Gets feelings out on the table. Draws people into relationships. Avoids making enemies.
Vocational Strengths	Coordinates practical projects. Works in "helping" professions. Does personnel work. Warm counselor. "Soft-sell" salesperson.
Wants Others To . . .	Give recognition — every day. Show warm appreciation. Accept their help with gratitude. Trust them. Let them "talk out" problems.

Pattern VI

Lead Strengths	Risking	Theoretical Thinking	Dependent Risking
Supporting Strengths	Thinking	Practical Thinking	Independent Risking
Flex-Patterns	III	V	VIII

Personality Characteristics	Diplomatic, humorous, gracious, cheerful, hospitable, soft-hearted, sympathetic, expressive, open, liberal, responsive, idealistic, compassionate, hopeful, warm, affectionate, trusting, demonstrative **Gives self to relationships — wears heart on sleeve.**
Relationship Strengths	Focus of attention on relationships. Trusts others. Shows feelings openly. Seeks "closeness" and "intimacy". Makes others feel warm and accepted. Leaves self unprotected and exposed.
Vocational Strengths	Entertains people. Works in public relations. Active in volunteer organizations. Diplomat. Performer.
Wants Others To . . .	Be receptive. Show warmth and compassion. Share feelings. Help them feel good about themselves. Give them compliments.

Pattern VII

Lead Strengths	Risking	Practical Thinking	Independent Risking
Supporting Strengths	Thinking	Theoretical Thinking	Dependent Risking
Flex-Patterns	II	VIII	V

Personality Characteristics	Self-assertive, forceful, decisive, ambitious, action-oriented, vigorous, resourceful, adventurous, enterprising, self-starting, self-confident, competitive, outspoken, active, doer, energetic **Has strong drive to accomplish — stimulated by a challenge.**
Relationship Strengths	Focus of attention on personal goals. Full dedication to winning. Never gives up. Expresses thoughts and feelings. Takes charge. Impatient to get into action.
Vocational Strengths	Takes calculated risks. Gives leadership to practical projects. Starts new ventures. Tackles difficult challenges. Effective in personal sales.
Wants Others To . . .	Respond!! "Don't just sit there — do something, even if it's wrong." Say what you think — come on straight. Give loyalty and active support. "Lead, follow, or get out of the way."

Pattern VIII

Lead Strengths	Risking	Theoretical Thinking	Independent Risking
Supporting Strengths	Thinking	Practical Thinking	Dependent Risking
Flex-Patterns	IV	VII	VI

Personality Characteristics	Dynamic, eloquent, spirited, enthusiastic, convincing, inspirational, dramatic, charismatic, optimistic, persuasive, impulsive, exciting, innovative, imaginative, versatile, colorful, impelling, exuberant **Has vision — stimulates change.**
Relationship Strengths	Focus of attention on own vision. Courage to risk all — "bet the farm". Wants to influence others. Seeks the spotlight. Enlivens relationships. Talks.
Vocational Strengths	Gives dynamic leadership to a "cause". Sells a dream. Promotes an idea. Puts deals together. Public speaker.
Wants Others To . . .	Notice them and react. Show excitement and enthusiasm. Be influenced. Follow them. Be supportive.

3.

Innate Capacities

In the Bi/Polar theory of personality, the second force that contributes to the formation of the human personality is identified as innate capacities. The purpose of this chapter is to define the nature of this force and discuss its role in shaping one's personality.

Our innate capacities and our pattern of core strengths are similar in that both are genetically based. They are the two stable and enduring forces in our personality that determine our natural way of being. These forces come into being at conception and maintain a constant influence on shaping our personalities throughout our lifetimes.

These two stable forces are different in that the pattern of core strengths refers to how the core strengths relate to one another in forming a particular bundle of strengths in the personality core, while innate capacities refers to how much potential strength there is in this bundle compared to other people. In other words, the pattern refers to the shape or configuration of the bundle itself, and innate capacities refers to a measurement of how much strength is there when compared to some outside standard.

In the development of the Bi/Polar System, the focus within the two stable forces has been on the pattern of core strengths — not on innate capacities. As a result, the Bi/Polar System has much less to offer the serious student wanting to learn about innate capacities and how to measure them.

What the Bi/Polar System does offer is a theory of personality that affirms the validity of individual differences in innate capacities and a recognition that these differences produce different personalities. The other possible contribution could come from a better understanding of the basic nature of innate capacities — the understanding that these capacities are actually Bi/Polar in their fundamental nature.

In general psychology, the force of innate capacities is dealt with most fully in studies that deal with individual differences. The principles and disciplines associated with tests and measurements are particularly important. Tests that measure mental abilities, drive, or energy potential would tend to measure what is referred to as innate capacities in the Bi/Polar System.

Mental Abilities

Psychologists have been attempting to identify and measure the mental abilities of people for many years. Much progress has been made: many different kinds of mental abilities have been identified, and many professionally validated tests have been designed to measure them.

Probably the best known and most researched concept in the field of mental capacities is general intelligence. Alfred Benet did the pioneering work in 1905, and intelligence, as a specific capacity, has been studied extensively since that time.

One of the most vexing problems in trying to measure intelligence has been to devise a testing instrument that could measure the power of the brain itself as opposed to the quantity of knowledge it has absorbed. Many of the criticisms of so-called I.Q. tests stem from the recognized difficulty of constructing a valid instrument that measures the innate capacity of the brain itself rather than the fruits of that capacity (knowledge).

The split-brain research of Nobel Prize-winner Roger Sperry and the related theories of the late Aleksandr Luria are providing some new hope to those who are addressing the problems in measuring intelligences. Sperry's research has provided a radical new departure from the methodology that has dominated I.Q. testing since its beginning. The Kaufman Assessment Battery for Children (K-ABC) is a good example of a test using this new methodology.

Kaufman's three-part intelligence test is designed to measure how children process information, not what they already know. The focus is on the difference between sequential and simultaneous information processing. Sequential processing, as Sperry confirmed in his prize-winning experiments, tends to predominate in the brain's left hemisphere and simultaneous processing in the right. In sequential processing, the brain solves a problem by dealing with information one bit at a time (corresponds to practical thinking in Bi/Polar). Contrasted with this, simultaneous processing occurs when one integrates many stimuli at once (corresponds to theoretical thinking in Bi/Polar). It is also assumed that everyone uses both modes of thinking, but some tend toward sequential thinking, and in others simultaneous thinking dominates.

The conclusions reached by Sperry in his split-brain research and the new methodology used in such testing instruments as the K-ABC are very much in harmony with the Bi/Polar concepts and philosophies.

"Drive" or "Energy Potential"

Much less work has been done in an attempt to scientifically measure emotional drive. In recent years, progress has been made in measuring this important variable in our personalities, but much more work needs to be done to clearly identify the nature of "drive" and to measure it in individual people. In the Bi/Polar approach, the assumption is made that the amount of "drive" a person has is an innate capacity, along with general intelligence. It is also assumed that the amount of drive within individuals will be distributed along a normal probability curve in much the same way as intelligence. Beyond this, "drive" seems to have some relationship to the risking strength identified in the Bi/Polar System. The nature of this relationship is not at all clear at this time, and much work needs to be done before the differences and similarities can be clearly identified.

Summary

In the last two chapters, the two stabilizing forces in our personality have been discussed. They have been identified as (1) our pattern of core strengths and (2) our innate capacities. These two forces are composed exclusively of strengths. They are inherently positive, and there is nothing in their nature that may be regarded as negative or destructive to the creative process. Although we all possess the same strengths, we are different in that we have different patterns of these strengths, and we have different amounts of these strengths. The Bi/Polar System has no basis on which to evaluate these differences as either more or less desirable. Each of us has been given our own unique bundle of strengths. We need to feel good about our own bundle, whatever it may be, and through its expression make our own unique contribution to the world.

In the next two chapters, the two dynamic forces that produce changes in our personalities will be discussed. They are (1) environment and (2) personal choice. These two forces are not all positive. They may be expressed in constructive ways that release our creative potential, or they may be expressed in negative ways that interfere with and block out our natural creativeness. They are the two forces that determine how our pattern of core strengths and innate capacities are expressed in the world. Through them we enter the growth process that produces our personalities.

4.

Environment

This chapter deals with environmental influences, the third force that produces the human personality. The environment has received much more attention from psychologists and social scientists that have the other three personality forces. It has been investigated more extensively, and much more is known about its specific effects on personality development. The best-known and most widely-accepted psychological systems of our day tend to focus on the effects of the environment. Possibly because of the emphasis given to this force by the professionals, the environment is commonly regarded as the dominant and most influential force that determines our personalities. This chapter presents a different view.

Nature of the Environmental Force

Our environment is composed of external forces that are dynamic and in a constant state of flux. It is the only personality force that is external to us. Our environment is created by outside sources — our own power is limited to how we respond to it.

The environmental force is essentially an agent for change. If we are to continue our existence as individuals and as a species, we must adapt and adjust to the changing conditions in our environment. Our capacity to make flexible and adaptable responses to changing environmental conditions is what enables us to survive.

Our changing environment demands that we exercise our adaptive capacities. In the process, we develop a creative human personality. It is important for our discussion here to note that being creative calls for a flexible, adaptive response to our environment, not a radical change in our basic make-up as individuals. To be more specific, responding creatively to our environment does not require a change in our structured pattern of core strengths or a change in our innate capacities. It simply requires that we express our natural pattern of strengths and innate capacities in adaptive ways that fit the need of the situation.

Broadly speaking, the environmental forces that influence personality development may be classified into two main categories: (1) natural forces and (2) forces that are set in motion by conscious choices made by human beings.

The natural forces in our environment are manifestations of the creative process at work in the universe and, as such, contribute in a positive way to the healthy development of each unique personality. Through the action of these natural forces, we are encouraged to fill our niche in the creative process and make our contribution to the whole. There is nothing negative or destructive about the natural forces in our environment.

In the Bi/Polar System, a destructive force is defined as a force that is inhibitive to the creative process. It is a force that "blocks" or "distorts" the natural processes emanating from the primordial creative force. This potential for turning a natural, positive force into a negative force is born with the advent of personal consciousness — the seat of our personal freedom to make conscious choices. People can make "good" conscious choices that contribute to the creative process, or they can make "bad" choices that are destructive to the process. These good and bad choices made by people create good and bad influences in our environment — influences that either contribute in a positive way to our personality development or are destructive to it.

The influence of particular personal choices can be passed on from generation to generation. This applies to both good choices and bad choices. The difference is that the good choices maintain their influence because they are a living part of the creative process, whereas bad or destructive choices, although they may live a long time, will eventually die because they are not a contributing part of the creative process.

How the Environmental Force Influences Personality Development

The environmental force begins its influence at the conception of an individual and is a continuing influence throughout the lifetime of that person. Although this influence varies at different times in a person's life, it is always there to some extent. We couldn't become individuals without an environment.

The natural environmental forces are wholly positive, tending to guide us in expressing our strengths constructively as part of the creative process. The environment created by others is a mixture of good and bad influences. Some are positive contributing influences to our personality development; others are inhibitive and destructive.

The influences coming from others are especially potent in the development of our attitudes, value systems, and self-concepts. The extent to which we develop these factors in our early years is largely dependent upon how other people relate to us, especially those who are closest to us. Since we are all exposed to a mixture of good and bad influences coming from other people, these factors will always have some negative elements within them. The people who have a rich and nourishing environment with few negatives tend to develop more positive attitudes, sound value systems, and healthy self-concepts. Those who are exposed to an environment in which there are many negatives tend to develop more negative attitudes, inadequate value systems, and destructive self-concepts.

The attitudes, value systems, and self-concepts we develop in our formative years are not set for life, however. They can be changed by two of the personality forces: a changing environment and our personal choices. A new environment with more positive influences and good personal choices about how we think and behave tends to heal the wounds inflicted by earlier negative influences. Although the scars made by these early negatives will probably remain on our psyches, the wounds themselves can be healed with the help of a good environment and good personal choices.

Although all of us are affected to some extent by the environment that surrounds us, some seem to be affected more than others. Those who lean toward dependent risking in their core pattern of strengths tend to be influenced more by environmental forces. Although they can and do exercise their power of personal choice, their environment tends to be the dominant influence in their personality development. For those who lean toward independent risking, the independent choices they make tend to be the dominant force in their personality development. They are still influenced by their environment, but their personal choices make a large difference in their development.

Not only does the influence of environment tend to vary with different individuals, but it also varies at different times with the same individual. At one time, the environment can be in the foreground and have the dominant influence on one's thinking and behavior. At other times, it may recede into the background and have the least effect. The environmental force is always there and having some effect, but the intensity of its influence is a dynamic variable, changing from moment to moment.

Limitations of the Environmental Force

In the Bi/Polar theory of personality, equal weight is given to the four personality forces. From a theoretical point of view, any of the four forces can have the dominant influence on a particular person. There is nothing within the forces themselves that would automatically or consistently make one more influential that another. Since the actual influence of each of the forces varies with different individuals and at different times within the same individual, it is important for us to keep an open mind regarding the relative influence of these forces on a particular person. The Bi/Polar theory allows us to keep this open mind and helps us to resist the temptation to focus too sharply on only one or two of the forces and neglect the others.

Although each of the four personality forces is limited by the other three, in this section the focus is on the limitations of the environmental force. I am focusing on the environment here because of the historical tendency to overemphasize its importance and consequently to de-emphasize the importance of the other three forces. My intent is to challenge the practice of overemphasizing the influence of environmental factors in personality development and neglecting our pattern of core strengths, innate capacities, and personal choice. The intent is not to depreciate the influence of environment, but rather to place it on an equal par with the others and give all four equal status.

The influence of our environment is limited by the stable structure inherent in our pattern of core strengths. The stabilizing forces that are a part of the creative process create a stable bundle of strengths at the core of every personality. This stabilizing force tends to keep the structure of our core pattern intact, regardless of the changes in our outside environment. With continued advancement in genetic engineering, more skill will likely be developed in changing genetic material. It is conceivable that, in the future, ways may be found to alter the genetic structures that produce a particular pattern of core strengths. Even if this is done, however, it will not lessen the stabilizing power of the new genetic structure on our personality. The force will simply be expressed through a new, stable, and structured form. We may alter the forms through which the stabilizing forces are expressed, but the forces themselves remain untouched.

The influence of our environment is also limited by the stabilizing forces in nature which create the genetic structures giving uniqueness to our innate capacities. Again, genetic engineering may find effective ways to alter the genetic materials associated with innate capacities, but, even if this is done, the stabilizing force will manifest itself through these changed genetic structures and still bring stability and constancy to our personalities. The important point to remember is that stability and structure are just as much parts of our personalities as are dynamism and change.

Our freedom to make personal choices is a third distinct limitation to the influence of environmental forces. We have some power to choose how a particular environment will influence us. An example comes to mind that illustrates this power.

In my work as a consulting psychologist to management, I frequently interview managers in an effort to understand them as individuals. During these interviews, I usually ask them to tell me about the people who have had the greatest influence in their lives. Usually they talk about a person who was a good model for them, or someone who encouraged them in some way. In some instances, however, a very different thing happens — the person I am interviewing talks about a father or mother who set a bad example. Frequently it is a father who was an alcoholic and turned out to be a dismal failure, both as a husband and a father. The surprising thing is that the one I am interviewing learns from the bad example set by his father and turns this negative environment into a positive learning experience. Sometimes the person says he is grateful to his father because he learned what not to do. A negative environment does not automatically have a negative influence — some people, through personal choice, make lemonade out of a lemon.

All psychological systems tend to focus on one or two of the four personality forces. Although the Bi/Polar System recognizes and places an equal value on each of the four forces, our application of the Bi/Polar System tends to focus on two of the forces: our pattern of core strengths and our freedom to make personal choices.

Most of the best-known systems of our day focus on the two dynamic forces: the environmental force and our freedom to make personal choices. One of the most popular — behaviorism — focuses exclusively on the effects of the environment. The danger inherent in focusing on one or two of the forces is that this can be interpreted to mean these one or two forces are consistently more important and influential in forming the personality. This tends to create a value system in which one or two of the forces are valued above the others.

It is this philosophical position with which Bi/Polar takes issue. When any of the four forces are depreciated or disregarded, the result is a view that is destructive to normal and healthy personality development. As an example, when the influence of environment is depreciated, it lessens our awareness of the important influence we can have on each other through social interaction.

The destructive effects of overemphasizing the environmental force come from the de-emphasis and neglect of the influences that come from the other three forces. When our natural pattern of core strengths is disregarded, everyone looks the same. Locke, an English philosopher, expressed this view many years ago in the statement: "At birth a person is a tabula rasa and through experience becomes whatever is writ on this blank sheet". In other words, the environment is the sole determinant of our individuality. It is hard to imagine how much destructiveness has resulted from such a statement.

When our unique bundle of core strengths is disregarded, we lose our stamp of self-identify as a person. We become copies of each other rather than our original and unique selves. We become pieces of putty to be molded into shapes that fit someone else's idea of what we should be, rather than a unique person with a destiny and a particular vocation to fulfill. We lose our individuality and our dignity as significant human beings.

Summary

This chapter has presented a discussion of the environmental force — one of the four forces that produces a healthy personality. Environment was defined as an external force that either contributes to healthy personality development or is destructive to it. Whatever destructive elements may be in the environment were seen as coming from the bad personal choices made by people. Environmental influences were seen as having a major effect on the formation of our attitudes, value systems, and self-concepts.

This chapter also presented a discussion on the limitations of the environmental force, primarily to counteract the overemphasis placed on the environmental force by the most influential psychological systems of our day. The intent was not to depreciate the important place of the environment on our personality development, but to place it on an equal par with the other three forces.

5.

Personal Choice

This chapter describes the fourth and last force that determines the human personality: our power to make personal choices. It has a special relationship to the other three personality forces in that it is produced by them. Our power to make personal choices is the fruit of the creative interaction of our core strengths with each other and a nourishing environment.

The force of personal choice is similar to the environmental force in that it produces changes — particularly a change in the direction of one's thinking and behavior. It is different from the environmental force in that personal choice is internal and controlled by the person, whereas the environment is external and controlled by outside sources.

Nature of Personal Choice

The power of personal choice became a force in the world when the evolutionary process produced the dawn of human consciousness, thus giving human beings the power to make conscious choices. It appears to be a uniquely human characteristic. As far as can be told, no other organisms in the world have reached the level of development which would produce the extent of personal awareness required to create consciousness at least as we know it.

As the polar strengths in our creative core feed each other, they produce an increasing degree of personal awareness. When this awareness reaches a particular level, we experience personal consciousness, and this consciousness is what creates our freedom to make personal choices. We don't choose this freedom; it is thrust on us by the creative interaction of the strengths within us. Although we are not responsible for the creation of our freedom to choose, we are accountable for the personal choices we make after we receive the power to choose.

When we develop consciousness and gain the power to make personal choices, we become conscious participants in the creation process. This is both an opportunity and a responsibility. The personal choices we make either contribute to the creative process at work in the world, or they work against it. This is what defines good and bad personal choices — good choices feed and enhance the creative process; bad choices distort and restrict the process.

Our power of personal choice gives us the ability to choose our focus of attention and to control our behavior. Although this ability is limited by the other three personality forces, it is still a very real power in our lives and in our development. In many ways, this power to make conscious choices appears to be an evolutionary development that enables us to respond in more flexible and adaptive ways to our environment. For example, if we focus our attention on the creative process, we can understand better how it works, and, by directing our behavior in line with its demands, we can participate more fully in it.

How Personal Choices Influence Personality Development

Our personal choices make a difference in who we become. If we make good choices that are in harmony with the creative process, we tend to mature and develop a healthy personality. If we make bad choices that go against the process, our personality tends to deteriorate and become a destructive force.

Our personal choices also make a difference in how we affect the people around us. If we make good choices, we tend to encourage their development into healthy personalities. If we make bad choices, we tend to become a negative and destructive influence on others.

Much of what Bi/Polar has to offer comes from its concepts of how the creative process works and the specific choices we must make to participate more fully within it. These specific choices and what we must do to make them is the primary subject matter in Part II (Expressing Your Strengths) and Part IV (Strengthening Your Relationships).

Limitations of the Power of Personal Choice

As with all of the personality forces, the power of personal choice is limited by the power in the other three forces. The influence of our personal choices may be great or it may be small — it depends on the person and the situation. No matter how powerful the influence of our personal choices may become, however, it will never become strong enough to totally overcome or do away with the power in the other three personality forces.

Our power to change through personal choice is limited by the stabilizing power of the genetic structures that give form and intensity to our core pattern of strengths. We cannot become anything we want to become simply by thinking and changing our behavior. We can modify the ways in which our pattern is expressed in the world, but we cannot, through the power of personal choice, do away with the stabilizing power in our pattern of core strengths.

Our power to make personal choices is also limited by the forces that create our environment. Within limits, we can modify the form and structure of our environment, we can remove ourselves from one environment and place ourselves in another, and we can choose how we will respond to a particular environment. However, the forces that actually create our environment are, by and large, beyond our control. Most of our ability to impact our environment comes through the exercise of our personal choice.

Transition

Up to this point, we have been focusing on the fundamentals of the Bi/Polar System. In the Introduction, the Bi/Polar Concept and its undergirding assumptions were discussed. In Part I, the first chapter presented the Bi/Polar theory of personality, and the next four chapters discussed each of the four forces that produce the human personality. For the most part, the basic concepts of the Bi/Polar System have been presented. Parts II, III, and IV will turn our attention to how these concepts may be put to practical use.

Part II deals with personality development — how we grow and mature as individuals. This part describes the growth process, discusses our tendencies and temptations, shows how we can become polarized, and, finally, identifies the growth choices we can make to take us toward personal maturity.

Part III is about understanding other people and the relationship dynamics between people. This part describes what is going on in a creative relationship between two people, discusses four distinct relationship tendencies human beings experience, and identifies the relationship characteristics each pattern tends to produce.

Part IV is about strengthening relationships — our one-to-one relationships with other people. It gives specific guidelines on how we may go about strengthening our relationship with a particular person. The final segment of Part IV deals with pattern relationships — how people tend to relate to each other according to their patterns of core strengths. There are 36 different pattern relationships described. In each description, the typical relationship problems that normally occur between the two patterns are identified, and suggestions are given for how to deal with these problems and strengthen the relationship.

II.

Expressing Your Strengths

6.

The Growth Process

The original impetus for the development of Bi/Polar came from my efforts to understand the process of growth (see Introduction). My desire to understand this process has remained the central driving force behind the development of the system. The Bi/Polar Concept was the first fruit of these efforts, and it continues to be the corner-stone concept for understanding the growth process. The under-standing of growth presented here is grounded in the assumptions and hypotheses presented in the earlier discussion on the Bi/Polar Concept. My intent in this chapter is to build on the Bi/Polar Concept and show you how the growth process works in personality development. The growth process and the creative process are interchangeable terms in the Bi/Polar System — they point toward the same process. Although I have chosen to use the growth process in this presentation, the creative process could be substituted without altering any of the basic concepts being discussed.

Fundamental Forces in the Growth Process

Understanding the Bi/Polar concept of growth requires us to distin-guish between the activity of the core strength itself and what is produced by that activity. In the basic pair of core strengths, our total thinking activities produce mental perceptions, and our total risking activities produce feelings. In the thinking pair, practical thinking activity results in perception of reality — we see the facts, how things really are. On the other hand, theoretical thinking activity yields perceptions of possibilities, and enables us to understand ideas and have a vision of how things could be.

In the risking pair of strengths, risking dependence allows us to experience the support and approval of others and build warm relationships. When we risk independence, we experience personal freedom and power and develop self-confidence. The six core strengths and the particular product each strength produces are summarized in Figure 5.

The six core strengths and their products are the fundamental forces that power the growth process. The core strengths themselves are continuously active and, for the most part, unconscious. The activity of these core strengths produces our conscious awareness. We are conscious of our mental perceptions and our feelings, but largely unaware of the activity that produces these perceptions and feelings.

The fundamental forces in the growth process are wholly positive — there are no negative forces within the process itself. A person may relate to these fundamental forces in a negative way, but the forces themselves are inherently positive — each force makes its own positive contribution to the process.

How the Growth Process Results in Personal Growth

The growth process works within us through the creative interaction between the two polar strengths in each pair. The activity of the polar strengths is natural and automatic. Each strength produces its own natural fruit and feeds on the fruit produced by its opposite polar strength. This Bi/Polar interaction allows for the increase we experience in growth. As each strength produces more fruit, more raw material is available for its opposite strength to use in producing even more of its own fruit — what increases in growth is the product

Your Creative Core

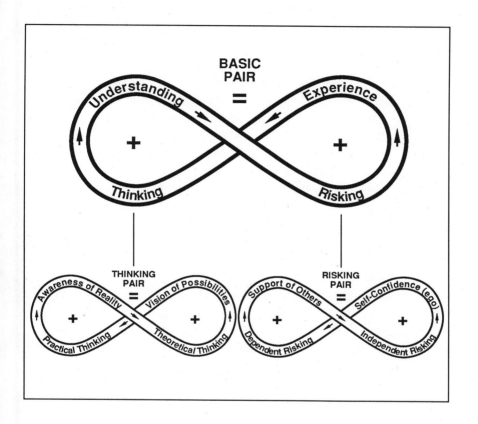

Figure 5

or fruit of the strength, not the core strength itself. This is in harmony with our original assumption that our pattern of core strengths and our innate capacities are constants in personality development.

In the growth process, both strengths in a Bi/Polar pair remain active and become more productive through their interdependent feeding relationship. In other words, when we grow, we gather strengths on both sides of a Bi/Polar pair. We have clearer perceptions and experience more courage to risk. We perceive reality more clearly and are more aware of alternatives. We experience stronger relationships with others and feel more self-confidence. This approach to growth affirms the idea that the two polar strengths operate together — each one fuels the other. If the activity of either one is blocked, it reduces the fruit both can produce. The two polar strengths either *grow* together or *decay* together — one cannot operate by itself.

This view of growth is contrary to the way most of us tend to think about how we can become stronger on one side of a Bi/Polar pair. For example, most people would accept the following statement as true: "One becomes more independent by being less dependent; one becomes more practical by being less theoretical; one becomes more of a risker by being less of a thinker". Sometimes this negative approach is expressed in personal evaluations such as "You are too dependent" or "You are too theoretical".

There are at least two things wrong with statements such as these — they imply that (1) a good strength is really a weakness and (2) you grow by blocking and fighting against a natural strength.

In contrast with the negative approach described above, Bi/Polar takes a positive approach that affirms the strength as a positive value and encourages a natural expression of all our strengths as essential for personal growth. What allows us to take this positive approach is the concept that distinguishes the activity of a core strength from the product this activity produces. Growth does require that we give up something and make sacrifices. Healthy, growing people learn that we must pay the price — there are no free lunches.

Conventional wisdom recognizes that we must give up something in growth, and that is what is behind the idea that we grow by blocking a strength. The mistake is in the belief that we give up the activity of a strength. The truth is, what we actually give up in growth is the fruit of the strength, not the natural activity of the strength itself.

Here is an illustration of how we grow by sacrificing the fruit of a strength rather than consciously blocking the activity of a strength. Let's take the people who have a natural lead strength in dependence. Out of being themselves, they naturally develop support and approval from others. This support and approval is a valued fruit of dependent risking and usually means a good deal to the people who tend to naturally favor dependent risking over independent risking.

It is also natural for people who have dependence as a lead strength to develop a felt need for more self-confidence — the fruit of independent risking. In using the Bi/Polar approach, we encourage those people to affirm their dependent strength as a good strength that produces valuable results, and not to consciously fight against or block out their natural inclination to be dependent. We avoid saying "You are too dependent" or "You have to stop being so dependent on other people". Rather, we take the positive approach and suggest that they consciously shift emphasis to a more active expression of their independent strength.

We also try to help them understand that becoming more active in expressing independence may require them to give up some of the support and approval they are now receiving from others, but they must stand ready to make this sacrifice. We give this advice with the conviction that standing ready to sacrifice the support and approval of others can free up a stronger expression of independence and result in an experience of personal growth. Their growth is manifested in their behavior through a stronger expression of both dependence and independence. They also experience more self-confidence and more support and approval from others — the fruits of independence and dependence. By sacrificing the support and approval of others to the process, they actually receive more support and approval in the future. To stay in the process, they must also sacrifice this additional support and approval that they receive in the future. The goal is to live in the process, not to indulge ourselves in our fruits, and this requires a continuing sacrifice of the fruits that we produce.

Participation in the Growth Process

The primordial force that creates all existence expresses itself in the growth process described in the preceding section. As individuals, we are created by this force — we are natural participants in the process. We are not the process ourselves, nor do we create on our own apart from the process. The process was here before we came into being as individuals and will continue to exist after we die. We were created to give all we have to the process.

Although we are natural participants in the growth process, with the advent of human consciousness our participation took on a new dimension. Now it becomes a matter of human choice — both our own personal choice and the choices made by other people. With the emergence of our own personal consciousness, we must choose our participation in the growth process. No longer is it simply "natural" and "automatic" — now we must make some hard choices and be willing to "pay the price". Once this power to choose is thrust upon us, there is no turning back — we cannot choose "not to choose". Any effort to get rid of consciousness is still a personal choice that affects our participation in the process.

The conscious choices we make are either good or bad. They are good choices when they contribute to the growth process, and they are bad when they fight against or block the process. The better we understand the process and our role in it, the better equipped we can be to make good choices. The remainder of this section is devoted to a discussion of three basic choices that determine the extent of our participation in the growth process and the development of our individual potential.

Our first choice is between being ourselves or trying to be something we aren't. The choice to be true to our natural way of being makes us participants in the growth process. The choice to reject our natural way and try to be something different makes us phony and takes us out of the process.

All of us have our own unique bundle of strengths at the core, and this bundle of core strengths gives us a niche to fill in the creative process. The constant demand of the growth process is for us to "fill our niche" by contributing in ways that fit our natural talents and strengths.

In Bi/Polar, the eight patterns of core strengths are used as conceptual tools to help people identify their natural way of being. What makes us participants in the growth process is the choice to express our pattern, whatever it may be. Although the Bi/Polar philosophy holds that the eight patterns have equal value and all are required by the creative process, this is not necessarily the value system held by the society in which we live. In most societies, some patterns are valued more highly than others, and the favored pattern can vary from one society to another. If our own natural pattern happens to be in disfavor in our own society, we are under a good deal of pressure to show a different pattern and hide our real selves. This is a hard choice: to be accepted by others, we must be something other than what we really are; to be participants in the growth process, we must be ourselves and risk the rejection of others.

This problem also crops up in sexual stereotypes — men are expected to show certain patterns of strengths, and women are expected to show other patterns. When people discover their natural pattern doesn't fit the stereotype held by their culture, they have to make a painful choice about their behavior. On the one hand, they are rejected if they don't fit the mold, and on the other hand, they lose themselves if they try to be something they aren't.

How does a person solve this dilemma in a creative way? I will give a short answer here and reserve a more complete answer for the discussion in Chapter 9 entitled Personal Growth. The short answer is that people having this problem need to go ahead and be themselves and risk the rejection that is likely to come, but, at the same time, be flexible enough to use their supporting strengths to deal with the problems caused by being themselves.

Our second choice has to do with being flexible and deliberately emphasizing the strength required by differing situations. In a sense, it is the polar opposite of being true to ourselves. Here we choose to be true to a situation and express the strength that will further the growth process in that particular situation. This adaptation is a creative response to our environment.

I would like to use a personal example to illustrate the nature of this choice. My natural way of being is to lead with theoretical thinking and emphasize theory rather than the practical application of the theory. When I started giving seminars on the Bi/Polar System about 24 years ago, I gave my presentations in my natural way — highly theoretical and conceptual. I recall presenting a seminar to a group of bank executives during these early years. After the seminar was over, the bank president confided in me with this observation, "Jay, I really think you have some good ideas, but it seems to me that you overkill them".

He got my attention with this comment, and I began to reflect on my presentation. It became painfully obvious that my lectures were highly theoretical and very abstract. For the practical manager, my presentations were probably dull and boring. My friend was saying to me that I needed to be more practical and talk about how these ideas could be put to practical use in solving some of their management problems. Now I had a choice to make: I could continue to emphasize theory out of my natural leanings, or I could adapt to their needs and bring more practicality to my presentations. Since my livelihood was dependent upon my having successful seminars, I decided to change my lectures by giving more practical examples and talking about ways to put the concepts to practical use in solving their people problems.

Immediately this enlivened my seminars and made them more effective and useful. In addition, shifting emphasis to my practical thinking strength had the effect of giving me more facts and information about reality. In turn, this factual data gave me more raw material to use in developing even better theory. My adaptive response put me in the growth process. I could have chosen to blame them for not having enough interest in theory and continued to overkill my ideas, but I suspect that would have resulted in my finally giving my lectures to empty rooms.

At first blush it may appear that the choice to be one's natural self and to emphasize one's supporting strengths is in conflict—that you can't do both. However, in the Bi/Polar approach, this is precisely what mature people do well. The flavor of their natural way is unmistakable and always there, but, at the same time, they show flexibility in expressing the strength required by the situation, even if it happens to be one of their supporting strengths.

Our third choice has to do with the sacrifice we must make when we choose to be ourselves, and when we choose to be flexible and adapt to the situation. In both instances, we must give up something that has great personal value to us. The growth process requires that we give up the fruits of our strengths and let them be used up in the creative process. Our choice is either to give them up to the process or to hang on to them for our personal use. If we choose to give up these valued fruits and invest them in the creative process, we become participants in the process. If we choose to indulge ourselves in these fruits and refuse to let them go, we take ourselves out of the process.

This choice to sacrifice our fruits is painful because it involves giving up those things that have the most value to us. Take me, as an example. My best products are my ideas (coming from my natural lead strength — theoretical thinking) and my self-confidence or ego (coming from my lead strength in independent risking). My ideas are very dear to me, and I have a tremendous ego investment in them. The hard choice I must make if I am to be involved in the creative process is to put these ideas out into the world and let them be tested by reality. The threat I feel is that my ideas may be wrong and found wanting, and, if that turns out to be true, I lose something that has great value to me, and my ego is bruised.

But the growth process demands that I make this sacrifice. If I indulge myself in my ideas and refuse to let them be used up in the creative process, I become polarized on my own ideas and take myself out of the growth process. Not only do I take myself out of the process, but I become involved in a process that is the opposite of growth — a process of psychological decay. On the other hand, if I choose to make the sacrifice, I put myself in the growth process and position myself to have more practical effectiveness and to have new and even better ideas in the future.

7.

Personal Tendencies

A personal tendency is an inclination to favor a particular polar strength. We all have tendencies. They are a natural part of being human. They need to be understood, affirmed, and expressed. They also need to be dealt with when they get us into trouble and cause us pain. In the Bi/Polar approach, we do not seek to get rid of our personal tendencies. If we did, we would get rid of ourselves and our distinctiveness as individual persons. We should seek only to become aware of our tendencies and gain skill in dealing with the problems they bring about.

We have two kinds of tendencies: (1) natural tendencies and (2) learned tendencies. Our natural tendencies come from our core pattern of strengths. We naturally favor our lead strengths, and this bias will express itself naturally in our personal tendencies. Many of our tendencies come from our natural way of being — how we are put together at the core.

Our learned tendencies come from our interactions with our environment, particularly with other people. Although we have been taught many valuable and good things by our parents and the society that nurtured us, much of what we have learned has been imperfect, incomplete, and one-sided. Other people have given us many of our prejudices, a good deal of inaccurate information, and a number of wrong ideas. We all experience many distortions in our personal value system because of what we have been taught by others. Many of our tendencies to regard one polar strength as more valuable than another have come from a poorly conceived value system we have picked up from other people.

Sometimes a learned tendency can be in opposition to a natural tendency. Here is an example which illustrates this fact. A professor at a southwestern university used the Bi/Polar concepts to discover he had the Pattern III combination of natural lead strengths. He naturally favored theoretical thinking, but felt that he actually favored practical thinking. In reflecting upon his earlier years, it became apparent that he had a natural tendency to favor theoretical thinking, but the West Texas culture in which he grew up so depreciated theory and put so much emphasis on practicality that he had developed a learned tendency to favor practicality.

Developing this learned tendency to favor practicality did not change his basic nature, but it did rob him of some of his sense of self-worth. As he became acquainted with the concepts of Bi/Polar and developed a greater appreciation for his natural bent toward theoretical thinking, his sense of self-worth increased, and he became more productive by feeling more free to express his theoretical thinking. The learned tendency to depreciate his theoretical thinking will always be with him, but its negative effect has been lessened.

The most mature and effective people are aware of their tendencies and usually develop a sense of humor regarding them. I first became aware of this through my interviews with business managers. During these interviews, I would usually ask these executives to tell me the most important lesson they had learned during their life. I discovered that those who were the most mature would rather quickly tell me about what they had learned.

A typical example was a lesson in which people had learned the importance of listening to other people. Usually they wanted to talk about how they had learned this lesson, and, in doing so, they would talk about their tendency — in this case, their tendency to talk when they should be listening. Then a surprising thing would frequently happen. As they talked about their tendency, they would smile, get a twinkle in their eye, and sometimes give a little chuckle. Sometimes, they would say, "You know, I don't know if I have really learned that lesson, because I still talk too much and don't listen enough".

Having this kind of experience over and over again with psychologically healthy people brought me to my first realization that mature, growing people do have natural tendencies they really never get rid of. What they learn to do is to accept these tendencies as a natural part of who they are and develop skill in dealing with them when they cause problems. All this seems to involve a relaxed acceptance of their tendencies and an ability to laugh at themselves.

Figure 6 presents a list of common tendencies normal, healthy people experience. As you read these tendencies, you probably will find that you experience a number of them. During our seminars on Bi/Polar, we ask the participants to read this list of tendencies and circle those they feel fit them. Most people circle from 5 to 15 tendencies.

We enter the creative process by being ourselves — by being who we were created to be as unique, imperfect, out-of-balance persons. In this way, we find our place and make our own unique contribution to the whole. We are being ourselves when we express our natural tendencies. So the first step in entering the growth process is to follow our natural tendencies. Mature people go ahead and show who they are by following their natural tendencies, in spite of the realization that at some point they will develop a problem with the outside world. In other words, healthy, growing people go through life "at a tilt", and this is what keeps them vital and effective.

The second step in living creatively is to deal effectively with the pains and problems that naturally come to us as a result of following our natural tendencies. Our awareness of the problems our tendencies can cause and our skill in dealing creatively with these problems is just as much a part of our maturity as is being true to ourselves.

We can polarize on either of these two steps and take ourselves out of the creative process. We can become so intent on being ourselves

Common Tendencies

Tendency to . . .

1. . . . *talk* when it's time to be listening.
2. . . . *avoid confrontation and conflict* when it's time to express real thoughts and feelings.
3. . . . *say "yes"* when it's time to say "no".
4. . . . *withdraw into own self-sufficiency* when it's time to draw on the strengths of others.
5. . . . *imagine the possibilities* when it's time to get the facts.
6. . . . *wait for the other person to make the first move* when it's time to take the initiative.
7. . . . *compete with others* when it's time to be cooperative.
8. . . . *hold on to established ways* when it's time to change and try new things.
9. . . . *keep emotionally involved* when it's time to back off and be more objective.
10. . . . *go along with others* when it's time to go own way.
11. . . . *think about the problems* when it's time to look for solutions.
12. . . . *make the decision* when it's time to think more before deciding.
13. . . . *hold feelings inside* when it's time to express them more openly.
14. . . . *drive hard to accomplish own goals and ambitions* when it's time to find out how others are thinking and feeling.
15. . . . *think about theory* when it's time to be practical.
16. . . . *depend on others* when it's time to be more independent and self-sufficient.
17. . . . *do things personally* when it's time to trust others to do them.
18. . . . *be sympathetic and supportive* when it's time to require others to be more responsible.
19. . . . *change things* when it's time to hold steady and keep things the way they are.
20. . . . *emphasize the realities* when it's time to emphasize the possibilities.
21. . . . *be impatient* when it's time to be more understanding of others.
22. . . . *do things that please others* when it's time to pay more attention to own needs and desires.
23. . . . *be quiet and listen* when it's time to speak out.
24. . . . *take risks* when it's time to be more conservative and take fewer chances.
25. . . . *speculate about future possibilities* when it's time to look at present realities.
26. . . . *think own thoughts* when it's time to listen to what others are saying.
27. . . . *analyze the problem* when it's time to take action.
28. . . . *assertively express thoughts and feelings* when it's time to be more reserved and quiet.
29. . . . *be tolerant of others* when it's time to be more firm.
30. . . . *be practical and realistic* when it's time to be more imaginative.

Figure 6

that we fail to develop skill in being flexible and adapting to our environment. On the other hand, we can become so flexible and adaptable that we lose ourselves. When we continue to do one without the other, we enter a process of psychological decay. This process tends to feed on itself and become increasingly destructive and painful until we make the painful choices required to break polarization.

Chapter 8 describes this process of polarization and how we experience its destructive effects.

8.

Polarization

Although Bi/Polar is basically a positive psychology that views strengths as the fundamental building blocks of the personality, it does affirm the reality of negative and destructive forces in human life. In the Bi/ Polar System, these negative forces come into existence with the advent of human consciousness — the source of our power to make conscious choices about how we think and behave. The nature of these negative and destructive forces is understood through the concept of polarization, the subject matter of this chapter.

Although we will be dealing with the negative and destructive in this chapter, I would not want this discussion to give the impression that proven therapeutic techniques have been developed to use Bi/ Polar with people who are severely disabled, mentally or emotionally. The concept of polarization presented here has gradually emerged out of my experiences working with psychologically healthy people. I am not trained nor have I practiced as a clinical psychologist or psychiatrist. On occasion, I have found myself in a professional relationship with a person who appears to be in need of therapy. When this happens, I refer this person to a professional who is competent to deal with illness. I am hopeful that the basic concepts of Bi/Polar, including those regarding polarization, can make a contribution to a better understanding of what may be going on within a person who is severely disturbed psychologically, but, at this point, the techniques for its successful application to mental and emotional illness have not been developed.

The Creative Process Within

Our core strengths naturally interact and feed each other creatively in an orderly process. This creative interaction between our polar strengths goes on all the time, as long as we are alive. Let's look at this process as it occurs naturally in our creative core.

Although we may start with any of our core strengths, for the sake of illustration, let's start with practical thinking. As our practical thinking strength is active, we become aware of a problem in reality. This automatically stimulates an emphasis on our theoretical thinking to look for a possible solution. These two kinds of thinking, working creatively together, produce a clear perception of the problem and a concept of what we need to do to solve it. This creative perception gives us confidence, and this confidence gives us courage to move into action.

Let's speculate about how the process may work on the risking side. We may start with an expression of independence. In expressing independence, we separate from others and experience a sense of personal freedom and self-worth. Before long, however, we experience this separation as a pain and feel a need to be related to other human beings. Out of this need, we seek to be with other people. In these relationships, our dependent risking strength becomes more active, and its expression results in an experience of support and approval from others. Out of the creative interaction of independence and dependence, we experience both more self-worth and stronger supporting relationships from others. This gives us more basic confidence that allows us to face the reality of problems more directly and dream bigger dreams.

Although this is a somewhat simplistic description of a very complex process, I hope it communicates the idea that the creative process is going on naturally within us and that we need only to make the conscious choices that keep our strengths naturally interacting and contributing to this creative process.

Polarization

Every human being is creative at the core. The positive strengths in the personality core naturally feed each other in a continuous process of creation. How do negatives enter into this process? They enter when one of our strengths in a Bi/Polar pair is blocked. This blockage sets up a process of psychological decay within the individual that becomes increasingly painful with the passage of time. This process is referred to as polarization. We get stuck on one side and continue to emphasize one strength in a Bi/Polar pair while, at the same time, blocking the expression of strength in its polar opposite.

There are two forces that take us toward polarization. One force comes from the negative influences in our environment. The other comes from our own natural out-of-balance nature as human beings.

One of the most common negative environmental influences is that of being taught a value system in which one of our core strengths is depreciated or perhaps even regarded as a negative. This negative view of one of our positive strengths tends to cause us to block its expression and, to that extent, take us out of the creative process and toward polarization. The negative influences in our environment that tend to take us toward polarization are very important, and becoming aware of them can be helpful in our efforts to deal creatively with them. In spite of the importance of becoming aware of these negative environmental influences, the focus in the Bi/Polar System is on the personal choices we may make after we become aware of the influence our environment is having on us.

Our own out-of-balance nature is manifested most basically in our core pattern of strengths. It is natural for us to favor our lead strengths and express these strengths more strongly than we do our supporting strengths. This being the case, we tend to be more aware of the good fruits coming from our lead strengths, and, out of this awareness, we tend to polarize more frequently on the fruits of our lead strengths.

Let me give a personal example. Since one of my natural lead strengths is independent risking, I have a tendency to experience and enjoy the values of being alone. Because of this, I am tempted to withdraw from other people. To say it in another way, I enjoy the values of being alone so much that I am tempted to disregard or depreciate the values of being involved with other people. On the other hand, a person who has natural lead strength in dependent risking may have an opposite tendency and temptation. They may enjoy the values of being with people so much that they are tempted to avoid being alone.

I do not want to give the impression that we tend to polarize only on the fruits of our lead strengths. The fact is, we can polarize on any of our strengths — even if they are our supporting strengths. Our environmental situation may place such a demand on the expression of our supporting strengths that we become more aware of their good fruits and, as a result, have a tendency to polarize on our supporting strengths.

We can also polarize on one side of a Bi/Polar pair, then make the shift and become polarized on the opposite side at a later time. We can shift back and forth, alternately polarizing on one then the other — never really blending the strengths in creative interaction. When this happens, the two strengths become disassociated and function separately, rather than as a creative whole. This alternating shift from one strength to its opposite without the integrity of blending may be one explanation of what is going on in some types of personality disorders (particularly in the disorder that has come to be known as bipolar).

The Results of Polarization

Our negative feelings and distorted perceptions come out of the polarization process. Since we live in an environment that has some negative influences, and we all have natural tendencies that take us into the early stages of polarization, it is normal to experience some negative feelings and distorted perceptions. This is human nature.

However, it is the extent of polarization that determines our maturity and quality of life. The more polarized we become, the more we experience such negative feelings as: depression, fear, guilt, anxiety, resentment, hostility, jealousy, inferiority, and despair. Not only do our negative feelings become more intense as polarization deepens but our perceptions become even more distorted. As our negative feelings and distorted perceptions intensify, we experience a corresponding increase in the pain associated with them. In turn, the increasing pain of polarization becomes a motivating force that tends to turn us back to creativity and psychological health.

Although the increasing problems and pain associated with the polarization process create a motivating force tending to turn us toward growth, they are never enough to do the job alone. We must sacrifice the fruits on which we are polarized and change our thinking and behavior through a conscious personal choice before we can break polarization. This sacrifice and change of thinking and behavior is what relieves our pain and puts us back in the creative process.

Becoming Polarized on a Basic Strength

Thinking and risking are the two basic strengths in the personality core that together create our existence as individuals. Each requires the other for its own creative fulfillment. Creative thinking requires risk and exposure. Creative risking requires reason and judgment. Neither can be creative without the other.

As we shift emphasis back and forth between thought and action, sometimes we get stuck in one or the other. As individuals, we tend to get stuck more easily on our lead strength. Those who lead in thinking will more easily polarize on thinking than risking. Those who lead in risking will more easily polarize on risking than thinking. Since we can't solve our problems with either thinking or risking alone, getting polarized on either one inevitably leads to failure.

In Figure 7, a spiral of decay is drawn in both the thinking and risking loops, giving a visual image of what happens when we get hung up in either loop. Below each loop, a series of statements describes how we think and behave when we polarize on each of the two strengths.

Six of the common tendencies listed in Figure 6 may be identified as personal tendencies that may take us toward polarization on the thinking strength. They are listed below:

2. *avoid confrontation and conflict* when it's time to face the person directly and express real thoughts and feelings.
6. *wait for the other person to make the first move* when it's time to take the initiative.
8. *hold onto established ways* when it's time to change and try new things.
13. *hold feelings inside* when it is time to express them more openly.
23. *be quiet and listen* when it's time to speak out.
27. *analyze the problem* when it's time to take action.

There are also six common tendencies listed in Figure 6 that may take us toward polarization on the risking strength. They are listed below:

1. *talk* when it's time to be listening.
9. *keep emotionally involved* when it's time to back off and be more objective.
12. *make the decision* when it would be better to think more before deciding.
19. *change things* when it's time to hold steady and keep things the way they are.

Becoming Polarized on a Basic Strength

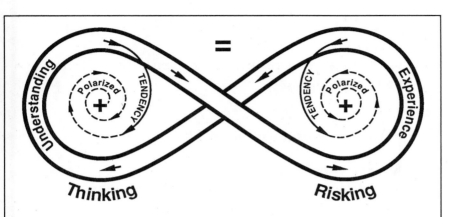

Signs of Becoming Polarized on Thinking	Signs of Becoming Polarized on Risking
Continues to think when it's time to get into action.	Continues to engage in action when it's time to stop and think.
Build-up of ideas and plans.	Build-up of activity and movement.
Stability and order become increasingly important.	Action becomes increasingly important.
Takes fewer and fewer risks.	Thinks less and less.
Holds feelings inside.	Expresses feelings aggressively.
Resists change.	Resists thoughtful analysis.
Holds onto established ways.	Quick to change things.
Procrastinates.	Makes quick decisions.
Feels more and more depressed and anxious.	Feels increasingly exposed and agitated.
Becomes more and more "removed" and "out of it".	Becomes more and more emotional.
Immobilized.	**Out of control.**

Figure 7

24. *take risks* when it's time to be more conservative and take fewer chances.
28. *assertively express thoughts and feelings* when it's time to be more reserved and quiet.

Becoming Polarized on a Thinking Strength

Not only can we become polarized on one of our basic strengths, but we can also become polarized on one of the four individual strengths that come out of our two basic strengths. We can get stuck on one type of thinking, and we can get stuck on one type of risking. In this section, we deal with polarization on one type of thinking.

What happens when we polarize on our practical thinking strength? Practical thinking deals with facts and reality. It enables us to see things as they are and identify real problems. Sometimes, we get stuck on identifying problems. It's like a broken record—we identify the problem, then we identify the problem, and then we identify the problem some more. It is way past time to start looking for solutions, and there we are still identifying the problem. The longer we stay stuck on the practical side, the more frustrated, unhappy, and nonproductive we become. In Figure 8, a spiral of decay is drawn in the practical thinking loop to give visual image of what happens when we polarize on the practical side.

Also in Figure 8, there is a series of statements below the practical thinking loop. As you read down the page, the statements suggest increasing pain, frustration, and unhappiness. They describe how we feel and behave as polarization deepens. At the bottom, we use the terms depression, no hope, and despair to describe how we feel when we polarize deeply on the practical side. Most of us find some way to shift gears before we reach despair, but we all experience some degree of pain and frustration before we make the shift. This is the way a normal person experiences life. If you have a tendency to

Becoming Polarized on a Thinking Strength

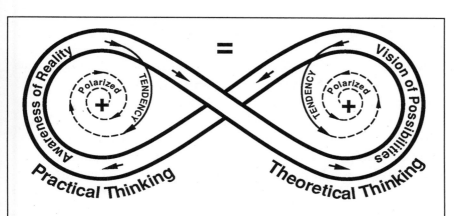

Signs of Becoming Polarized on Practical Thinking	Signs of Becoming Polarized on Theoretical Thinking
Continues to think about the problem when it's time to look for solutions.	Continues to imagine possibilities when it's time to look at the facts.
Build-up of facts.	Build-up of ideas and possibilities.
Facts become increasingly important.	Possibilities become increasingly important.
Sees all the rocks in the road.	Sees the pot of gold at the end of the rainbow.
Holds onto status quo.	Eager to try something new.
New ideas are a threat.	Facts are a threat.
Sees all the reasons why an idea will not work.	Sees all the reasons why an idea will work.
Uses facts as clubs to destroy ideas.	Disregards facts.
Pessimistic and gloomy.	Unbridled optimism.
Sour outlook.	Imagination runs wild.
Depression.	Flights of fantasy.
No hope.	Loses contact with reality.
Despair.	**Lives in a dream world.**

Figure 8

emphasize practical thinking, it is very normal for you to hold to the "status quo", experience new ideas as a threat, and be tempted to depreciate and reject new ideas. Whether or not you experience depression, no hope, and despair depends upon how deeply you get stuck on the practical side.

Now let's take a look at what happens when we polarize on our theoretical side. The process is the same as we just described for practical thinking. The difference is that now we are emphasizing theoretical possibilities and refusing to use our practical thinking abilities — we are stuck on the theoretical side. The broken record is playing a different tune now — we imagine possibilities, then we imagine possibilities, and then we imagine some more possibilities. The deepening process is indicated by both the spiral of decay in the theoretical loop and the sequence of statements under it. As we go down the right-hand side of the chart, the statements suggest more and more rejection of reality. At the bottom, we have the statement: Lives in a dream world. Most of us make the shift to the practical side before we reach the lower levels; however, those of us who tend to polarize on theoretical thinking can usually identify with the first few statements.

Listed below are some common tendencies from Figure 6 that may take us toward polarization on practical thinking:

11. *think about the problems* when it's time to look for solutions.
20. *emphasize the negatives* when it's time to emphasize the positives.
30. *be practical and realistic* when it's time to be more imaginative.

These tendencies may take us toward polarization on theoretical thinking:

5. *imagine the possibilities* when it's time to get the facts.
15. *think about theory* when it's time to be practical.
25. *speculate about future possibilities* when it's time to look at present realities.

Becoming Polarized on a Risking Strength

When we use our strengths defensively, we can also get polarized on one type of risking. When we do, we disregard and depreciate the other type. This causes us to enter into a tightening spiral of decay that becomes increasingly painful — we get "up-tight". As polarization deepens, we become more defensive and less productive. We experience more and more frustration, unhappiness, and failure.

Figure 9 gives a visual picture of how we can polarize on either type of risking. Below each of the risking loops, a series of statements is listed. These statements describe what happens to us when we polarize. First, read down each of the two lists separately to get a feel for the progressive nature of the decay process. Next, go down the page a second time, reading the corresponding statements opposite each other on the two lists.

Six of the common tendencies listed in Figure 6 may take us toward polarization on dependent risking, and six others may take us toward polarization on independent risking. They are listed below.

Tendencies that may take us toward polarization on dependent risking:

3. *say "yes"* when it's time to say "no".
10. *go along with others* when it's time to go own way.
16. *depend on others* when it's time to be more independent and self-sufficient.
18. *be sympathetic and supportive* when it's time to require others to be more responsible.
22. *do things that please others* when it's time to pay more attention to own needs and desires.
29. *be tolerant of others* when it's time to be more firm.

Tendencies that may take us toward polarization on independent risking:

Becoming Polarized on a Risking Strength

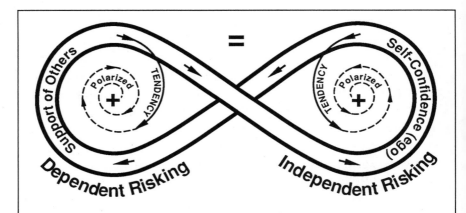

Signs of Becoming Polarized on Dependent Risking	Signs of Becoming Polarized on Independent Risking
Continues to depend on others when it's time to depend on self.	Continues to depend on self when it's time to depend on others.
Build-up of support and approval of others.	Build-up of ego and self-confidence.
Support and approval of others becomes increasingly important.	Personal power and freedom becomes increasingly important.
Fewer and fewer expressions of independence.	Fewer and fewer expressions of dependence.
Says "yes" when should say "no".	Talks when should be listening.
Becomes less and less responsible.	Assumes more and more responsibility.
Loses self-confidence.	Loses confidence in others.
Loses awareness of self.	Loses awareness of others.
Loses the respect of others.	Loses the support and approval of others.
Finally, loses the support and approval of others, the very thing that is most dear.	**Finally, loses personal power and freedom, the very thing that is most dear.**

Figure 9

4. *withdraw into own self-sufficiency* when it's time to draw on the strengths of others.

7. *compete with others* when it's time to be cooperative.

14. *drive hard to accomplish own goals and ambitions* when it's time to find out how others are thinking and feeling.

17. *do things personally* when it's time to trust others to do them.

21. *be impatient* when it's time to be more understanding of others.

26. *think own thoughts* when it is time to listen to what others are saying.

In this chapter, I have attempted to describe where negative and destructive forces come from, and how we experience them in our lives. In the next chapter, we will be discussing how we can respond to the problems and pains that are inherent in human life. Our approach will be to regard these pains as growth challenges and to describe ways in which we may blend our strengths to keep us in the growth process and experience the rewards that come from being a part of the process that is creating our world.

9.

Personal Growth

The Bi/Polar System is based on the assumption that it is natural for people to grow and develop their potential. We are natural participators in the growth process throughout our lifetime. And when we develop a particular level of conscious awareness, we also become conscious participators in the process. Our conscious awareness gives us the power to make personal choices that tend to either keep us in the process or take us out of it. The nature of these conscious personal choices is the focus of this chapter.

At the end of Chapter 6 (The Growth Process), three growth choices were identified: (1) the choice to be ourselves, (2) the choice to be flexible and adapt to the needs of the situation, and (3) the choice to make the sacrifice that is inherent in doing both (1) and (2). The human condition requires that we make a positive choice in all three in order to stay in the growth process. It is a forced choice situation — we either make the positive choices required or we find ourselves spiraling into polarization. There is no middle ground. With the emergence of human consciousness, human beings must either choose participation in the process or eventually experience the painful effects of psychological decay.

The eight patterns of core strengths and the concepts on which they are based gives us a conceptual system that may be used to be more specific about how we make these three growth choices. We may use the patterns as a more specific definition of our natural way of being and, from this foundation, be ourselves even more fully. We may use the concept of flex-patterns to develop a better idea of how we can become more flexible in expressing our supporting strengths and still remain true to ourselves. Finally, we may use our awareness of our strengths and the values they give us as a means to identify more clearly what we need to sacrifice in order to stay in the growth process and, as a result, grow as individuals.

Being True to Ourselves

In the Bi/Polar approach, being true to ourselves is equivalent to being true to our pattern of core strengths. We are true to our pattern when we express our natural blend of lead and supporting strengths. Our lead strengths are in the foreground, giving us a self-identify and a unique individuality. Our supporting strengths are in the background, giving us the flexibility to deal creatively with the outside world. Actually, our core pattern is a blend of our lead strengths and our supporting strengths. Although our lead strengths are dominant, our supporting strengths are there and contributing to making us a whole person.

In being true to ourselves, we do what comes naturally and show the world who we are. We follow our natural way, in spite of outside pressures that may influence us to do otherwise. We follow our natural tendencies and stand ready to deal with the problems they may cause. We have no desire to be someone else, nor do we wish to change our basic nature.

When we are being ourselves, we seek opportunities to use our natural talents and do those things we do the best. We feel good about who we are and have a strong sense of self-worth. Our basic core pattern "flavors" whatever we do. Although we may display a good deal of flexibility and gain considerable skill in expressing our supporting strengths, the identity of our basic pattern shows through.

Being True to the Situation

We are true to the outside situation when we emphasize the strength that is appropriate, regardless of our own pattern of core strengths. Becoming effective in expressing the strength appropriate to the situation requires a ready willingness to express our supporting strengths. We use the concept of *flex-patterns* to show how we can shift emphasis to any of our three supporting strengths and still remain true to ourselves.

The concept of flex-patterns assumes that not only do we have a natural blend of core strengths (our basic core pattern), but we also have the capacity to express a different blend of these strengths when it is appropriate to the situation. This capacity gives us flexibility in expressing our strengths and the ability to adapt and adjust to the demands of our environment. When we emphasize one of our supporting strengths, we express a changed blend of strengths and display the characteristics of a pattern that is different from our natural pattern. By emphasizing each of our three supporting strengths one at a time, we can express three different patterns that have two lead strengths in common with our basic core pattern. These patterns are what we refer to as our three flex-patterns.

Since flex-patterns are those having two lead strengths in common with our basic core pattern, they are the ones most similar to our basic pattern. In expressing a flex-pattern, we shift emphasis to one of our supporting strengths, while maintaining our natural leanings in the other two pairs. This enables us to be flexible and meet the need of the situation, while still expressing a strong "flavoring" of our core pattern.

Being flexible and gaining skill in expressing our three flex-patterns at appropriate times is one of the measures of our personal maturity. As we become more adept in expressing our flex-patterns, we develop more effectiveness in dealing creatively with a variety of situations. However, there is a limit to our flexibility. Beyond this limit, we become so flexible and adaptable that we begin to lose ourselves. We may extend the flex-pattern concept to show there is a limit to how flexible we can be and still remain true to our basic nature.

Our three flex-patterns are only one step away from our natural pattern. In our flex-patterns, we have the same lead strength in two of the pairs and opposite lead strength in only one pair. This makes our flex-patterns relatively similar to our natural pattern and relatively easy for us to express.

There are three other patterns that are two steps away from our natural pattern. These three patterns have opposite lead strengths in two of the pairs and only one lead strength in common with our natural pattern. This makes these patterns considerably different from our natural pattern and, as a result, more difficult for us to express and still keep our natural way. In order to show these patterns, we must shift emphasis to two supporting strengths at one time and still be true to ourselves. We tend to find this awkward, and, if we keep it up for a long period of time, we can begin to lose the vitality and productivity of our natural way. We tend toward becoming "phony". We are certainly faced with situations that require an emphasis on two of our supporting strengths. We need to deal with these situations as creatively as we can, but we need to be aware of the difficulty we face in maintaining the integrity of our basic pattern and the risk we run in losing ourselves.

There is one pattern that is our pattern opposite, and expressing it requires us to emphasize all three of our supporting strengths at one time. The difficulty and risk we run in trying to express our opposite pattern are extreme. We may be able to do it for short periods of time, but to try to maintain such a mask of our true nature for any extended period will almost surely result in problems for us and the world around us. We rob the world of the finest contributions we have to make and deprive ourselves of the fulfilling experiences that accompany the expression of our natural talents and strengths.

In personal growth, the ultimate goal is to be a full, contributing member in the growth process. We make our fullest contribution to the process when we value it more highly than anything else. With it at the center of our awareness, we give all that we have to it — our strengths and the fruits our strengths produce. When we make the choices that benefit the process, we discover that we are growing as persons.

Personal growth is much like happiness. If we try to be happy, it never happens. When we are doing the right things and forget about trying to be happy, happiness comes to us. The same is true with personal growth. When we forget about trying to grow and go about using our strengths for the positive benefit of the creative process, then, as an afterthought, we look back and discover we have grown.

The growth process requires the fruits of our strengths. If we are to remain in the growth process, we must sacrifice the fruits of our strengths and let them be used up in the process. If we fail to make the positive choice to give up the fruits we have produced, we become polarized on them and enter a process of psychological decay. In this process, not only do we experience the increasing pain and anguish associated with deepening polarization, but we eventually lose the very fruit we sought to save. It decays into nothingness because it is no longer a part of the process.

Making the sacrifice is the really hard part of staying in the growth process, because it involves a free choice to give up something that has great value to us. In fact, the most important sacrifices we need to make are those involving the things that mean the most to us. The one thing we never sacrifice is our commitment to and involvement in the creative process. We hold fast to the process and sacrifice all we have to it.

The idea of sacrifice seems to go against the grain with most of us. It seems that we are forever trying to get something for nothing. The desire to avoid paying the price appears to be part of being human. We all have tried to have our cake and eat it too. As normal healthy people grow and mature, one of the lessons they tend to learn is that you do have to make sacrifices to live a worthwhile life. You have to pay the price, and there are no free lunches. This doesn't mean that we won't still wish we could get something we want without making the sacrifice, but the more personal maturity we develop, the more willing we become to pay the price. We learn that any pain we experience in making the sacrifice is temporary and overshadowed by the rewards of participating in the process. On the other hand, the pains we experience in polarization get worse and inevitably take us toward even more pain.

One point needs to be re-emphasized: personal growth requires that we meet the demands of all three growth choices. When we are in the process, we (1) are true to ourselves, (2) express the strength that is appropriate to the situation, and (3) willingly sacrifice the fruits of our strengths. The most mature people I have known appear to do all three things well. First, their natural pattern of strengths is distinctive and unmistakable — not only do their leads strengths show clearly, but their natural leanings create problems for them — they are not perfect people, never making a mistake. Second, they are highly flexible — they shift quickly and skillfully to their supporting strengths when the situation requires it, and they do it without a hint of phoniness. When they express their flex-patterns, they do it in their own way — the "flavor" of their core pattern is still there. Third, they are willing to go through the pain of sacrifice and pay the price that is an integral part of being in the process and living a creative life.

Dealing Creatively With Our Personal Tendencies

Each of the eight Bi/Polar patterns tends to produce particular personal tendencies. Those who have Pattern I strengths have different natural tendencies than those who have Pattern VIII strengths. Although the different patterns produce different tendencies and growth challenges, having one pattern or the other does not make it easier or harder for us to grow. One pattern produces just as many growth challenges as another, and they are equally difficult — they are just different challenges. So we have no cause to feel fortunate or unfortunate about having our own pattern of strengths. Those who have a different core pattern from our own are having just as difficult a time dealing with their growth challenges as we are having dealing with ours.

Now it is time to be specific about the growth challenges that each pattern tends to produce, discuss how we may respond to these challenges creatively, and, as a result, grow as individuals. We can do this by selecting a typical tendency for each of the eight patterns and discussing the growth choices we must make to deal creatively with that tendency.

Pattern I

Lead Strengths	Supporting Strengths	Flex-patterns
Thinking	Risking	V
Practical thinking	Theoretical thinking	III
Dependent risking	Independent risking	II

Typical Tendency: *avoid confrontation and conflict when it's time to express real thoughts and feelings.*

Being True To Oneself

People with Pattern I strengths are naturally quiet, respectful, and accepting in their relationships. They are good listeners and tend to wait for the other person to make the first move. These are excellent strengths and essential ingredients in warm relationships and good communication. Their first growth choice is to express these strengths and follow their natural tendencies.

As those with Pattern I strengths follow their natural tendencies, before long they begin to experience problems. Sometimes they discover that others are invading their territory and taking advantage of their "good" nature. Others may regard them as weak and tend to disregard and ignore them. These depreciating attitudes from others in turn tend to cause Pattern I's to feel bad about themselves. The pain of polarization has begun and will continue to deepen and stimulate even more intense negative feelings until something is done to bring more equality to the relationship.

Being Flexible

To solve the problem caused by their tendency to avoid confrontation and conflict, those with Pattern I strengths need to shift to their Flex-pattern II and express more independence. By shifting to their Flex-pattern II, they can maintain the force of their natural way, in both thinking and practicality, and consciously focus their energies in blending more independence into their behavior.

   To be most effective in expressing their own thoughts and feelings, they need to plan their actions carefully, and, in the actual confrontation, do it in a stable, organized way. The painful emotions they are experiencing will be obvious and have a strong impact on the other person, but the expression of these emotions will be controlled and directed by their thinking strengths. In other words, this type of person will look much like a Pattern II when they confront another person with their real thoughts and feelings. The extra ingredient will be the warm background of acceptance that comes from the natural lead strength in dependent risking. These people express real independence, but do it in their own way — as Pattern I's with natural leanings toward acceptance of others.

Paying the Price

When those with Pattern I strengths express their own thoughts and feelings in a more independent and forceful way, what price must they be ready to pay? One of the most important sacrifices they make is that of a stable relationship. The confrontation and conflict they initiate will change the relationship into a dynamic and emotional interaction. The outcome is highly uncertain, and the emotional components of the relationship are accentuated. They must be willing to give up the "status quo" and the stability of the relationship.

In order to effectively express their independence, they must also stand ready to sacrifice the support and approval of the person they are confronting. There is a distinct risk that, in the confrontation, a serious conflict will be generated, and the other person will withdraw support. If the one initiating the confrontation is prepared to give up this support, their ability to express independence in a more forceful way is enhanced.

Payoff

What is the payoff to people with Pattern I strengths when they effectively express their thoughts and feelings, even if it means the possibility of confrontation and conflict? Probably the biggest payoff is an immediate increase in self-esteem and self-confidence. They experience a real sense of personal impact and power. Another is that of being relieved of bottled-up hostilities and resentments that usually have built up over time and created a heavy burden for them to carry. A final payoff that usually occurs is of an increased respect from other people.

What about the payoff for the other people in the relationship? Almost invariably the others feel good about the people with Pattern I strengths having responded in an open way and come on straight about their real feelings. It clears the air and provides a strong basis on which to build a deeper and more creative relationship in the future.

Pattern II

Lead Strengths	Supporting Strengths	Flex-patterns
Thinking	Risking	VII
Practical thinking	Theoretical thinking	IV
Independent risking	Dependent risking	I

Typical Tendency: *hold feelings inside when it's time to express them more openly.*

Being True to Oneself

People with Pattern II strengths are naturally calm and self-controlled in their relationships. Their objectivity and cool rationality bring stability and order to their interactions with other people. These are excellent strengths, and they contribute essential ingredients to a healthy, productive relationship between two people. The first growth choice for people who have these leanings is to go their natural way and bring rationality and stability to their relationships.

As people with Pattern II strengths follow their natural tendency to emphasize rationality and control over their feelings, before long their relationships begin to suffer due to a dearth of emotional expression. They begin to feel a need for closer and more satisfying relationships that only an expression of real feelings can bring about. Others may feel rejected and shut out from them. This need for an expression of feelings and a show of genuine emotion sets the stage for their second growth choice.

Being Flexible

The second growth choice involves a willingness to relinquish some of the tight control they are exercising over their feelings. This is done by shifting to their Flex-pattern VII and risking an expression of their feelings. Then they can maintain the force of their natural way by continuing to be practical and independent but, at the same time, engage in a more active expression of their real feelings.

To be most effective in expressing their feelings more openly, those with Pattern II strengths still need to maintain a good deal of control on their feelings (their natural way), but, at the same time, let their guard down a bit and tell the other person how they are feeling. They loosen their tight grip on their feelings and let them bubble up to the surface so they are revealed in a semi-controlled way.

Paying the Price
What price must those with Pattern II strengths be ready to pay when they express their feelings? The possible loss of control over their own feelings and over the relationship itself. The relationship could become explosive and dynamic when the intensity of the feelings is brought out in the open. They must be willing to sacrifice a stable, somewhat distant relationship for the potential of developing a closer emotional relationship that could flower into a close friendship.

Payoff
What is the payoff when people with Pattern II strengths risk expressing their real feelings in their natural way? First, it feels good to get your feelings out in the open. It clears the air and relieves the tension. Second, the other people in the relationship feel relieved, because now they know where the Pattern II people are coming from. Third, it creates a solid and honest basis on which to build a productive and satisfying relationship that deepens with time.

Pattern III

Lead Strengths	Supporting Strengths	Flex-patterns
Thinking	Risking	VI
Theoretical thinking	Practical thinking	I
Dependent risking	Independent risking	IV

Typical tendency: *be quiet and listen when it's time to speak out.*

Being True to Oneself

People with Pattern III strengths are naturally quiet, respectful, and supportive in their relationships. They are mild-mannered and usually wait for others to take the initiative. They are thoughtful of others and are usually good listeners. When they follow their natural way, they bring stability, acceptance, and warmth to a relationship. Their first growth choice is to be true to themselves and bring these strengths to their relationships.

As they follow their natural, quiet way, before long they discover it is time for them to take the initiative and speak out. The relationship begins to suffer because others may be taking them for granted or running over them. In any event, there always comes a time when the relationship demands they speak out and let others know what they are thinking and how they are feeling. This need to speak out presents them with their second growth choice.

Being Flexible

In speaking out, those with Pattern III strengths must emphasize their risking strength by shifting to their Flex-pattern VI. They still maintain their natural warmth but become more active in expressing their thoughts and real feelings. In doing this, they display many of the characteristics associated with the Pattern VI combination of strengths. They are deliberately more outgoing, active, and expressive. They get more involved and display more feeling and emotion.

Paying the Price

What gives those with Pattern III strengths the courage to risk speaking out? It is the willingness to sacrifice the comfort and protection they receive by being quiet and not being noticed. If they speak out, they draw attention to themselves and lose their protective cover. A willingness to let go of this protective cover gives them the courage to expose themselves by speaking out.

Payoff

What is the payoff when Pattern III people screw up their courage and speak out when the situation requires it? The first is a feeling of involvement and a sense of aliveness. Life becomes more interesting and dynamic. Second, there is an enhanced feeling of closeness with other people and an increase in personal impact and self-esteem. The big payoff is in their relationships. With the introduction of stronger emotional elements, their relationships become much more dynamic and emotionally satisfying.

Pattern IV

Lead Strengths	Supporting Strengths	Flex-patterns
Thinking	Risking	VIII
Theoretical thinking	Practical thinking	II
Independent risking	Dependent risking	III

Typical Tendency: *withdraw into own self-sufficiency when it's time to draw on the strength of others.*

Being True to Oneself

The people with Pattern IV strengths tend to feel self-sufficient and able to take care of themselves. They tend to be strongly independent and go their own way. They have strong internal convictions and tend to feel a good deal of confidence in their ability to figure things out on their own. Usually they make their greatest contributions by coming up with new and innovative ideas.

The first growth choice for those with Pattern IV strengths is to be themselves and rely on their own strengths to develop fresh and new approaches to solving old problems. They need to be self-sufficient and figure things out on their own. As they follow their natural inclination to work alone and rely on their own strengths, after awhile they develop a need to interact with other people and draw on their strengths. The emergence of this need to be dependent on others is what creates their second growth choice. Now they must choose between continuing their natural self-sufficiency or making a conscious choice to depend more on others.

Being Flexible
When those with Pattern IV strengths deliberately shift emphasis to their supporting strength in dependent risking, they show many of the characteristics of their Flex-pattern III. Although there is a strong flavor of independence and self-confidence, they become warmer and more accepting, more understanding and supportive of others. They listen more carefully to other people and try to understand their point of view. They develop more patience and build stronger ties with others. They become more caring and participate more fully in the strength of the group. By shifting to their Flex-pattern III, those with Pattern IV strengths still maintain the strengths of their natural way in two of their lead strengths (thinking and theoretical thinking) and make the shift in one pair (the risking pair). The result is that there is still a strong "flavoring" of their natural Pattern IV strengths but with an obvious effort to blend in more of their dependent strength.

Paying the Price
What must those with Pattern IV strengths sacrifice when they deliberately emphasize their dependent risking? One of the most important values they must give up is their own self-importance. Now they must use their self-confidence to run the risk of depending more on others. They must put their own ideas out on the table and let them be criticized and judged by others. If they are willing to let go of their ideas and let them be used up in the creative process, this sacrifice gives them the courage to depend on other people and listen to what others have to say.

Payoff

What's the payoff for those with Pattern IV strengths when they let go of some of their ego and depend more on the strengths of others? One of the greatest benefits is that they receive more data and information from others. This information gives them more raw material to use in developing even better ideas. Another benefit is on the emotional level. As they interact more with others and make themselves more vulnerable through depending on other people, they feel and actually receive more support and approval from others. This gives them a stronger base of confidence. They still keep their basic thrust as innovators of fresh ideas, but they have more information to deal with and more courage to let their ideas be tested by reality.

Pattern V

Lead Strengths	Supporting Strengths	Flex-patterns
Risking	Thinking	I
Practical thinking	Theoretical thinking	VI
Dependent risking	Independent risking	VII

Typical Tendency: *say "yes" when it's time to say "no".*

Being True to Oneself

People who have the Pattern V combination of strengths are naturally outgoing, friendly, and supportive of other people. They tend to feel warm toward others and are inclined to help others. Although we all want the support and approval of others, those with Pattern V strengths have a particularly strong need to be well liked and recognized by others. They want to please others, and frequently find themselves saying "yes" when really they should say "no". They can find they are so intent on pleasing others that the demands of others are running their lives.

Those with Pattern V strengths need to be true to their natural way and express their warm relationship strengths. They need to keep these natural strengths working in their relationship, even when they discover that these strengths have created a problem. To solve the problem, they need to blend in some of their supporting strengths, but they must keep the flavor of their natural way even while emphasizing a supporting strength.

Being Flexible
When the people with Pattern V strengths find saying "yes" when they should say "no" is causing problems, they need to shift to their Flex-pattern VII and emphasize their independent risking strength. In doing this, they tend to show many of the characteristics associated with the Pattern VII. They become more self-directed and show more independence in their relationship. They relate to others on a more nearly equal basis and bring their own needs into the equation more forcefully. They learn to say "no" in a nice way but do it with firmness. Their natural acceptance and warmth toward the other person gives a background flavor to their interactions, but the deliberate expression of their independence introduces a self-interest that needs to be taken into account.

Paying the Price
What price must Pattern V people pay when they deliberately emphasize their independent strength? By far the most important sacrifice is the possible loss of the support and approval of others. When they express independence by saying "no", they run the distinct risk of losing the other person's support. When they are able to consciously let go of this support and give it up to the process, they gain the courage to go ahead and express the independence that is required for them to say "no".

Payoff

In most instances, the biggest payoff from dealing creatively with this tendency is an immediate experience of freedom — the freedom to be oneself and see after one's own interest. The next benefits include more self-respect, enhanced feelings of self-worth, and more self-confidence. This increase in self-esteem enables them to relate to others on a more objective basis and with a stronger sense of equality. This personal growth provides the basis for healthier and even stronger relationships with other people.

Pattern VI

Lead Strengths	Supporting Strengths	Flex-patterns
Risking	Thinking	III
Theoretical thinking	Practical thinking	V
Dependent risking	Independent risking	VIII

Typical Tendency: *try to stay close and intimate when it's time to back off and be more objective.*

Being True to Oneself

People with Pattern VI strengths are naturally active and outgoing. They are caring people who want to get involved with others. They are more oriented to feelings than facts. They live in a world of people and enjoy being close and intimate with others. They identify strongly with others and feel a great deal of compassion toward them.

Those who have these valuable relationship strengths need to express them and be true to their natural way. This is their first growth choice. As with all normal and healthy people, those with Pattern VI strengths also find that following their natural way will eventually create a problem. Sometimes they find they have become so close and involved with others they are causing a problem for themselves and perhaps even the other person. It is time for them to back off and be more objective. This kind of problem presents the second growth choice for them.

Being Flexible

When those with Pattern VI strengths become aware that being so close and intimate is causing a problem, it is time for them to emphasize their thinking strength by shifting to their Flex-pattern III. They need to back off, take time to think about the situation, and develop a better rational understanding of what is going on. When they shift to their Flex-pattern III, they become quieter and more reflective. They are more reserved in their relationships and don't come on so strong. Their natural leaning toward warmth and compassion is in the background, "flavoring" their actions, but they are more thoughtful and wait longer for the other person to respond on his or her own initiative.

Paying the Price

What must those with Pattern VI strengths sacrifice in order to bring more objectivity and healthy distance into their relationships? They must be willing to give up some of the warm emotional feelings they experience in close, intimate relationships with other people. They must stand ready to sacrifice these warm feelings to the process and bring more objectivity, rationality, and respect for individuality into their relationships. Being convinced that healthy relationships include separation and independence as well as closeness and intimacy helps them to make this sacrifice.

Payoff

What is the payoff when people with Pattern VI strengths bring more objectivity and distance into their relationship? The first comes to them personally. No longer do they feel burdened by problems that can be solved only by the other person. The second comes to the other person in the relationship. No longer does he or she feel invaded and smothered by so much closeness. These two results help to strengthen the relationship and make it healthier and more productive for both parties.

Pattern VII

Lead Strengths	Supporting Strengths	Flex-patterns
Risking	Thinking	II
Practical thinking	Theoretical thinking	VIII
Independent risking	Dependent risking	V

Typical Tendency: *to be impatient when it's time to be more understanding of others.*

Being True to Oneself

Those with Pattern VII strengths are naturally self-assertive and goal-oriented. They are competitive, ambitious, and experience a good deal of self-confidence. They take the initiative and are action-oriented. They are doers and out-front leaders. These are all positive strengths and contribute to the creative process. The first growth choice for those with Pattern VII strengths is to be true to themselves and express their natural leadership strengths.

Pattern VII's naturally feel a high drive to accomplish their goals, which tends to cause them to feel a good deal of impatience with any delay. So it is natural for people with this combination of strengths to display impatience and, as a result, to experience the problems that impatience can bring about. When they become aware of these problems, they are faced with their second growth choice — to deliberately express the supporting strengths that will solve the problems being caused by their impatience.

Being Flexible

Impatience has its most destructive effects on one's relationships with other people. As those with Pattern VII strengths express their impatience, others tend to develop negative attitudes and feelings toward them. The usual result is that Pattern VII's find it even more difficult to accomplish their goals, because others are fighting them rather than trying to help. To solve this problem, they need to shift to their Flex-pattern V and emphasize their dependent risking. They need to shift their attention away from their own personal goals and pay more attention to the other person in the relationship. This concentrates their attention on the other person and helps them to understand what they are thinking and how they are feeling. They ask questions and listen rather than talk and give orders.

Paying the Price
What must those with Pattern VII strengths sacrifice if they are to deal effectively with their impatience? The answer is that they must sacrifice immediate self-gratification in accomplishing their personal goals and ambitions. They must give up taking immediate action and take time to plan a course of action that gives due consideration to the needs and desires of the other person in the relationship.

Payoff
What is the payoff when Pattern VII's learn to deal creatively with their natural impatience? Probably the most important is an increase in personal productivity and effectiveness. By maintaining their natural drive and intensity to accomplish and through expressing more dependence on others, they become highly effective leaders with increasing personal impact and influence on the world around them. A second benefit comes from the good relationships they create with other people. By expressing their dependence on others, they experience more support and approval from others, and others are more loyal to them.

Pattern VIII

Lead Strengths	Supporting Strengths	Flex-patterns
Risking	Thinking	IV
Theoretical thinking	Practical thinking	VII
Independent risking	Dependent risking	VI

Typical Tendency: *talk when it's time to be listening.*

Being True to Oneself

Those with Pattern VIII strengths are highly dynamic. They naturally seek to have a strong influence on other people. They are natural promoters who can capture a vision and sell it to others. They are exciting, enthusiastic, and persuasive. They initiate action and stimulate change.

Their first growth choice is to express these dynamic strengths and influence other people. In the process of being themselves, it is natural for them to be in the spotlight and do a lot of talking. Their second growth choice comes when they become aware that their talking is causing a problem, and it becomes time for them to do less talking and more listening.

Being Flexible

What strengths are Pattern VIII's emphasizing when they talk less and listen more? The first shift they make is to their thinking strength. When they do this, they show the characteristics of their Flex-pattern IV. They are more thoughtful and concentrate on trying to understand the situation. The second shift is to their courage of dependence. In making the shift to dependence, they express their Flex-pattern VI. They pay more attention to the other person and try to put themselves in the other person's shoes.

Paying the Price

What enables those with Pattern VIII strengths to deliberately stop talking so much and begin to listen more? It is the giving up of their personal impact — something that they value very highly. If they can let go of their egos and forego the experience of influencing others, they can easily shift into more reserved behavior and let themselves be influenced more strongly by other people.

Payoff
What is the payoff when Pattern VIII's learn to deal creatively with their tendency to talk when it is time for them to be listening? One of the most important is that they enhance their positive influence on others. When they talk somewhat less, other people pay more attention to what they have to say. Another benefit is that they learn more and develop a deeper understanding of what is going on in their relationships with other people. These two benefits combine to produce even better relationships with others.

Summary

This chapter has presented the Bi/Polar concept of personal growth. The diagram in Figure 10 may be used to summarize the essential elements of the concept.

In Figure 10, the lop-sided infinity symbol at the top represents the assumption that every person has a lead strength and a supporting strength in each of the three Bi/Polar pairs of strengths — we are naturally out-of-balance.

The vertical dotted line represents perfection — a perfect balance between the two polar strengths. The vertical line labeled "Personal Line of Productivity" is set off to the side of the line of perfect balance. This indicates that mature people don't seek perfection or perfect balance within themselves. Rather, they seek to contribute their natural talents and deal creatively with the problems that come their way. They recognize that their natural way takes them off to one side of perfection but affirm this as a part of the creative process at work in the world.

Personal Growth

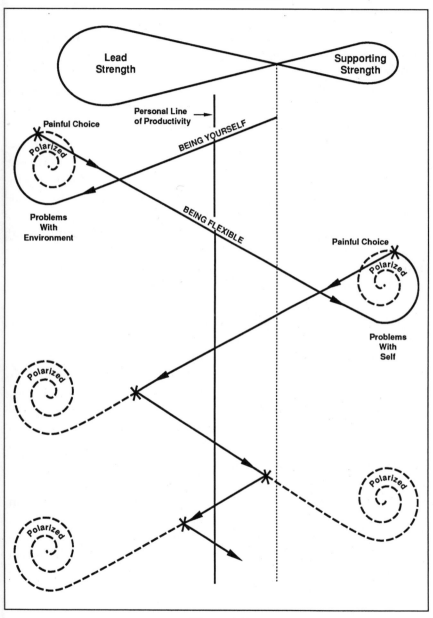

Figure 10

The painful choice at the "X" in the polarization spirals represents the place where we sacrifice our fruits and feed them into the creative process.

Mature people express their psychological health by doing two things well. First, they show their natural bias toward their lead strengths. In other words, they show who they are as real, out-of-balance human beings. They freely express their core pattern. Second, they adapt quickly to problems by deliberately emphasizing their supporting strengths. In other words, they display flexibility by consciously emphasizing their supporting strengths when the situation requires it.

Creative and effective people do both of these things and avoid becoming "polarized" on either one. The "flavor" of their core pattern is there and showing itself; yet, at the same time, they display flexibility by expressing their supporting strengths when appropriate.

Through experience, they become more sensitive to the problems caused by going too far either way. On one hand, they become more aware of the problems caused by expressing their natural way of being and disregarding the needs of the situation. On the other hand, they become more aware of the problems caused when they become so flexible they disregard their own natural way of being. In the first instance, they lose effectiveness in dealing with the real world. In the second instance, they tend to "lose themselves". Both are painful experiences and pave the way for a creative response.

The creative response is a painful choice to change directions and move to the opposite side. Through practice, they gain skill in making the appropriate shift at an earlier time and with more effectiveness. As they learn and grow, they spend more time bracketing their "Personal Line of Productivity" and less time polarized on one side.

III.

Understanding Other People

10.

Dynamics of a Creative Relationship

Some of the most useful concepts in Bi/Polar deal with relationships between people. Because that is how we get to know other people — through our one-to-one relationships.

There are three chapters in this part on understanding other people. The first chapter lays the foundation for understanding one-to-one relationships by discussing the dynamics of a creative relationship. The second describes the four fundamental relationship tendencies that people experience and express. The third chapter describes the relationship characteristics that each of the eight core patterns tends to produce.

Relationship Dynamics

What are the dynamics of a creative and productive relationship between two people? What is actually going on when two people have good communication and a strong relationship? The purpose of this section is to answer these questions.

The straightforward answer is to say there are three basic dynamics that make a relationship creative. All are essential, and each one makes its own contribution to the creativeness of the relationship. First, the two people have an attitude of equality toward each other; second, they are self-assertive and take initiative to move toward each other; third, they are respectful of each other's territory.

In an effort to more fully define the nature of these three dynamics, it may be helpful to diagram how they would be manifested in a perfect relationship. Of course, a perfect relationship never exists between two real people, but a concept of a perfect relationship may help us understand what is going on in our real relationships and see more clearly what we may do to strengthen them.

Figure 11 depicts a perfect relationship. The two ellipses represent two people. The arrows coming from each person and meeting at the vertical line between them may be used to describe the three dynamics in a perfect relationship.

A Creative Relationship

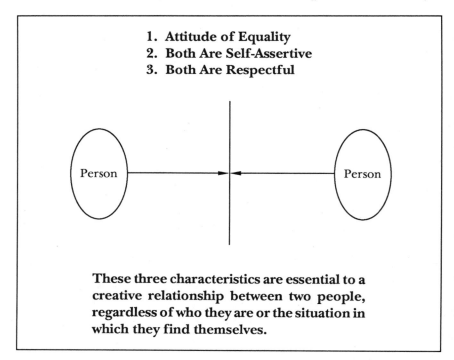

1. **Attitude of Equality**
2. **Both Are Self-Assertive**
3. **Both Are Respectful**

Person   Person

These three characteristics are essential to a creative relationship between two people, regardless of who they are or the situation in which they find themselves.

Figure 11

First, the horizontal positioning of the arrows suggests a level relationship — the two people look straight across at each other. They value themselves and each other on an equal basis. There is no "looking up" nor "looking down" in the relationship. This *attitude of equality* is an essential dynamic in a perfect relationship.

Second, the arrows going up to the line suggest that each person faces and approaches the other. There is a movement toward the other, an effort to make contact and enter into a relationship. This kind of assertion is required not only to make contact, but also to maintain and strengthen an ongoing relationship. *Being assertive and moving toward the other person* is the second dynamic in a perfect relationship.

Third, the arrows stopping at the vertical line between the two ellipses suggest that each person refrains from going over into the territory of the other. They respect each other's space, and each is careful not to go across the line and violate the rights of the other person. *Being respectful of the other person's territory* is the third dynamic in a perfect relationship.

Although we can never achieve a perfect relationship with another person, we do approximate it when we have a close friend. I have asked many people what a close friend means to them. Although people respond differently and tend to emphasize one of the dynamics discussed above, the thread of each of the three dynamics usually appears in some form. Many people describe a close-friend relationship as one in which they feel comfortable. They can be themselves and still be accepted. They don't have to be on guard because they know the other person will not take advantage of them. The idea of mutual concern is usually there also. Many people say "a close friend is someone I would help if needed and someone I know would help me if I needed it". The word trust is frequently used — "a close friend is someone I can trust — someone I can confide in and know it won't go any farther".

Guidelines that have stood the test of time seem to combine these three characteristics in some way. Our Judeo-Christian heritage gives us two excellent examples: "Love your neighbor as yourself" and "Do unto others as you would have them do unto you". Both of these sayings suggest equality and a balance between self-assertion and respect for the other person.

In summary, there are three dynamics in a perfect relationship. One, the two people are looking straight across at each other, affirming their own worth and the worth of the other person on an equal basis; two, both are being assertive and moving toward the other person, seeking to establish and deepen the relationship; and three, both are respectful of the other person's space and careful not to go across the line into the other's rightful territory.

The Line of Creativity

In Figure 11, the vertical line drawn between the two people is referred to as the line of creativity. In a perfect relationship, it represents the point to which each person goes, and stops, when they are expressing a perfect balance between assertiveness and reserved behavior. Meeting at the line of creativity represents the most creative, productive, and mutually-satisfying relationship two people can have.

In a perfect relationship, the vertical line between the two people is drawn in the middle, suggesting that we are dealing with two hypothetical people who are always in the same situation. In other words, the individual differences of the two people and the changing situation in which real people live are not taken into account.

In our real relationships, the only thing equal is our worth as individuals — all other comparisons are unequal. We have different patterns of strengths, different amounts of strength, different levels of maturity, different degrees of authority, and different sets of tendencies. In addition to these individual differences, the situation in which two people find themselves is continually changing. Because of these natural differences between two real people and the changing situation in which they live, the line of creativity is never in the middle. It is closer to one side than the other, depending upon who the people are and the situation in which they find themselves.

For example, in the relationship between a father and son, normally the father is more mature and has more strength and authority. A diagram of their relationships could be drawn as shown in Figure 12a. The line of creativity, being closer to the son, suggests that their most creative, productive, and satisfying relationship is one in which the father exerts more power, freedom, and authority. Although they have equal worth as individuals and both look straight across at each other (suggested by the two horizontal arrows), the father is the dominant influence in the relationship. When the son grows up and is taking care of his aged father, their relationship may be diagrammed as shown in Figure 12b. They still have equal worth as individuals, but the son is now the stronger one and has the dominant influence in the relationship.

When two people are working together in a team effort, their individual contributions to the accomplishment of a common objective are never equal. One is always contributing more than another. These differences can find expression in the corporate structure of an organization. In Figure 13, the line of creativity being closer to the subordinate suggests that the supervisor has more power, freedom, and authority. They still look straight across at each other and have equal worth as individuals, but the position of the line of creativity between them is determined by their relative power, freedom, and authority.

Two Father-Son Relationships

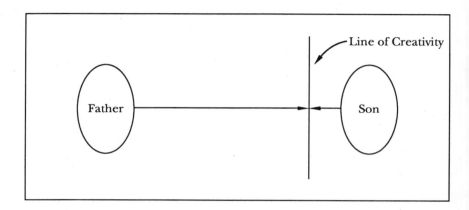

Figure 12a

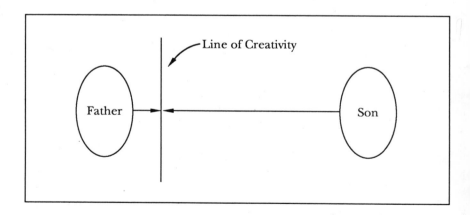

Figure 12b

Supervisor - Subordinate Relationship

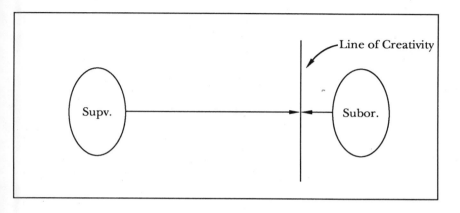

Figure 13

The Zone of Creativity

In our real relationships, we don't come up to the line of creativity and stop. First, we don't know where the line is until we experiment some in the relationship — perhaps going too far across the line and then not going far enough. Second, none of us is good enough to relate that perfectly to another human being. We actually relate to another person in a zone of creativity rather than on a line of creativity.

Figure 14 illustrates how two people actually relate to each other when they have a productive relationship. Each one is continually undershooting and overshooting the line. As the relationship becomes stronger and more creative, the zone of creativity narrows. But the zone never narrows to a line. That would be a state of perfection that real people aren't equipped to reach. The line of creativity can be a goal toward which we strive but not something we expect to achieve in reality.

Zone of Creativity

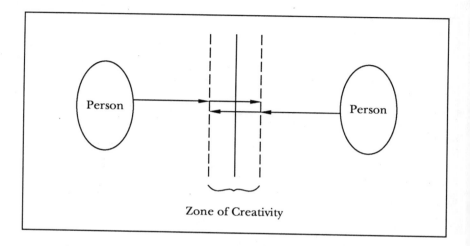

Figure 14

11.

Relationship Tendencies

Human beings experience and express four distinct kinds of tendencies in their relationships with one another. These four tendencies may be identified as follows:

1. Reserved and relational tendency
2. Reserved and independent tendency
3. Assertive and relational tendency
4. Assertive and independent tendency

All four of these tendencies are expressions of positive, constructive strengths, and each makes its own contribution to a productive and satisfying relationship between two people.

These four tendencies are very normal and a natural part of every human relationship. As individuals, it is natural and normal for us to express some more frequently than others. When we consistently express one of these tendencies more frequently than the others, it becomes a distinguishing feature of our personality.

It is important for us to realize that our own inclination to express one of these tendencies more than the others is a very normal and natural thing. The intent here is not to encourage people to get rid of their tendencies, but rather to help them become aware of their tendencies and develop skill in dealing creatively with them when they cause problems. We assume that tendencies are a natural part of being a healthy and creative person, and we need to express them as a natural part of our own individuality. With experience, we become aware of the problems they can cause us and, out of this awareness, develop skill in dealing creatively with them.

When the Bi/Polar approach is used as an aid in strengthening our relationships, a good understanding of the four basic tendencies is essential. Because of the importance of this understanding, each tendency is discussed in some detail below.

Diagrams illustrating how these tendencies are expressed in our relationships and how we may be perceived when we express them are presented in Figure 15.

Reserved and Relational Tendency

Two important Bi/Polar strengths stand behind the reserved and relational tendency: the thinking strength and the dependent risking strength. These two strengths combine to provide stability and warmth to a relationship. The thinking strength brings a quiet reserve characterized by thoughtfulness, understanding, and respect; the dependent strength gives a "warm glow" expressed in quiet appreciation, devotion, and loyalty.

The reserved and relational tendency is expressed in quiet, "watchful-waiting" behavior. An expression of this tendency is more of a reaction to what the other person does than a self-generated action. Behavior expressing this tendency is mild-mannered, reserved, cautious, tentative, and respectful.

Bi/Polar Patterns I and III tend to experience and express the reserved and relational tendency most frequently (although all patterns can and do express this tendency at times).

The reserved and relational tendency is illustrated in the top section of Figure 15. The short, drooping arrow coming from the ellipse on the left represents the expression of the reserved and relational tendency. The reserve quality is represented by the arrow being drawn short of the line of creativity—a hesitancy to be assertive

| Relationship Tendency: | May Be Perceived by Others as: |

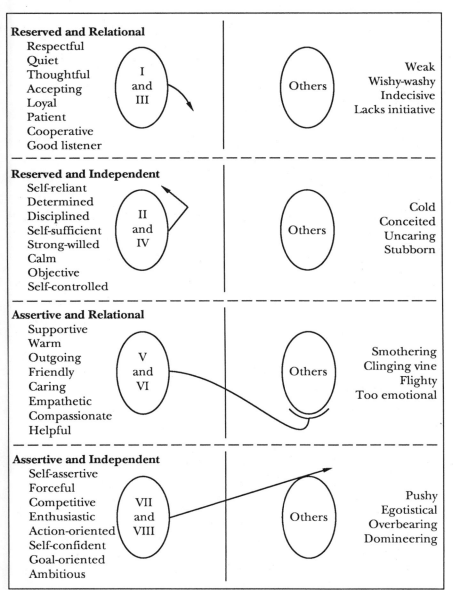

Reserved and Relational
Respectful
Quiet
Thoughtful
Accepting
Loyal
Patient
Cooperative
Good listener

I and III → Others

Weak
Wishy-washy
Indecisive
Lacks initiative

Reserved and Independent
Self-reliant
Determined
Disciplined
Self-sufficient
Strong-willed
Calm
Objective
Self-controlled

II and IV → Others

Cold
Conceited
Uncaring
Stubborn

Assertive and Relational
Supportive
Warm
Outgoing
Friendly
Caring
Empathetic
Compassionate
Helpful

V and VI → Others

Smothering
Clinging vine
Flighty
Too emotional

Assertive and Independent
Self-assertive
Forceful
Competitive
Enthusiastic
Action-oriented
Self-confident
Goal-oriented
Ambitious

VII and VIII → Others

Pushy
Egotistical
Overbearing
Domineering

Figure 15

and move toward the other person. The relational or dependent quality is represented by the drooping of the arrow — suggesting a tendency to depreciate oneself in the relationship.

Because the thinking and dependent strengths are emphasized in an expression of the reserved and relational tendency, the assertive and independent strengths are automatically de-emphasized. This relatively "weak" expression of assertiveness and independence can create an impression of personal "weakness". Because of this, those who express this tendency are sometimes inaccurately described with derogatory terms such as weak, passive, indecisive, submissive, timid, gives in easily, doesn't stand up, lacks initiative, no backbone, won't speak up, etc. However, if the individual is actually polarized on thinking and dependent risking, then these terms take on more validity in describing that person's behavior.

In dealing creatively with this tendency, it is important for people to realize the solution is neither to depreciate these strengths nor to refuse to express them. The creative solution lies in shifting emphasis to their polar strengths — in this case, a shift to more assertiveness (risking) and more independence (independent risking). This is the flexing concept — a change of behavior that still retains its reserve and relational qualities but blends in more assertiveness and more independence.

Reserved and Independent Tendency

In the reserved and independent tendency, the thinking strength and the strength of independence are emphasized. The expression of these two strengths gives the impression of intellectual competence and self-sufficiency. The thinking strength contributes rationality, stability, logic, and structure to the relationship. The independent strength provides leadership in defining and establishing objectives and brings confidence, discipline, and determination to accomplish them.

The reserved quality in this tendency comes from an internal marshaling of strength to understand and solve the problem. Behavior expressing this tendency is usually characterized by intense concentration and detachment from the immediate surroundings. This intense mental activity gives an impression of strength and stability much like the whirling gyroscope — a great deal of activity within but practically no movement relative to the outside world. The independent quality comes from the emphasis on internal strengths — looking to resources within rather than outside. This orientation gives the impression of quiet self-confidence, self-sufficiency, self-directedness, and substantial internal strength.

People who frequently express this tendency are usually highly task-oriented, quality minded, dedicated to efficiency, and show a good deal of bull-dog tenacity. They are essentially private people who feel comfortable being alone — they are the original loners.

Bi/Polar Patterns II and IV tend to naturally experience and express the reserved and independent tendency. Of course, other patterns may express this tendency because of what they have learned from their life's experiences. But in those instances it is a learned tendency, not a natural or innate tendency for them.

The reserved and independent tendency is illustrated in the second section of Figure 15. The line coming out of the ellipse on the left represents the expression of the reserved and independent tendency. The reserved quality is represented by the line's abrupt change of direction, moving away from the other person. The independent quality is represented by the upward movement of the line, suggesting self-confidence and self-sufficiency.

Because the thinking and independent strengths are emphasized in an expression of the reserved and independent tendency, the assertive and dependent strengths are automatically de-emphasized. This relatively "weak" expression of assertiveness and dependence causes people who express this tendency to be inaccurately described in such negative terms as: cold, prudish, conceited, snobbish, priggish, uncaring, suspicious, distrustful, withdrawn, insensitive, stubborn, hard-headed, etc. However, if an individual becomes polarized on thinking and independent risking, then these descriptions begin to more accurately describe that individual.

How does one deal creatively with the reserved and independent tendency when its expression is causing a problem? First, these people must realize they are expressing two good strengths — the thinking strength and independent risking strength. They shouldn't feel they need to give up these strengths or even hold back using them; rather, they should make a conscious effort to express more of their own assertiveness (risking) and risk more dependence (dependent risking). In terms of the flexing concept, those with a natural tendency toward being reserved and independent should continue to affirm and express their thinking and independence, but consciously and deliberately blend in more of their assertive and dependent strengths. However, they should do this only after becoming aware their natural tendency is causing a problem. If they try to catch it too early, before it causes a problem, they tend to become something other than who they really are and lose the force and creativity of their natural lead strengths.

Assertive and Relational Tendency

The assertive and relational tendency comes from emphasis on two important Bi/Polar strengths: (1) the dynamic, moving, action-oriented risking strength and (2) the courage to risk dependence on another person. These two basic strengths together bring a good deal of warmth and active caring to a relationship. People who express this tendency move toward others in an assertive way, seeking to initiate contact and create a close relationship.

The assertive and relational tendency is expressed in active, reaching-out behavior, characterized by friendliness and helpfulness. People with this tendency are supportive, sympathetic, and self-sacrificing. The center of attention is the other person rather than self. They seek communication, sharing, and closeness. Usually they are highly social, emotionally expressive, and feel at home dealing with feelings.

Bi/Polar Patterns V and VI tend to naturally experience and express the assertive and relational tendency. Other patterns may express this tendency, but for the V's and VI's it is a natural tendency, coming from their basic make-up.

The assertive and relational tendency is illustrated in the third section in Figure 15. The curved line coming out of the ellipse on the left and going across the line of creativity shows the assertive strength becoming an aggressive strength when it invades the territory of the other person. The downward, swooping line that ends up cradling the other person in active support shows that interest and concern tends to center on the other person.

Because the assertive and dependent strengths are emphasized in an expression of the assertive and relational tendency, the thinking strength and the independent risking strength are automatically de-emphasized. This relatively "weak" expression of thinking and independence sometimes causes people who express this tendency to be inaccurately described with such negative terms as: smothering, clinging vine, flighty, burdensome, mushy, emotionally unstable, sentimental, copy cat, impressionable, too friendly, etc. However, if the individual is polarized on risking and dependent risking, then these terms begin to take on more accurate meaning.

Those who have a problem with the assertive and relational tendency can deal creatively with it by blending more thinking and more independence into their behavior. This requires a personal choice to shift emphasis to the thinking and independent risking strengths at appropriate times. The appropriate times are usually very specific and obvious, because those are the times when the tendency is causing the most problems. Although the deliberate and conscious shift of emphasis to the thinking and independent strengths involves the risk of losing some of the fruits of action and warm dependence, it does not stop the activity of these strengths. Those who deal creatively with this tendency remain true to their natural way of being by keeping their natural assertiveness and dependence active in the background. Dealing effectively with a tendency does not involve changing one's basic nature.

Assertive and Independent Tendency

Two important Bi/Polar strengths are emphasized in the expression of the assertive and independent tendency: (1) the dynamic, moving, action-oriented risking strength and (2) the courage to be independent. These two basic strengths stimulate enthusiasm, initiate action, and provide out-front leadership in a relationship.

In the expression of the assertive and independent tendency, the center of interest and concern is the self. Behavior expressing this tendency is characterized by self-confidence, self-awareness, and self-interest. Those who consistently express this tendency are self-starters, highly competitive, forceful, ambitious, and energetic. They drive hard to accomplish and usually have a strong impact on other people. They continually seek to expand their sphere of influence.

Bi/Polar Patterns VII and VIII tend to experience and express the assertive and independent tendency most frequently. All patterns have the assertive and independent strengths and emphasize these strengths at times. But VII's and VIII's have a natural tendency to lead with these strengths.

The bottom section in Figure 15 illustrates the assertive and independent tendency. The arrow coming out of the ellipse on the left represents the expression of the assertive and independent tendency. The portion of the arrow going across the line of creativity into the territory of the other person shows the aggressive element in the tendency — the tendency to invade the territory of the other person and establish dominion over it. The upward slant of the arrow suggests self-confidence.

In the expression of the assertive and independent tendency, the assertive, action-oriented strengths and the independent, self-oriented strengths are emphasized with a resulting de-emphasis on two important Bi/Polar strengths — thinking and dependence. Because of this, the following negative terms are sometimes used (inaccurately) to describe those who consistently express the assertive and independent tendency: pushy, domineering, impatient, egotistical, selfish, obnoxious, braggart, arrogant, presumptuous, combative, overbearing, loud-mouth, bully, etc. As was the case with the other tendencies, if the individual becomes polarized on the strengths being emphasized (in this case, risking and independent risking), then these negative terms begin to be more accurate in describing the individual.

The assertive and independent tendency is dealt with most effectively and creatively by consciously and deliberately thinking more about the other person and expressing more dependence upon them. This involves centering one's attention on the other person, looking straight across as an equal, asking questions and listening to what the other person has to say. When this is done creatively, the high internal drive to accomplish and the strong independent strength remains, but there is more awareness and concern for the other person and more active dependence is placed upon them. As with the other three tendencies, this shift of emphasis to neglected strengths does not get rid of the tendency but brings balance and creativity to one's relationships.

12.

Relationship Characteristics of Each Pattern

This chapter describes the relationship characteristics the eight patterns of core strengths tend to produce. Each of the eight descriptions is presented separately.

Pattern I

Lead Strengths	Supporting Strengths	Flex-patterns
Thinking	Risking	V
Practical thinking	Theoretical thinking	III
Dependent risking	Independent risking	II

Relationship Strengths

People with Pattern I core strengths normally bring a good deal of stability and warmth to a relationship. Their consistent and organized approach to the world can contribute much to a team effort, and their natural inclination toward cooperation makes them good team members. They are very dependable and can be counted on to keep things running smoothly on a consistent basis. Their natural warmth and concern for other people contributes to an atmosphere of acceptance and frequently pours oil on the "troubled waters" of a relationship. They are good listeners and very supportive in their relationships. Loyalty is one of their finest strengths.

They can bring other values to their relationships by deliberately emphasizing their three supporting strengths. First, they can bring a spark of dynamism by emphasizing their risking strength (Flex-pattern V). Second, they can bring more conceptual understanding by emphasizing their theoretical thinking (Flex-pattern III). Third, they can bring stable leadership by emphasizing their independent strength (Flex-pattern II).

Natural Tendencies
Normally those with Pattern I strengths express the reserved and relational tendency more frequently than any other relationship tendency.   They tend to be quiet, unassertive, supportive, and accepting in their relationships. The personal tendency that usually gives them the most trouble is avoiding confrontation and conflict by not expressing their thoughts and feelings. They tend to understate their needs and desires, and feel uncomfortable standing up for their rights. Sometimes they are so quiet and respectful that other people don't know how they feel or what they want.

They have a natural urge to respond to the needs of others. Although this is an admirable and creative thing, when the urge is given free rein, they find that they are letting the needs and desires of others rule their lives. They no longer have time or energy for their own needs and desires.

Another tendency that frequently has an adverse effect on their relationships is to polarize on their problems and dwell on the negatives. When they fail to deal creatively with this tendency, they develop a negative attitude and become depressed. In turn, these negative feelings and attitudes can sour their relationships and drive people away from them.

What Those With Pattern I Strengths Want From Others
All patterns want to be accepted and respected by other people, but those who have Pattern I strengths usually experience this as an especially strong need. How others feel about them makes a great deal of difference in how they feel about themselves. They want

recognition and encouragement, and they don't want to have to demand it from other people.

They also want to receive stimulation from others. They feel most comfortable when others are taking the initiative and causing things to happen, and they are being called on to help out. They want to be included and feel the support of other people.

They want to be needed by others, and they want others to help them feel good about themselves. They want others to take the leadership role, but they want to be recognized and appreciated for their own contributions.

Pattern II

Lead Strengths	Supporting Strengths	Flex-patterns
Thinking	Risking	VII
Practical thinking	Theoretical thinking	IV
Independent risking	Dependent risking	I

Relationship Strengths

Those with Pattern II core strengths bring stable leadership to their relationships — particularly in rationality, practicality, and realistic planning. They take the initiative to organize and stabilize situations.

They also bring a sense of excellence to their relationships. They are quality-minded and set high standards for achievement. They provide objectivity, efficiency, discipline, and practical reasoning to a team effort.

They are self-confident and bring a solid feeling of power and confidence to their relationships. They provide motivation to see things through and "stick with it" when the going gets tough. They have a high internal drive for tangible accomplishment and give confidence to other people who are working with them in a team effort.

People who have Pattern II strengths can bring other values to their relationships by deliberately emphasizing their three support-ing strengths. First, they can stimulate more interaction and action by becoming more self-assertive (Flex-pattern VII). Second, they can bring an expanded awareness of possibilities by emphasizing their imaginative strengths (Flex-pattern IV). Third, they can bring more warmth and appreciation by emphasizing their dependent strengths (Flex-pattern I).

Natural Tendencies
Those who have Pattern II strengths are naturally reserved and independent in their relationships. Sometimes they are referred to as loners. They are self-confident and have a tendency to withdraw into their own self-sufficiency. They are very much "do-it-yourself" people — they rely on their own strengths. Usually, it is a real chore for them to delegate authority and depend upon other people. Many who have this combination of strengths feel as if dependence on others is really a "weakness", not a strength.

They have a tendency to be overly critical of other people. They tend to see other people's faults and shortcomings much more clearly than they see their potential. Failure to deal creatively with this tendency can be very damaging to their relationships.

Perhaps the most frequently expressed tendency of people who have Pattern II strengths is that of holding their feelings within. Usually they find it very difficult to be emotionally expressive and show people their real feelings — particularly warm, dependent feelings. Sometimes they feel very unsure of themselves when dealing with these feelings — either their own or someone else's. Because of this, they tend to keep a tight rein on their own feelings and feel awkward and threatened when others are showing their feelings — particularly dependent feelings.

What Those With Pattern II Strengths Want From Others
They want space. Normally, they want other people to be objective
and rational in the relationship. When they are aware the relationship
needs an expression of warmth, they prefer the other person to take
the initiative to express it. They want to be respected and particularly
dislike other people trying to get too close. They want others to listen
to them when they have something to say.

People with Pattern II strengths prefer a relationship where the
two people involved are working together to achieve a tangible result.
They prefer a relationship that is task-oriented rather than rela-
tionship-oriented. They want others to be logical and rational and,
above all, to make sense.

Pattern III

Lead Strengths	Supporting Strengths	Flex-patterns
Thinking	Risking	VI
Theoretical thinking	Practical thinking	I
Dependent risking	Independent risking	IV

Relationship Strengths
People who have Pattern III core strengths contribute conceptual
clarity in their relationships. They usually have a depth of understanding regarding ideas and theories — particularly those that are
proven and well-established. Usually they are an excellent source of
information on a wide variety of subjects. Their sensitivity and insight
into moral issues can contribute a good deal to a particular relationship.

They bring approachability and quiet warmth to a relationship.
They are supportive, agreeable, and tend to play the role of peace-
maker. They can be a good communication link between two people
who are having problems in their relationship. They make good
team members.

They are usually very conscientious. They bring stability, consistency, and dependability to their relationships. They tend to be respectful and thoughtful of others and are usually very sensitive to the feelings of others. Usually they get along very well with other people and sometimes are cooperative to a fault.

Those who have the Pattern III combination of strengths can bring other values to their relationships by deliberately emphasizing their three supporting strengths. First, they can stimulate more dynamic interaction by emphasizing their assertive strengths (expressing their Flex-pattern VI). Second, they can bring more practicality and realism by emphasizing their practical thinking (expressing their Flex-pattern I). Third, they can bring more leadership to the relationship by emphasizing their independent strength (expressing their Flex-pattern IV).

Natural Tendencies
People who have Pattern III strengths are naturally reserved and relational in their relationships. They tend to be unassertive and wait for others to make the first move. A number of those who have these strengths find their most troublesome tendency is to be quiet and not speak up when they should. This is particularly true in their relationships with self-confident and assertive persons. Closely related to this tendency, they find it hard to say "no" and sometimes end up letting the demands and wishes of others rule their lives.

They tend to avoid confrontation and conflict if at all possible. Their tendency to exaggerate the importance of others and depreciate their own importance makes it difficult for them to stand up strongly for their own rights.

Another tendency they tend to experience is procrastination. This tendency to re-think a problem rather than commit themselves to a course of action is a common and recurring problem for most people who have this combination of strengths.

What Those With Pattern III Strengths Want From Others
They want to be appreciated and respected, without having to ask for it or demand it. They want others to help them feel good about themselves and give them encouragement.

Those who have Pattern III strengths like for others to take the initiative and provide dynamic stimulation. They are most comfortable when others take the leadership role and ask them for their help. They want to know they are needed and appreciated.

They want support and approval from other people. Although all patterns want this support and approval, with them it is a critical need. A good deal of their self-confidence comes from the support and approval they receive from others.

Pattern IV

Lead Strengths	Supporting Strengths	Flex-patterns
Thinking	Risking	VIII
Theoretical thinking	Practical thinking	II
Independent risking	Dependent risking	III

Relationship Strengths
People who have Pattern IV core strengths are the most introverted of all the eight Bi/Polar patterns. All three lead strengths of this pattern point inward — (1) thinking, (2) theoretical, and (3) independence. The combination of these three strengths results in a creative and innovative thinker — particularly in the realm of ideas and abstract concepts. One of the most important contributions they make to their relationships is that of new ideas and innovative approaches to solving old problems.

They tend to be leaders in the realm of new ideas and innovations, but normally are not leaders of people in the emotional sense. Neither are they emotional followers of people. Rather they tend to follow ideas which are either their own, or ideas of others they have thought through and made their own. They usually express their leadership most effectively in writing. Usually they are less effective in face-to-face activities such as debating.

They tend to be very intense and insightful people. Their enthusiasm, imagination, unpredictability, and self-confidence can bring a dynamic spark to a relationship. Their ideas and concepts can sometimes provide powerful motivation for human accomplishment.

Those with Pattern IV strengths can bring other values to their relationships by deliberately emphasizing their three supporting strengths. First, they can make the relationship more dynamic and exciting by emphasizing their assertive strengths (Flex-pattern VIII). Second, they can bring more practicality and realism by emphasizing their practical thinking (Flex-pattern II). Third, they can bring more warmth and appreciation into the relationship by emphasizing their dependent strength (Flex-pattern III).

Natural Tendencies
People who have Pattern IV strengths are characteristically reserved and independent in their relationships. Their major tendency is to withdraw into their own self-sufficiency and work out their problems alone. Expression of this tendency usually causes real problems in their relationships, because it tends to make others feel rejected, left out, and depreciated.

Another tendency that frequently gives them a problem in their relationships is their tendency toward perfection. This causes them to be overly critical and demanding of other people, thus effectively putting people on the defensive and tending to drive them away.

Still another problem they sometimes experience in their relationships comes from their tendency to become married to their own ideas. They feel personally threatened if anyone questions or belittles their ideas. This threat can cause them to experience a good deal of resentment and hostility. They tend to reject those who don't appreciate their ideas and can become very critical of them.

What Those With Pattern IV Strengths Want From Others
The most important thing people with Pattern IV strengths want from others is respect. They value their independence and autonomy very highly and are supersensitive to violations of their territory. Although they want and need relationships with others, it is important that they have space and distance in these relationships.

They want to be independent and self-sufficient and want others to be the same in their relationships with them. The most difficult thing for IV's to handle in a relationship is an expression of dependence. They have difficulty expressing their own dependence and tend to feel restricted and violated when others depend too heavily on them.

They feel threatened when others try to get too close or personal. They feel very uncomfortable when others push too hard, demanding an emotional reaction from them. They want respect but are easily embarrassed if put in the limelight or bragged on. They usually feel awkward in accepting compliments.

Pattern V

Lead Strengths	Supporting Strengths	Flex-patterns
Risking	Thinking	I
Practical thinking	Theoretical thinking	VI
Dependent risking	Independent risking	VII

Relationship Strengths
Pattern V core strengths tend to produce people who are very extraverted. Their three lead strengths are (1) risking, (2) dependence, and (3) practical thinking — all outer-directed. Relationships with others are most important for people who have this combination of strengths. They are assertive in establishing relationships and continually seek closeness with other people. Although all people need and want the warmth of human companionships, with them,

interaction with other people is at the center of their lives. All other values are secondary to the warmth of human relationships.

They are usually very much aware of other people — especially their feelings. They are very interested in the personal lives of other people and invite others to share their feelings with them. People generally feel comfortable with them and are motivated to "let their hair down" and talk about their personal problems. Pattern V's are easy to talk to.

They are usually good coordinators of practical affairs. It is easy and natural for them to express affection, warmth, and acceptance — the natural emotional bridge for communication. Generally speaking, V's are excellent communicators. Frequently they are highly effective as one-to-one counselors.

Those who have Pattern V strengths can bring other values to their relationships by deliberately emphasizing their three supporting strengths. First, they can bring rationality and reserve by emphasizing their thinking strengths (Flex-pattern I). Second, they can bring dynamic leadership to the relationship by emphasizing their independent strength (Flex-pattern VII). Third, they can bring a vision of possibilities by emphasizing their imaginative strengths (Flex-pattern VI).

Natural Tendencies
People who have the Pattern V strengths are naturally assertive and relational in their relationships. One of their strongest tendencies is to go overboard in pleasing other people. Sometimes this causes them to get so involved in helping others they find they have no time for themselves. They find their lives ruled by the wants, needs, and demands of others. They are no longer running their own lives.

They live on recognition and compliments. In an effort to be well-liked and approved by others, they sometimes avoid confrontation and conflict when they should stand up for their own rights. One of their most troublesome tendencies is to say "yes" when they should say "no".

What Those With Pattern V Strengths Want From Others
They want others to react to them — show their feelings and tell them what they are thinking. They especially want others to tell them how they are feeling toward them. It is not enough to tell them how you feel about them only occasionally. They want you to tell them every day.

When they make an overture of friendliness, they want a response! They much prefer a warm friendly response, but even bad news is better than no news at all. They want to be noticed and recognized. It is hard to give them too many compliments.

They want to be needed. They want others to ask for their help and accept what they have to give. Their greatest fulfillment comes when they are doing something for someone else.

Pattern VI

Lead Strengths	Supporting Strengths	Flex-patterns
Risking	Thinking	III
Theoretical thinking	Practical thinking	V
Dependent risking	Independent risking	VIII

Relationship Strengths
People who have Pattern VI core strengths bring a good deal of emotional warmth to a relationship. Their outgoing, people-oriented strengths are frequently expressed in an easy social grace that makes others feel warm and accepted. Their emotional feel for people and situations helps to lubricate human relationships and bring people closer together.

They initiate communication and bring a dynamic spark to a relationship. They like to see people happy and having a good time. Frequently they take the lead in group activities and get people involved and reacting together. They like to entertain and please other people. VI's have the natural strengths that contribute life, sparkle, and warmth to group activities.

They bring trust and openness to a relationship. They display their emotions openly and encourage others to be open with them. They are usually effective in encouraging others to talk and share their feelings.

Those who have Pattern VI strengths can bring other values to their relationships by deliberately emphasizing their three supporting strengths. First, they can bring rationality and calm by emphasizing their thinking strengths (Flex-pattern III). Second, they can bring dynamic leadership by emphasizing their strength of independence (Flex-pattern VIII). Third, they can bring practicality and realism to the relationship by emphasizing their practical thinking strength (Flex-pattern V).

Natural Tendencies
People who have Pattern VI strengths are naturally assertive and relational in their relationships. Probably the tendency that gives them most problems is that of going overboard to please other people. They can get so involved in making other people happy they can't say "no" to them when it needs to be said. Thus, they can arrive at the point where the needs and demands of others are ruling their lives, and they become a doormat for other people to walk on rather than self-directed individuals.

Another tendency that sometimes gives them a problem is trusting people too much. They have the tendency to trust and idealize people beyond the reality of their trustworthiness, causing them to become overexposed, where other people can easily take advantage of them.

Their tendency to come on too strong and smother the other person with too much attention, concern, and affection can also cause major problems in their relationships. Usually this causes the other person to run away, reject, or attack them. Any of these responses is bad for the relationship and is distressing to the Pattern VI.

What Those With Pattern VI Strengths Want From Others
How other people relate to them is of critical importance to those who have Pattern VI strengths. Relationships with others are important to everyone, but with them it is the most important single force in their lives. Since relationships are so critically important to them, they are highly sensitive to the quality of their relationships and tend to be affected greatly by them.

They want to be needed. They want others to ask them for their help and trust them to be a friend. They want others to be open with their feelings and share their problems with them.

They want to be recognized and appreciated in very obvious ways. They want others to tell them how much they appreciate them and lay it on heavy. They don't want to guess how other people are feeling toward them — they want to be told!

They want other people to interact with them in a warm and accepting way. Perhaps their greatest enjoyment comes when other people respond to them in an active way, displaying a good deal of warm appreciation and sincere friendliness.

Pattern VII

Lead Strengths	Supporting Strengths	Flex-patterns
Risking	Thinking	II
Practical thinking	Theoretical thinking	VIII
Independent risking	Dependent risking	V

Relationship Strengths
People who have Pattern VII core strengths bring initiative, confidence, enthusiasm, and dynamic movement to a relationship. They stimulate action and get things moving. They are natural emotional leaders. They tend to step out front and say "follow me".

They energize a relationship. They bring a high drive to accomplish and a full dedication to winning. They bring the excitement of

186 U N D E R S T A N D I N G   O T H E R   P E O P L E

competitive challenge and the courage to move and do, in spite of the risk. The quote from an early American naval hero — "Damn the torpedoes, full speed ahead" — is very descriptive of the leadership and courage they can bring to their relationships.

Practicality is another strength they bring to a relationship. They risk on a calculated basis and are usually realistic about what can be accomplished. They encourage others to look at the facts and seek out practical ways to accomplish their objectives.

Those who have Pattern VII strengths can bring other values to their relationships by consciously emphasizing their three supporting strengths. First, they can bring more rationality and planning by emphasizing their thinking strengths (Flex-pattern II). Second, they can bring more warm encouragement and support by emphasizing their dependent strengths (Flex-pattern V). Third, they can bring more vision of possibilities by emphasizing their theoretical thinking strength (Flex-pattern VIII).

Natural Tendencies

People who have Pattern VII strengths are naturally assertive and independent in their relationships. They tend to move assertively into the other person's territory and sometimes move on past them as they actively pursue their personal goals.

From their high drive to accomplish, they tend to experience a good deal of impatience with other people. They usually have clear and compelling goals they want to accomplish, and quickly become impatient with anything that interferes with or slows down the process of achieving them. They tend to be much more aware of what they are trying to accomplish that they are of the other person in the relationship.

They also have a strong tendency to talk when they should be listening. Frequently, when they are not saying anything in a relationship, they are not really listening but figuring out what they are going to say when the other person stops talking.

Their tendency to rely more on themselves than other people can become a serious problem in their relationships. If this tendency takes them to the point where they are trying to do it all themselves and refusing to trust or rely on other people, their relationships deteriorate rapidly. Those who are relating to them tend to feel depreciated, put down, and unworthy.

What Those With Pattern VII Strengths Want From Others
Those with Pattern VII strengths want an active relationship where there is a lot of excitement and give-and-take going on. They want a response more than anything else. The kind of response is not too important — they just want a response.

They want people to come on direct and straightforward, saying what they mean, with force. They enjoy others being competitive, even to the point of conflict. Sometimes a good fight is just what they want.

They want recognition and enjoy being in the spotlight. They want to be leaders and have others follow them. They want the relationship to be productive and accomplish something.

Pattern VIII

Lead Strengths	Supporting Strengths	Flex-patterns
Risking	Thinking	IV
Theoretical thinking	Practical thinking	VII
Independent risking	Dependent risking	VI

Relationship Strengths
People who have Pattern VIII core strengths bring excitement, enthusiasm, confidence, and imagination to their relationships. They fire people's imaginations and stir their emotions. They are emotional leaders who sell and promote their ideas and dreams. Many political and religious leaders have the Pattern VIII configuration of strengths.

They take the initiative in their relationships. They willingly make the first move and get the interaction started. If the relationship becomes dull and boring, they find ways to liven it up. They step out front, take a strong position, and expose themselves on their own initiative. They contribute energy, spontaneity, and dynamic action — things happen in their relationships.

They can bring other values into their relationships by consciously emphasizing their three supporting strengths. First, they can bring more rationality and stability into the relationship by shifting to their Flex-pattern IV and emphasizing their thinking strengths. Second, they can bring warm encouragement and support by shifting to their Flex-pattern VI and emphasizing their dependent strengths. Third, they can bring realism and practicality by shifting to their Flex-pattern VII and emphasizing their practical thinking strengths.

Natural Tendencies
Those who have Pattern VIII strengths are naturally assertive and independent in their relationships. One of their most obvious tendencies is to move assertively toward other people and seek to have a strong impact on them. In their effort to strongly influence others, they frequently overstate, exaggerate, and make extreme statements. Sometimes they take an extreme position in order to shock people and draw attention to themselves.

They tend to talk when they should be listening. Their normal orientation tends to make them so intent on influencing others, they don't have time to be influenced themselves. Sometimes, others give up and leave the relationship because they find it so difficult to actually influence them.

Another tendency that sometimes gives them problems in their relationships is taking action too quickly — before they get all the facts. Although their intuitive feel is very valuable and sometimes very accurate, without a solid rational basis their actions become suspect to most people.

To the extent they fail to deal creatively with their tendency to overemphasize their intuitive feel, others tend to lose confidence in them and withdraw their support.

What Those With Pattern VIII Strengths Want From Others
Those with Pattern VIII core strengths want the spotlight. They like to be highly visible and noticed by other people. They want others to recognize them and respond to their leadership.

They want to see the impact they are having on others. They want others to show them how they are influencing them. The most difficult thing for them to handle is "no response". A person who "just sits there" and refuses to interact is an enigma for them. Without some kind of response, they have no place to go — they don't know what to do next to try to influence the person.

They want other people to be influenced strongly by them and interact on the basis of that influence. They want to maintain control of the relationship and have it focus on their own interest and concerns.

IV.

Strengthening Your Relationships

13.

How to Strengthen Relationships

This chapter presents some practical guidelines for using Bi/Polar concepts to strengthen relationships. It is divided into three sections.

The first presents a discussion on how we can deal creatively with our natural tendencies when they give us problems in our relationships. It shows how we can blend in a stronger expression of our supporting strengths, yet still remain true to our natural way of being.

The second gives some practical suggestions on how we can discover another person's core pattern of strengths.

The third discusses how we can strengthen our relationships by relating to other people in terms of their core patterns.

A chart at the end of the chapter gives some specific suggestions on how to relate to individual people according to their particular patterns of core strengths.

Dealing Creatively With Our Own
Relationship Tendencies

In the previous discussion on personal growth, mature people were described as those who do two things well. First, they are true to themselves — they express their natural way of being. Second, they are flexible and adaptable — they emphasize their supporting strengths when the situation requires it. The same creative duality operates in people who develop strong relationships with others.

First, they show who they really are by expressing their natural way of being; second, they deliberately shift emphasis to their supporting strengths when the relationship requires it. It is important to emphasize that they do both of these things. Although doing these two seemingly opposite things may appear to be a paradox, this is precisely what people do when they have a creative and productive relationship with another person. They show their true nature and, at the same time, express the strengths needed to strengthen the relationship.

We may use Figure 16 to illustrate how we can, in actual practice, remain true to our natural way of being and, at the same time, consciously blend in a stronger expression of our supporting strengths. The four diagrams in Figure 16 are the same ones used in Figure 15 to depict how the four relationship tendencies are expressed in our relationships. A dashed arrow has been added in each of the four diagrams to illustrate how we can move into the zone of creativity with another person by keeping our natural way of being and emphasizing our supporting strengths at the same time.

The diagram at the top of Figure 16 shows how a person who tends to be reserved and relational can move into the zone of creativity by being a little more assertive and independent in the relationship. Those who have core Patterns I or III tend to experience this tendency the most. The dashed arrow goes closer to the line of creativity and moves closer to the horizontal. This indicates more assertiveness and more equality in the relationship. The dashed arrow is still back from the line of creativity and still droops down somewhat, but not as much as before. In this way, the person still shows the characteristics of reserve and dependence, but at the same time blends in a stronger expression of assertiveness and independence. People who deal with their reserved and relational tendency in this way create the best opportunity to strengthen their relationships with another person, regardless of who the other person may be.

The second diagram illustrates how those with the reserved and independent tendency can blend in more assertiveness and depen-

Dealing Creatively With Our Relationship Tendencies

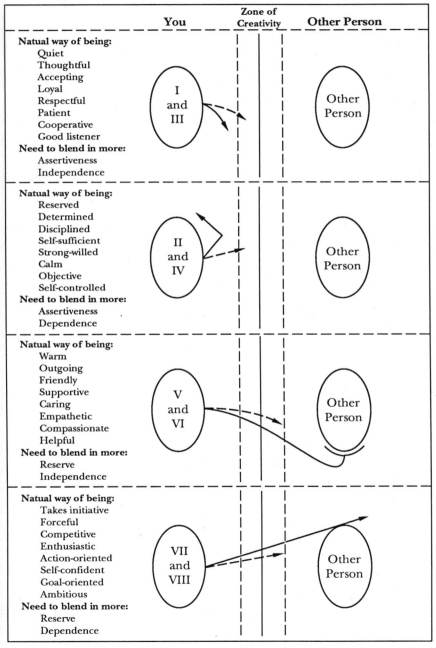

	You	Zone of Creativity	Other Person

Natual way of being:
Quiet
Thoughtful
Accepting
Loyal
Respectful
Patient
Cooperative
Good listener
Need to blend in more:
Assertiveness
Independence

I and III

Other Person

Natual way of being:
Reserved
Determined
Disciplined
Self-sufficient
Strong-willed
Calm
Objective
Self-controlled
Need to blend in more:
Assertiveness
Dependence

II and IV

Other Person

Natual way of being:
Warm
Outgoing
Friendly
Supportive
Caring
Empathetic
Compassionate
Helpful
Need to blend in more:
Reserve
Independence

V and VI

Other Person

Natual way of being:
Takes initiative
Forceful
Competitive
Enthusiastic
Action-oriented
Self-confident
Goal-oriented
Ambitious
Need to blend in more:
Reserve
Dependence

VII and VIII

Other Person

Figure 16

dence, thereby strengthening their relationships. Those with core Patterns II and IV tend to experience this tendency. The dashed arrow shows that their natural way of being is still there but is modified to a degree by their being somewhat more assertive and dependent. The arrow moves closer to the line of creativity and moves down somewhat, indicating a more level relationship with the other person. In actual behavior, they show more awareness and concern for others and move closer to them. Those who have this tendency still show the "flavor" of reserve and independence, but make a conscious, obvious effort to be more assertive and dependent.

The third diagram illustrates how those with assertive and relational tendencies can blend in more reserve and independence, thereby building stronger relationships. Those with core Patterns V or VI tend to experience this tendency. As indicated by the dashed arrow, those with this tendency still express their natural assertiveness and warmth toward the other person, but they moderate the expression of these strengths by blending in more thinking and self-sufficiency. In actual behavior, they become more thoughtful and depend more on their own internal strengths to solve their problems. Their natural warmth and caring for others is still there and functional, but it is expressed with more respect for others and in a quieter way.

The fourth diagram at the bottom of Figure 16 illustrates how those with assertive and independent tendencies can modify their expression of these strengths and create stronger relationships with others. Those with core Patterns VII or VIII tend to express this tendency. The dashed arrow indicates that those who have this tendency become more thoughtful and reserved, and focus their attention more on the other person in the relationship. Their natural assertiveness and self-confidence is still there, but made more creative by a stronger blend of basic thinking and courage to depend more on the other person.

Knowing the Other Person

In our efforts to strengthen a relationship, it is important not only that we understand ourselves, but equally important that we understand the other person in the relationship. The Bi/Polar System and its concepts may be used to deepen our understanding of another person and, out of that understanding, strengthen the relationship. Our knowledge of a person's core pattern of strengths gives us dependable guidelines for what we must do to build a strong relationship and good communication with that person.

How can we go about discovering another person's core pattern of strengths? There are at least three distinct avenues we may pursue. First, we can use the results of the *Bi/Polar Inventories of Core Strengths*. Second, we can talk with them about their own perception of their core pattern of strengths. Third, we can observe them and make a subjective guess about their pattern.

Using the Results of the *Bi/Polar Inventories of Core Strengths*
The most dependable way for an individual to accurately identify their pattern of strengths is through using the results of the *Bi/Polar Inventories of Core Strengths* along with the experience of attending the seminar *Bi/Polar: Foundations of Productivity*. If you are reading this book, the chances are that you have done (or are planning to do) just that.

The best use of Bi/Polar in terms of strengthening relationships is done between two people who have had that experience. They know what their respective patterns of core strengths are, and, when they discuss their relationship, they can both speak a common language.

Talking With Other People About
Their Own Perceptions of Their Core Pattern
Beyond just observing and thinking about others, we can gather additional information directly. We can engage them in a discussion

about the Bi/Polar concepts and ask what they see as their core pattern. An interaction of this sort is usually a very satisfying and productive experience for both parties. Frequently, it results in getting to know others much better, and usually we end up having a much better idea about their core patterns.

However, if that person has not been through the experience of the seminar on Bi/Polar, then that lack of a background of knowledge will hinder any effective use of the knowledge of the patterns.

Making a Subjective Guess About Another Person's Pattern

As we observe the personality characteristics displayed by other people, we can begin to associate them with a particular pattern. For example, if a person tends to be quiet and reserved, it suggests a lead strength in thinking — hence the guess that their core pattern is I, II, III, or IV. If, on the other hand, the person is active, outgoing, and assertive, it would suggest one of the risking patterns — V, VI, VII, or VIII. As we observe other characteristics being expressed, we pick up additional clues that suggest a leaning toward a particular polar strength. As we gather information, we make an educated guess regarding the person's basic pattern, then look for evidence to either confirm that pattern or bring it into question.

There are at least five important limitations to this approach. The first is that the knowledge of the patterns and all that is behind it cannot be freely shared between the two people in the relationship. The second is that the tendency is to "type" that individual and box them in rather than bring in all the factors that make a person who he or she is. The third is that one person's perception of another is subject to all kinds of factors that produce inaccurate perceptions of that other person (most importantly, the relationship we have with that person). The fourth is that, if we have only a superficial understanding of the patterns, our guesses are not very educated. A fifth factor that also influences the accuracy of our guess regarding another person's pattern is our own needs, desires, and prejudices.

Our perception of another person's core pattern is always distorted to some degree by our own wants. We can very easily perceive a person as we want them to be, rather than who that person is in reality.

Relating to Others in Terms of Their Bi/Polar Pattern of Core Strengths

Being aware of other people's core patterns of strengths gives us some valuable information about how we can go about strengthening our relationships with them. Figure 17 presents some specific suggestions about how to be most effective in our relationships with people when we know their patterns of core strengths.

However, everyone should keep in mind that the pattern is only a conceptual tool to help understand people — everyone is more than just a pattern.

How to Relate to People According to
Their Core Pattern

PATTERNS I & III	PATTERNS II & IV	PATTERNS V & VI	PATTERNS VII & VIII
1. Take initiative in a quiet way.	1. Take initiative but let them make their own decisions.	1. Get involved and interact with them.	1. Respond! React to their initiative.
2. Involve them in working out the details.	2. Consult with them in defining problems and objectives.	2. Rely on their ability to initiate relationships and make others feel at ease.	2. Challenge them.
3. Ask them to help in specific ways.	3. Challenge them to suggest solutions to problems.	3. Expect them to help — tell them how they can help.	3. Identify the objective then let them accomplish it in their own way.
4. Stay close enough to give support when needed.	4. Give them space, don't crowd.	4. Stay close and let them talk through problems.	4. Stay close enough to interact and respond as new challenges emerge.
5. Give encouragement.	5. Stay rational, objective, and task-oriented.	5. Express your feelings and share your concerns.	5. Come on straight and with force.
6. Show appreciation by being a friend.	6. Show appreciation through a quiet respect for their competence.	6. Show appreciation by giving recognition and lots of compliments.	6. Show appreciation by recognizing their leadership and giving your support.
Pattern I only: Draw on their practical down-to-earth thinking.	**Pattern II only:** Draw on their analytical thinking abilities.	**Pattern V only:** Draw on their ability to coordinate practical projects.	**Pattern VII only:** Draw on their ability to give leadership to practical projects.
Pattern III only: Draw on their knowledge about proven ideas.	**Pattern IV only:** Draw on their ability to conceive new ideas.	**Pattern VI only:** Draw on their ability to entertain and enliven social interaction.	**Pattern VIII only:** Draw on their ability to stimulate change and promote new ideas.

Figure 17

14.

Pattern Relationships

Caution in Using Bi/Polar Pattern Relationships

It is important to recognize the limitations of the pattern relationships presented in this section. One must keep in mind that they describe pattern relationships — not real people relationships. It is true there is a good deal of congruence between pattern relationships and real people relationships — that is where the value lies. But the other forces that affect a relationship must be taken into account if one is to understand any particular relationship. Sometimes these other forces are even more important than the Bi/Polar patterns of the people themselves. Personal differences in cultural and experience backgrounds, value systems, innate capacities, and maturity levels are certainly important variables in a relationship between two people. One of the most potent influences in a relationship is the immediate situation in which the two people find themselves. For example, the authority elements in a relationship between a superior and subordinate have a great deal of effect on that relationship; a marriage relationship brings forth a whole new set of situational influences. The 36 pattern relationships presented here deal only with those forces arising from the core pattern and do not take into account other personal characteristics or any situational factors.

The advantage of pointing up the limitations of these pattern relationships is to put their true value in bold relief. The outstanding value in understanding the pattern relationship between two real people in that we are dealing with something in the relationship that is stable, constant, and basic. The pattern dynamics are fundamental elements that are always at work — they were at work in the past, they are at work in the present, and they will be at work in the future. A clear concept of the pattern dynamics in a relationship can provide a stable foundation on which to build a more complete understanding that takes into account other influences beyond the pattern.

How to Interpret the Pattern Relationship Drawings

The solid arrows in the drawings represent the natural relationship tendencies produced by the patterns. The dashed arrows represent the adjustment each person can make to enter the zone of creativity and strengthen the relationship.

How to Find a Particular Pattern Relationship

Figure 18 presents a locator chart as an easy reference to locate the page number on which each of the 36 pattern relationships may be found. It works in the same way as a mileage chart.

Locator Chart for Pattern Relationships

(By Page Numbers)

	I	II	III	IV	V	VI	VII	VIII
I	204	207	210	214	217	221	224	228
II	207	231	235	238	242	245	249	252
III	210	235	256	259	262	265	268	272
IV	214	238	259	275	278	281	285	288
V	217	242	262	278	292	294	297	301
VI	221	245	265	281	294	304	307	311
VII	224	249	268	285	297	307	314	318
VIII	228	252	272	288	301	311	318	322

Figure 18

Bi/Polar Pattern Relationship I-I

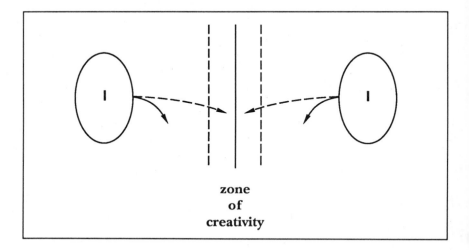

zone
of
creativity

Description

In a relationship between two Pattern I's, both tend to stay back from the line of creativity and hesitate to move toward each other. They reach out to one another in a very quiet, tentative, and hesitant way. Both are approachable and want the relationship, but each waits for the other to make the first move.

The relationship is very susceptible to outside influences. It is usually influenced more by outside forces that it is by forces within the relationship. It is normal for two Pattern I's to look outside the relationship for stimulation and direction.

Interactions between I's tend to be more intellectual than emotional. Neither is assertive in expressing feelings. Their conversations tend to center around practical matters and tangible things. They deal with facts and immediate situations. Together they are usually quite proficient in seeing things as they are and identifying what is wrong in a situation.

Typical Problems

It is natural for two Pattern I's to be unassertive and express reserved dependence with one another. Each wants the other to take the initiative. Since neither wants to make the first move, their relationship tends to suffer from lack of dynamism. This can cause them to feel dull, uninteresting, and bored with each other. If nothing is done to bring some life into the relationship, each can begin to resent the other because he or she is not more dynamic and assertive.

Another problem sometimes occurs between two Pattern I's when they polarize on their greatest strength — practical thinking. Through the use of this reality-oriented thinking strength, they naturally stimulate one another to see more and more negatives. This can set up a negative feedback, causing them to perceive a darker and darker picture. They can go hand-in-hand toward pessimism, depression, and despair.

Strengthening the Relationship

The relationship between two Pattern I's is usually strengthened by an expression of more dynamic strengths — more assertiveness, more imagination, and more independence. These strengths may come from the Pattern I's themselves or from other people outside the relationship. It can work either way; however, in practice it seems to be most effective when the strengths are brought in from the outside.

If two Pattern I's feel their relationship is dull and boring, one way to solve the problem is for them to join a dynamic, assertive, active group and participate in its activities. Another avenue is to seek out a naturally assertive and dynamic individual and bring this person into the relationship. Still another approach is for them to express their own dynamic potential without outside help. This involves a deliberate expression of their Flex-pattern V and an assertive expression of their feelings — they "let their hair down" with one another and share their real feelings. This shift to the emotional side can bring new life to the relationship and tap their potential for dynamic interaction.

If they find that together they develop negative attitudes and work themselves into a depressed state, they can draw on the outside world for positive solutions and a vision of new possibilities. They can do this by attaching themselves to groups or individual people whose thinking is more positive and optimistic. Another possibility is for them to shift into their Flex-pattern III and draw on each other's potential to imagine positive possibilities. After all, theoretical thinking is an intermediate strength of Pattern I's and, when stimulated, can be quite productive.

Two Pattern I's can achieve a very creative and deeply satisfying relationship. It requires following their natural reserved and relational tendency and dealing creatively with that tendency when it causes problems. A creative relationship between two Pattern I's is characterized by reserve, stability, and warmth, "sparked" at appropriate times with assertiveness, imagination, and dynamic interdependence. The "spark" can come from inside the relationship, outside the relationship, or from a combination of both sources.

Bi/Polar Pattern Relationship I-II

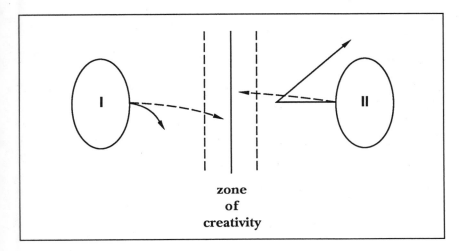

zone
of
creativity

Description

Patterns I and II are similar in that both lead with thinking and
practicality. They are different, however, in that they are at opposite
ends on the risking scale. Pattern I's lead in dependent risking;
Pattern II's lead in independent risking. Both have their greatest
strength of all in practical thinking — they are usually very good in
seeing things as they are.

Since both patterns lead in thinking, they tend to emphasize
rationality in their relationship and de-emphasize the expression of
feelings. This natural emphasis on rationality tends to make their
relationship stable and task-oriented rather than dynamic and feeling-oriented.

Neither moves assertively toward the other; however, Pattern II's
tend to take the initiative if they are working together to accomplish
a task. Pattern I's have a natural tendency to wait for Pattern II's to
provide leadership and usually feel comfortable following Pattern
II's.

Typical Problems

The tendency of Pattern II's to be task-oriented and have a lesser interest in people can cause them to appear "cold" or at least "cool" to Pattern I's. It is likely that Pattern II's will not be as sensitive to the feelings of Pattern I's as would be desirable. Out of this insensitivity, Pattern II's tend to communicate a lack of appreciation and acceptance for Pattern I's, easily generating discouragement and negative feelings within Pattern I's.

On the other hand, Pattern I's' tendency to be more people-oriented than task-oriented can cause a problem from the viewpoint of Pattern II's. Sometimes Pattern II's are pained and frustrated because Pattern I's do not take the initiative to get things done. Additionally, Pattern II's can feel frustrated because Pattern I's are not as task-oriented as they feel they ought to be. Since Pattern II's like to run a tight ship, the loose ship operation of Pattern I's can be very frustrating to them.

Another problem Patterns I and II can experience in their relationships comes from their common tendency to continue identifying the problem when they should be looking for solutions. When they are polarizing on the problems, they tend to identify all the things wrong in a situation and work themselves into a depressed state characterized by negative thinking, procrastination, and inaction.

Strengthening the Relationship

In general, the relationship between Patterns I and II suffers because of a need for more dynamic interaction. Both tend to hold their feelings within and not let the others know what is going on inside. The solution to most of their problems requires a conscious effort on both sides to get their feelings out in the open and let others know how they really feel. This is not easy, and it takes courage to pull it off, but the potential rewards for the relationship are great.

When Pattern I's feel unappreciated and "put down" by Pattern II's, they need to express their Flex-pattern V and tell the Pattern II's how they are feeling, to become assertive in sharing their discouragement and depressed feelings. This immediately brings an emotional dynamic into the relationship and stimulates an emotional response from Pattern II's. Once the interaction is sparked, Pattern I's need to shift emphasis to thinking by going into their Flex-pattern III and planning a deliberate expression of more independence. Finally, they need to move into their Flex-pattern II and express a greater measure of independence and self-sufficiency. Not only does this generate respect and appreciation for Pattern II's, but it also gives Pattern I's more self-confidence.

When Pattern II's find they are carrying an increasing load of negative feelings toward Pattern I's, it is time to get those feelings out in the open. II's express these feelings most naturally by expressing their Flex-pattern VII and sharing with Pattern I's the negative feelings they are experiencing because of the relationship. This sparks an emotional response from Pattern I's and gets the relationship moving. Once they have made emotional contact and have an interaction going, Pattern II's should shift into their Flex-pattern IV and plan a course of action expressing more dependence on Pattern I's — particularly an expression of dependence that is supportive, shows appreciation, and gives encouragement to Pattern I's. Finally, Pattern II's actually express this new blend of dependence by expressing their Flex-pattern I — they become more understanding and warm. Pattern I's have a special need for encouragement and support, and, when Pattern II's give it to them, it usually does wonders for the relationship.

When Patterns I and II become aware they are polarizing on their problems, they need to find some way to bring more imagination into their relationship. They can do this by deliberately stimulating their own strengths in theoretical thinking, or they can get other people involved with them.

If they choose to break polarization on their problems by using their own assertive and imaginative strengths, the first thing they must do is shift to their dynamic flex-patterns and get an interaction going — I's shift to their Flex-pattern V and II's shift to their Flex-pattern VII.

Frequently it is much easier and more effective for them to break polarization on their problems by interacting with other people outside the relationship. By relating to others who are naturally more dynamic and imaginative, they are relieved of the burden of consciously emphasizing those strengths that are not their natural lead strengths. Not only is it sometimes easier, but frequently it is more effective to draw on others, because those who have the needed strengths in natural dominance usually bring a stronger expression of them into the relationship.

Bi/Polar Pattern Relationship I-III

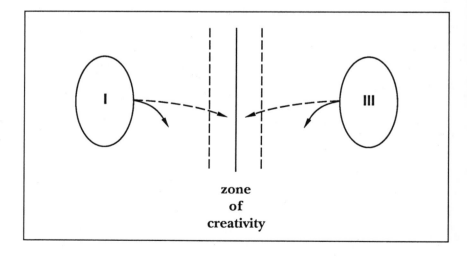

Description

Patterns I and III have two lead strengths in common: they both lead in thinking and dependent risking. They are different, however, in the way they think. Pattern I's lead in practical thinking, and Pattern III's lead in theoretical thinking. When Pattern I's recognize the values of Pattern III's' abilities in dealing with theories and ideas, and Pattern III's recognize the values in the practicality of Pattern I's, it becomes a highly positive factor in their relationship. This awareness of their complementary strengths enables them to draw on each other's strengths and create a feeding interaction. They become more creative in their thinking and more effective as a team.

Since Patterns III and I both lead in thinking and tend to have a need for greater self-confidence, they have very similar feelings toward themselves and other people. They have a common tendency to stay back from the line of creativity in their relationships — to be quiet and wait for others to take the initiative. Both shy from strong emotional expression — particularly expressions that could cause conflict or confrontation. Their relationship is likely to be characterized by warmth, acceptance, and stability. They reach out to each other in a reserved, respectful, tentative way and tend to feel comfortable with each other.

Typical Problems

The major problem Patterns I and III face in their relationships comes from their common tendency to avoid confrontation and conflict by not expressing their real feelings and thoughts. This can lead to a serious rupture of their relationship, simply because neither takes the initiative to start talking about problems, and, as a result, misunderstandings grow. Small problems become big problems because of a hesitancy on both sides to air the problems and get them out on the table.

Another problem can arise as they follow their natural tendencies and wait for others to make decisions about what they should do.

Their relationship can lose vitality and direction because both want to follow and neither is willing to assume an initiative role. This can cause a good deal of frustration, and sometimes even resentment, because each wants the other to take the initiative — and neither does.

Sometimes Patterns I and III have a problem in their relationship because of how they view their differences. Pattern I's can view the theoretical thinking of Pattern III's as academic and having little value in the real world. On the other hand, Pattern III's can view the practicality of Pattern I's as superficial and short-sighted. When they hold these negative attitudes toward these two types of thinking, they effectively reject and depreciate each other. In turn, this destroys much of the creative potential their relationship has to offer.

Strengthening the Relationship
In a relationship between Patterns I and III, it is important they keep aware of their common tendency to avoid confrontation and conflict by not expressing their real thoughts and feelings. When they become aware this tendency is causing a problem, they need to find some way to bring more assertiveness into the relationship. There are two distinct avenues they can take.

First, they can deliberately emphasize their own dynamic risking strengths by making a shift to their appropriate flex-patterns. Second, they can bring these strengths into the relationship by interacting with other people outside the relationship — particularly people who are naturally oriented toward action and movement.

Patterns I and III can improve their relationships through the self-discipline of consciously emphasizing their own supporting strengths at appropriate times. If their problem centers around their common reluctance to express their real feelings, the first step is to consciously shift into their assertive flex-patterns — Pattern I's move into their Flex-pattern V and Pattern III's move into their Flex-pattern VI. In effect, they bite the bullet and get their thoughts and feelings out in the open. This interaction brings new life to the relationship. The next step is to shift to their supporting thinking strengths (Pattern I's shift to their Flex-pattern III, and Pattern III's shift to their Flex-pattern I) and formulate a plan to express more independence in their relationship. Finally, they actually express their independence by shifting into their independent flex-patterns — I's express their Flex-pattern II, and III's express their Flex-pattern IV. Not only does this process improve the relationship and make it more rewarding to both, but it also stimulates their own personal growth — both become stronger individually.

Patterns I and III can also improve their relationship and make it more creative by bringing in the needed assertiveness and dynamism from the outside. They can appropriate this action-oriented strength from another person, a couple, or even a dynamic group. Sometimes this approach works even better than trying to do it on their own, because they have the natural relational strengths that enable them to draw these needed strengths easily from other people. In practice, a blend of both approaches is probably the most effective. They draw on outside sources of strengths for stimulation and consciously emphasize their own assertive and dynamic strength at the appropriate times.

The greatest creative potential in the relationship between Patterns I and III is in their complementary orientation. Pattern I's can draw on the theoretical strength of Pattern III's, and, conversely, Pattern III's can draw on the practical strength of Pattern I's. This can make both a lot more creative in their thinking.

Bi/Polar Pattern Relationship I-IV

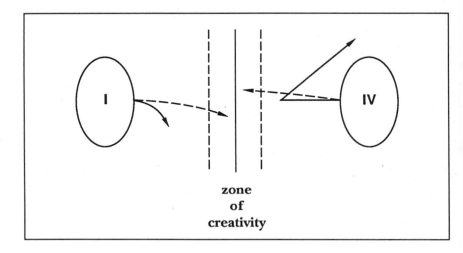

zone
of
creativity

Description

Patterns I and IV have one major strength in common: they both lead with thinking. Outside of that common lead strength, they are much different. They are at opposite ends on the thinking scale. Pattern IV's lead with theoretical thinking, whereas Pattern I's lead with practical thinking. They are also on opposite ends of the risking scale. Pattern IV's lean toward independence, and Pattern I's lean toward dependence on other people. If both identify their differences as opportunities to draw on each other, they can have a very satisfying and fulfilling relationship. When this happens, Pattern IV's draw on the practicality and warmth of Pattern I's, and, conversely, Pattern I's draw on the self-confidence and imaginative thinking of Pattern IV's.

Both tend to stay back from the line of creativity, but for different reasons. Pattern I's are quiet and unassertive out of respect for the other person, and Pattern IV's are quiet and unassertive because of their tendency to feel self-sufficient. Because of their common tendency to be unassertive toward each other, their relationship tends to be stable and somewhat reserved.

In the relationship between Patterns I and IV, Pattern IV's are natural leaders in discussing ideas and establishing objectives. Pattern I's are natural leaders in dealing with practical matters and relationships with other people.

Typical Problems

A frequent problem I's and IV's experience in their relationship with each other is brought about by their common lack of assertiveness and movement toward each other. They tend to hold their feelings within and not let the other know what is going on inside. This is a normal challenge in the relationship, and, if it is not dealt with creatively, they both can stay within themselves and let the relationship die for lack of interaction and communication.

The idealism of Pattern IV's and the realism of Pattern I's can also be a sore spot in their relationship. Pattern IV's usually have a high interest in philosophy, ideas, and "truth". On the other hand, Pattern I's have a high interest and concern with practical considerations. This can be painful and frustrating to Pattern IV's in that they tend to feel their idealism is depreciated by Pattern I's. On the other hand, Pattern I's can feel as if Pattern IV's are not giving enough consideration to the practical realities needing to be dealt with.

Another kind of pain and frustration that sometimes occurs in the relationship between I's and IV's comes from the different ways in which they express their risking strengths. I's like to risk dependently; IV's prefer to risk independently. I's enjoy and thrive on relationships with other people; IV's tend to be private people who enjoy being alone. This basic difference can sometimes cause a serious problem, especially in a marriage relationship. Pattern I's can feel that IV's are cold and antisocial, and IV's can feel that I's are overly dependent on relationships with other people.

Strengthening the Relationship
The first requirement for creating and maintaining a healthy relationship between Patterns I and IV is for both to be themselves and express their natural blend of strengths. The second requirement is for them to be alert to problems that normally develop because of who they are, then deal creatively with those problems.

When they discover that their common tendency to hold their thoughts and feelings within is causing a problem, it is time for them to deliberately become more assertive and get these thoughts and feelings into the open. Pattern I's become more assertive by expressing their Flex-pattern V and letting the IV's know how they are feeling and thinking. Pattern IV's become more assertive by expressing their Flex-pattern VIII and bringing their thoughts and feelings into the open. It is not easy for either to take the initiative in opening up in this way, and frequently a third person can be an effective catalyst in getting the process in motion. In any event, this kind of interaction between I's and IV's is usually the first step in improving the relationship, regardless of the problem.

There are other things Pattern I's can do to improve their relationships with Pattern IV's. If I's find they are tending to polarize on the problem, it is time for them to describe the problem to Pattern IV's, then shift to their Flex-pattern III and listen to the ideas expressed by the IV's. If I's are feeling depreciated and "put down" by Pattern IV's, it is time for them to shift into their Flex-pattern V, express their feelings, and get an interaction going. Once a give-and-take interaction is in motion, Pattern I's need to shift into their Flex-pattern II and express more independence.

There are additional things Pattern IV's can do to improve their relationship with Pattern I's. IV's need to make a conscious effort to pay attention to the feelings of I's and be aware of their tendency to feel unwanted and unappreciated. When Pattern IV's become aware that Pattern I's are suffering from self-depreciating feelings, they need to deliberately move into their Flex-pattern III and consciously give support and encouragement to them. It is critical to the well-being of the relationship for Pattern IV's to take the initiative in giving this support and encouragement. Also, IV's need to watch for those times when they are polarizing on the possibilities and suffering from an inadequate perception of how things really are. These are appropriate times for Pattern IV's to draw on the practical strengths of Pattern I's. IV's do this by shifting to their Flex-pattern II, asking Pattern I's to help out by giving their practical view, and then listening to what they have to say. Not only does this action on the part of the Pattern IV's help their thinking become more realistic, but it also improves their relationship with Pattern I's.

Bi/Polar Pattern Relationship I-V

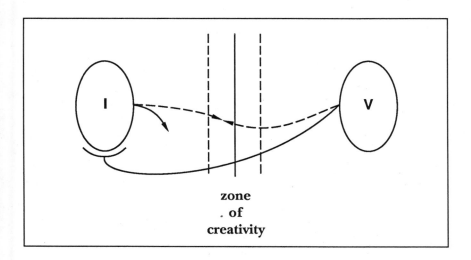

zone
. of
creativity

Description

Patterns I and V have many common characteristics. They have two lead strengths in common (practicality and dependent risking) and differ only on the basic pair (thinking and risking). Both patterns are extraverted, but Pattern I is only mildly so, whereas Pattern V is extremely extraverted (all three major strengths of Pattern V's point outward).

Pattern I's lead in thinking; Pattern V's lead in risking. This tends to make Pattern I's reserved in their relationships and Pattern V's assertive and relational. Both patterns tend to have a high interest in and concern for other people, but V's tend to be much more active and assertive in their relationships that are I's. Patterns I and V can be very creative together when they recognize that they naturally complement one another on the thinking/risking scale. With this positive attitude toward their differences, they can be stronger and more effective together than either would be by themselves.

Since both I's and V's are basically people-oriented and want relationships, they usually form a relationship quickly when exposed to one another. Pattern V's typically take the initiative, and Pattern I's are usually receptive. Their common orientation toward practicality and interest in other people provides a strong base for communication and interaction.

Typical Problems

A typical problem in a relationship between I's and V's comes from the fact that both lean toward practicality and have a supporting strength in theoretical thinking. When their relationship requires emphasis on theory and ideas, it usually poses a problem because neither has a natural tendency in this direction. They can experience failure or lack of effectiveness as a team because the theoretical side of their thinking is not as strong. Sometimes they even regard theory as unimportant and, as a result, neglect their own strengths in theoretical thinking.

Another problem they sometimes experience comes from their tendency to express heavy dependence on one another without enough independence and personal freedom. When this happens, both can feel weighted down and suffer from a lack of confidence, both in themselves and the other person.

Another problem likely to appear in a relationship between I's and V's is related to their difference in the basic pair of Bi/Polar strengths — thinking and risking. Pattern I's can become polarized on their thinking and continue to think and re-think the problem. When Pattern I's polarize on thinking, they withdraw from dynamic interaction — the very thing Patterns V's want the most. On the other hand, Pattern V's can become polarized on action and refuse to think things through on a rational and stable basis. When V's polarize on action, they tend to reject the values of stability and rationality — the greatest strengths of Pattern I's.

If polarization deepens on both sides, each takes a progressively more negative attitude towards the other. Pattern I's tend to describe V's as emotional, unpredictable, scatterbrained, and unreliable. On the other hand, V's can describe I's as dull, boring, an obstacle to progress, just plain uninteresting, and not any fun to be around.

Strengthening the Relationship
Patterns I and V can have a creative and satisfying relationship when they know and appreciate one another. They must be themselves in the relationship and deal with their tendencies when they cause problems.

They need to attune themselves to possible problems in their relationship because of their common leaning toward practicality and dependence. Being aware that they need to deliberately bring more independence and theoretical thinking into their relationship can set them on the road to being more creative together. They can bring these strengths into the relationship by consciously emphasizing their own strengths in theoretical thinking and independence, or they can reach out to other people outside the relationship and invite them to contribute the needed strengths. They emphasize their own strengths in these areas by shifting into their appropriate flex-patterns. As an example, when theoretical thinking is needed, I's move into their Flex-pattern III, and V's move into their Flex-pattern VI. When independence is needed, I's express their Flex-pattern II, and V's express their Flex-pattern VII. Sometimes it is easier and more effective if they relate to people outside the relationship and draw the needed strengths from them. It works best if they reach out to a person who has the needed strength in natural dominance.

When Pattern I's are polarizing on thinking and Pattern V's are polarizing on action, a basic attitude change can shift them from negative to positive. Rather than seeing Pattern V's as emotional, unpredictable, scatterbrained, and unreliable, Pattern I's need to look behind these negatives and appreciate the positive qualities of movement, action, and courage being expressed in the behavior of V's. Rather than seeing Pattern I's as dull, boring, and an obstacle to progress, Pattern V's need to look behind these negatives and appreciate the positive qualities of organization, thoughtful planning, and stability that I's bring to the relationship. With this shift of attitude, rather than fighting each other's strengths, they welcome them into the relationship and participate in the values that each has to give. Pattern I's participate in the dynamic action and movement V's provide, and Pattern V's participate in the stability and organized thinking I's bring to the relationship.

Bi/Polar Pattern Relationship I-VI

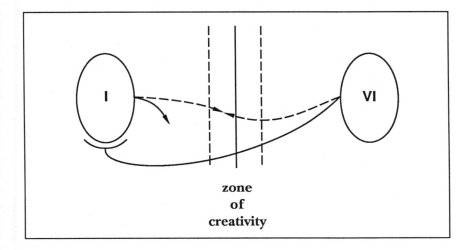

Description

Patterns I and VI have only one lead polar strength in common — dependent risking. They are at opposite ends on the other two pairs — Pattern I's are thought-oriented and practical while VI's are feeling-oriented and imaginative. Pattern I's are most comfortable in a world of practical reality, whereas Pattern VI's enjoy a world of emotional involvement with other people.

Patterns I and VI are more different than they are alike. If they appreciate their differences and each actively draws on the lead strength of the other, they can have a creative and personally rewarding relationship.

Pattern I's have a natural tendency toward thinking about the practical realities of life and constructing realistic plans to deal with them. On the other hand, Pattern VI's approach life from an emotional and intuitive point of view. Because of this fundamental difference, they tend to behave quite differently in their relationships. Pattern I's are quiet, thoughtful, and matter-of-fact, whereas Pattern VI's are emotional, personally involved, and demonstrative of their feelings. Pattern VI's tend to come on warmly, showing a good deal of active concern, where Pattern I's tend to show their warmth in a tentative and reserved way.

Pattern I's should normally take the lead to identify the problem and make a realistic appraisal of the situation. Pattern VI's should normally take the lead when there is a need for dynamic interaction and an open expression of feelings.

Typical Problems

The relationship between Patterns I and VI can deteriorate if they become polarized on their lead strengths and fail to appreciate the lead strengths of each other. For example, when Pattern VI's become polarized on dreams of possibilities and emotional involvement with other people, they tend to reject the values of reality, logic, and reason — the finest things Pattern I's have to offer the relationship. On the other hand, when Pattern I's become polarized on reason, logic, rationality, and practical considerations, they tend to depreciate the values of dreams, hopes, and emotional involvement, thus rejecting the greatest values Pattern VI's have to offer.

Another problem comes from their common tendency to over-emphasize the importance of relationships to the detriment of recognizing the values of independence and distance from one another. They can become so concerned and aware of each other that they are living more within one another than they are within themselves. In this kind of relationship, individuality tends to lose its sharpness and distinctiveness, sometimes resulting in a painful loss of self-identify.

Strengthening the Relationship

Patterns I and VI can have a very creative and rewarding relationship. In order to accomplish this, they need to first be themselves in the relationship — both must express their own patterns of natural strengths. Next, they need to recognize and affirm their differences. Pattern I's need to be aware of the values of imagination, dreams, and dynamic interaction and ask Pattern VI's to contribute these values to the relationship. Pattern VI's need to be aware of the values of practicality, reason, and rationality and ask Pattern I's to contribute these values to the relationship. In this kind of atmosphere, both are affirmed, feel appreciated, and experience being a contributing part of a creative relationship. Not only does this approach improve the relationship, but it also stimulates their individual growth. They rub off on one another, and each gains strength in the areas where they have their greatest need.

Sometimes Patterns I and VI polarize on their common lead strength (courage of dependence) and block out their own expressions of independence. To deal with this problem, either may take the initiative and deliberately shift emphasis to an expression of independence. Pattern I's go through the process of first moving into their Flex-pattern V to get the action going, then finally emphasizing their independence by expressing their Flex-pattern II. Pattern VI's follow a similar process in that they first move to their Flex-pattern III in order to plan their change of behavior, then finally emphasize their independence by expressing their Flex-pattern VIII. If one expresses more independence, it tends to automatically stimulate the other to do the same. Another way they may deal with this problem is to shift their dependence to a third party — preferably one who naturally leans toward independence. In this way they bring more independence into their relationship from the outside.

Bi/Polar Pattern Relationship I-VII

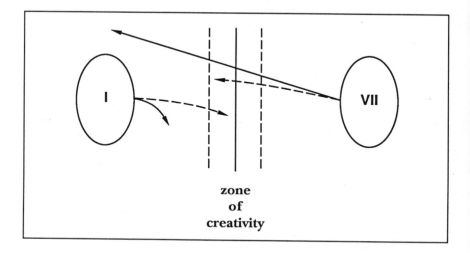

zone
of
creativity

Description

Patterns I and VII are more different than they are alike. They tend in the same direction on the thinking scale — toward the practical rather than the theoretical. But they are at opposite ends in the other two Bi/Polar pairs of strengths. In the basic pair, Pattern I's lean toward thinking, and Pattern VII's lean toward risking. In the risking pair, Pattern I's naturally lead with dependence, and Pattern VII's naturally lead with independence.

In a normal relationship between Pattern I's and Pattern VII's, Pattern VII's are the natural out-front leaders; Pattern I's are the natural followers. Pattern VII's are naturally assertive in their relationships. They tend to come on strongly and move across the line of creativity, invading the territory of the I's. Frequently they are so intent on accomplishing their objectives that they are not aware, or are only vaguely aware, that they have gone too far and moved into the territory of the Pattern I's. The assertiveness of Pattern VII's can be so strong on occasion that they just push the Pattern I's aside. On the other hand, I's tend to be quiet and unassertive in the relationship. Their tendency is to let VII's come into their territory, experience the onslaught, and accept it without protest. Generally, Pattern I's appreciate and respond positively to the assertive leadership of Pattern VII's. But if they feel violated and depreciated, they can become very hostile and resentful toward Pattern VII's.

Typical Problems
From the point of view of Pattern I's, the problem in the relationship is the assertiveness of Pattern VII's. If they feel violated and "put down", they develop an increasing load of negative feelings and attitudes toward Pattern VII's. They feel fearful, angry, resentful, and hostile. They see Pattern VII's as pushy, domineering, and obnoxious. They wish the Pattern VII's would stop pushing so hard and show them more respect. Although they are experiencing these negative feelings, they have a strong tendency to hold them within in order to avoid confrontation and conflict. This compounds the problem, because the longer these feelings are suppressed, the more intense they become.

From the point of view of Pattern VII's, the problem in the relationship is the lack of response from Pattern I's. If Pattern I's stay quiet and permit the Pattern VII's to take over, the VII's lose respect for them. When this happens, the Pattern VII's become very frustrated with the lack of response from Pattern I's and tend to either show more impatience with Pattern I's or "write them off" completely.

Sometimes Patterns I and VII can have a problem in their relationship because of their common leaning toward practicality. If they stimulate each other to be even more practical, it can result in polarization on the practical side and serve to block their theoretical thinking strengths.

Strengthening the Relationship

The relationship between Patterns I and VII can be very creative and satisfying for both. Both must work at it, however. They need to express their own pattern of strengths, follow their natural tendencies, and deal creatively with the challenges (problems) likely to develop in their relationship.

The first requirement for Pattern VII's is to be who they are and express their assertive and independent tendencies in their relationships with Pattern I's. They need to step out front and be natural leaders. This does not mean they deliberately invade the territory of Pattern I's, but it does mean they move assertively toward Pattern I's in an effort to discover the line of creativity between them. In a sense, someone needs to cross the line in order to find out where it is. We can't know where the line is until we have some give-and-take interaction. The second step for Pattern VII's is to deal creatively with their natural assertiveness and independence. The fundamental switch here is for Pattern VII's to deliberately put Pattern I's in the center of their attention — put themselves in the others' shoes, try to understand how they are feeling, and look for ways to actively encourage them. In making this switch, Pattern VII's demonstrate a sincere interest and concern for Pattern I's as individuals. No longer is it just a question of what the Pattern I's can do for them. This process requires Pattern VII's to first emphasize their thinking by moving to their Flex-pattern II and, at the same time, formulating a plan to express more dependence on Pattern I's. The final step is to shift to their Flex-pattern V and actually express their dependence on Pattern I's in face-to-face interactions.

Usually what Pattern I's need to do to improve their relationship with Pattern VII's is very simple — not easy, but simple. All they need to do is speak up and express how they are feeling in the relationship. Even a small step in this direction will frequently turn the relationship around and set it going in a creative direction. An assertive expression from Pattern I's tends to give them more self-confidence and, equally important, gets the attention of Pattern VII's. This is usually enough to dissipate some negative feelings and attitudes on both sides and build a positive base for developing a creative relationship in the future. The most effective procedure for Pattern I's to follow in expressing their independence is to first assertively move toward the Pattern VII by expressing their Flex-pattern V. This provides emotional contact and interaction. The next step is for Pattern I's to shift into their Flex-pattern II and emphasize their independent strength in their natural way.

If Patterns I and VII become aware they are polarizing on the practical side, they need to either make a deliberate shift to emphasize and stimulate one another's theoretical thinking or go to the outside and bring another person into the relationship. It works best if they bring in a person who naturally leans toward the theoretical side.

In a creative relationship between Patterns I and VII, they are both expressing their natural strengths and dealing with their natural tendencies when they become aware of the problems they are causing. Pattern VII's are providing initiative and out-front leadership, but, at the same time, they are deliberately working at becoming more aware of the Pattern I's and more concerned about them as being of equal worth to themselves. Pattern I's are depending on the Pattern VII's, contributing their thinking strengths, and at the same time deliberately shifting emphasis to more assertiveness and stronger expressions of stable independence.

Bi/Polar Pattern Relationship I-VIII

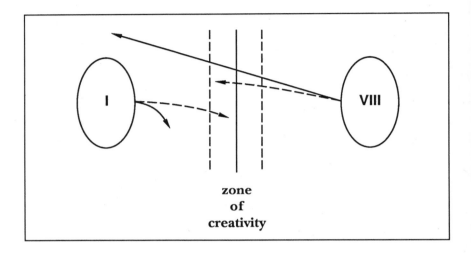

zone
of
creativity

Description

Patterns I and VIII are diametric opposites in all three pairs of polar strengths. Pattern I is the most stable of all the patterns, and Pattern VIII is the most dynamic. The three lead strengths of Pattern I's (thinking, practicality, and dependent risking) are all stability strengths. Conversely, the three lead strengths of the Pattern VIII (risking, independence, and theoretical thinking) all tend toward the dynamic end of the scale.

Since they are direct opposites in terms of the polar strengths, maintaining a creative relationship is difficult and challenging for both. However, on the positive side, there is a good deal of potential reward for both when they form a creative relationship — one in which they encourage each other to "be yourself". This enables them to contribute their natural strengths to the creativeness of the relationship.

Not only is there potential for a highly creative relationship, but there is also a potential for personal growth. Pattern VIII's can become more stable, realistic, and aware of other people by drawing on the lead strengths of Pattern I's. Conversely, Pattern I's can become more dynamic, imaginative, and self-confident by creatively drawing on the lead strengths of Pattern VIII's.

Pattern VIII's have a natural tendency to take the initiative and assume the leadership role. As VIII's move dynamically and assertively in pursuit of their personal goals, they tend to move across the line of creativity and invade the territory of the Pattern I's. Pattern I's, on the other hand, do the opposite — they tend to be quiet and unassertive and let the Pattern VIII's take over. In a normal relationship between Patterns VIII and I, the VIII's consistently invade the territory of the I's, and the I's consistently let this happen without putting up a fight.

Sometimes Pattern I's wish they were more dynamic and feel they would prefer to be more like Pattern VIII's. It is surprising to some Pattern I's when they find out that sometimes Pattern VIII's feel they would prefer to be more like Pattern I's by showing more calm rationality.

Typical Problems
The typical problems in a relationship between Patterns I and VIII come from their natural tendencies to emphasize their own lead strengths. When either begins to polarize on any lead strength, it automatically depreciates a lead strength of the other one in the relationship. For example, when Pattern I's polarize on thinking, they depreciate Pattern VIII's' lead strength in risking. When I's polarize on practicality, they depreciate VIII's' strength in imagination. Additionally, when they polarize on dependence, they depreciate VIII's' strength of independence and actually see this independence as a selfish, destructive force. It is just the opposite for Pattern VIII's. When VIII's polarize on their risking strengths, they depreciate the thinking strength of Pattern I's. When they polarize on their own self-confidence, they depreciate the values in the dependence

expressed by the I's and actually see dependence as a weakness rather than a strength.

If their polarization deepens, they can develop a good deal of hostility and rejection toward each other. When there is a severe polarization, Pattern I's view Pattern VIII's as "wild-eyed promoters" who are unstable, egotistical, and untrustworthy. On the other hand, Pattern VIII's view Pattern I's as "patsies" who are dull, uninteresting, and easily manipulated.

Strengthening the Relationship
Pattern I's need to watch for those times when they are polarizing on dependent risking and letting Pattern VIII's come into their territory unchallenged. When they become aware they are letting this happen, the most effective way to gain the respect of the Pattern VIII's and make the relationship more creative is to become more self-assertive and express more independence. The most natural way to do this is to first express their Flex-pattern V and share their real feelings in a face-to-face interaction with Pattern VIII's. This gets the attention of Pattern VIII's and has the overall effect of beginning to move Pattern VIII's back out of the Pattern I's' territory. Once this movement is started, Pattern I's need to shift into their Flex-pattern II and express their independence in their own natural way — with the undergirding force of rationality and logic.

Pattern I's also need to be alert to their tendency to overemphasize the facts of reality and devalue the visions of possibilities that Pattern VIII's are trying to promote. When I's become aware they are using facts as clubs to destroy the hopes and dreams of Pattern VIII's, it is time for them to find a way to activate their own capacities for seeing the possibilities by shifting into their Flex-pattern III and really listening to what the Pattern VIII's have to say. A realistic evaluation of these possibilities can come later, but first Pattern I's need to see and appreciate the possibilities before they can evaluate them. This procedure can create a communication bridge with

Pattern VIII's that Pattern I's can use later to communicate their own realistic evaluation of the possibilities.

Pattern VIII's need to watch for those times when they are polarizing on their own self-interest and not appreciating the strengths of Pattern I's. When Pattern VIII's become aware they are polarizing on their own egos, they need to first express their Flex-pattern IV and think about the potential values Pattern I's bring to the relationship. Then they need to shift into their Flex-pattern VI and exercise their dependent risking strengths by actively drawing on Pattern I's' strengths.

One of the most positive things Pattern VIII's can do to improve their relationship with Pattern I's is to be assertive in asking Pattern I's to contribute their natural strength in practical thinking.

Bi/Polar Pattern Relationship II-II

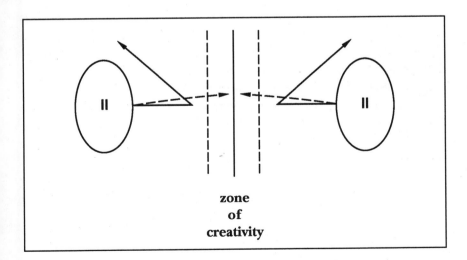

zone
of
creativity

Description

As two Pattern II's relate to one another, they share a common interest in having the relationship structured, stable, and somewhat formal. They keep their distance and studiously avoid displays of emotion — particularly feelings of dependence or warmth toward each other. They usually form a relationship out of their common desire to accomplish a particular task and have only a secondary interest in the relationship itself. The substance of their relationship is the task to be accomplished — not shared feelings. Since both tend toward independence and are usually ambitious, there is likely to be a competitive element in their relationship. They both have a natural tendency to feel responsible and follow their own convictions. Drawing strength from each other and working to accomplish a team goal is usually a disciplined response rather than a natural response.

Typical Problems

A common frustration in a relationship between two Pattern II's stems from the fact that neither feels comfortable sharing feelings with the other. Since shared feelings are an essential part of a dynamic and emotionally satisfying relationship, Pattern II's sometimes experience this lack of emotional communication as a frustrating and deadening element in their relationship.

Another frustration two Pattern II's sometimes experience is related to their common tendency to be problem-centered. Since their greatest strength is in their ability to see things as they are, it is easy for them to stimulate each other's practical thinking and end up with a picture of reality made up of all the things wrong with a situation. Their clear perception of all the facts, unblended with a vision of positive possibilities, tends to give them a negative attitude, and this, in turn, can make them unpleasant and sometimes difficult people to be around.

Another problem two Pattern II's can experience comes from their common leaning toward independence. If both become polarized on their independence and refuse to risk dependence on the other, their relationship can deteriorate and become destructive to both. When this happens, there are usually strong feelings of competitiveness and perhaps some resentment and anger (usually held within). If they stay in a relationship, these negative feelings are likely to increase until one of them risks some expression of dependence and the other responds in a like manner.

Strengthening the Relationship
A relationship between two Pattern II's can be strengthened from either inside or from outside the relationship. In order to improve it within, one must take the initiative to risk an expression of real feelings. The easiest and most natural way for Pattern II's to do this is to move into their Flex-pattern VII and express how they are feeling about the relationship. Sometimes this action serves as a release for a lot of suppressed feelings on both sides, and just getting them out in the open frequently gets rid of a lot of negative feelings and leaves them feeling much better about themselves and the relationship.

Frequently, the easiest way to break a logjam of unexpressed feelings between two Pattern II's is to bring a third party into the relationship. Although a mature person with any pattern of strengths can be helpful, a Pattern V or VII is frequently most helpful. V's and VII's usually have more developed skill in relationships and also provide a dynamic spark normally lacking in a relationship between two Pattern II's. A Pattern V or VII can be an effective catalyst to getting II's to express their feelings and get things out in the open where they can deal with them creatively.

If two Pattern II's find they are stimulating one another's natural tendency to polarize on problems, it is time to make a conscious shift to their Flex-pattern VII and challenge each other to look for possible solutions. This makes it easier for them to move into their Flex-pattern IV and emphasize their natural imaginative abilities. The final result is more creative solutions to their problems.

If two Pattern II's are polarizing on their independence and withdrawing into their own self-sufficiency, it is time to find effective ways to express dependence on one another. A natural way to do this is to first make emotional contact by shifting into their Flex-pattern VII and expressing their real feelings to each other. Next, they need to move into their Flex-pattern IV and identify the potential rewards of depending on one another. Finally, they need to express their Flex-pattern I and actually depend more on one another.

When two Pattern II's have a creative relationship, they affirm their own natural pattern of strengths and recognize how they must discipline themselves to keep their relationship creative and growing. They are true to themselves by keeping their relationship primarily task-oriented and, at the same time, seek to strengthen their relationship through a deliberate effort to express their feelings more fully at appropriate times. They also continue to affirm the importance of independence and distance in the relationship and, at the same time, develop skill in flexing to stronger expressions of dependence into their natural ways of being.

Bi/Polar Pattern Relationship II-III

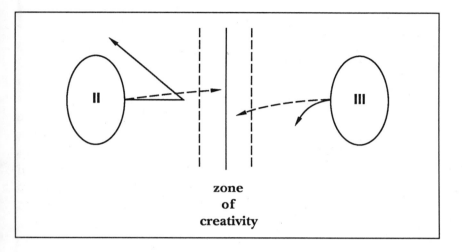

zone
of
creativity

Description

Patterns II and III are more different than they are alike. They are at opposite ends of two pairs of Bi/Polar strengths and at the same end on the other one. Their thinking is different. The II's naturally tend toward practicality while III's tend toward theory and ideas. They are also opposites on the emotional scale, with the II's favoring independence and self-reliance and III's tending toward warm relationships and dependence on others.

II's and III's are alike in that they both tend to feel more confident and effective in thinking than they do in risking. Since both are inclined toward the intellectual side, they have a common ground on which to meet and build a creative relationship. There is a great deal of potential for highly creative thinking in a healthy give-and-take relationship between them. II's can emphasize the facts of reality and III's can emphasize ideas and possibilities.

Typical Problems

Their common tendency to be reserved and unassertive toward each other makes it a challenge for them to initiate a relationship on their own. Since both have this reserved tendency, sometimes they never go far enough to discover the line of creativity between them and, as a result, lose much of their potential creativeness together.

Sometimes, the pains and pressure points in a relationship between Pattern II's and Pattern III's are tied to their natural differences. II's can become very frustrated with the tendency of III's to emphasize the importance of theory and ideas. II's want to know what will work in a particular situation. If Pattern III's emphasize general principles when Pattern II's are seeking to solve a practical problem, the II's can become upset and frustrated. On the other hand, Pattern III's can become frustrated with Pattern II's. Pattern III's want to understand the general principle and develop a theory that can apply to a number of practical problems. Having to deal with Pattern II's who are only concerned with solving an immediate problem can be a very frustrating experience for Pattern III's.

Their opposite orientations on the dependent/independent scale can also cause problems in their relationship. III's tend to experience a good deal of warmth and dependence in their relationships, whereas II's tend to feel more independent and usually want more privacy. It is easy for the III's to see the independence of the Pattern II's as coldness, lack of concern, or selfishness. On the other hand, it is easy for the Pattern II's to see the warmth and dependence of the III's as a weakness—a reluctance to make a decision on their own and to be personally responsible.

Strengthening the Relationship

If Patterns II and III find their relationship suffering because of a lack of dynamic interaction, they can either deliberately emphasize their own assertive strengths or look outside for other people to provide the missing dynamics. If they take the avenue of doing it on their own, then Pattern II's need to express their Flex-pattern VII, and Pattern III's need to express their Flex-pattern VI. Either one can take the initiative and bring new life to the relationship. Sometimes, it is easier and more effective to bring a third person into the relationship. It works best if the third party is a naturally outgoing and assertive person.

Problems can occur in a relationship between Pattern II's and Pattern III's because of their opposing tendencies. Pattern II's have a natural tendency to emphasize practicality and self-sufficiency; Pattern III's have a natural tendency to emphasize the polar values — theoretical thinking and relationships. They both need to deal creatively with their own tendencies in order for the relationship to improve and become more creative.

Pattern II's need to watch for those times when they are tempted to withdraw into their own self-sufficiency. To build their relationship with Pattern III's, they need to resist their temptation to withdraw and deliberately reach out to the Pattern III's for help. Pattern II's do this most naturally by first moving to their Flex-pattern VII and becoming more self-assertive in the relationship. The interaction stimulated by this assertiveness opens the way and creates a demand for an expression of dependence. Now Pattern II's can emphasize their dependence on Pattern III's by expressing their Flex-pattern I and asking Pattern III's for their help — particularly in areas of their competence. When Pattern II's take the initiative to draw on the strengths of Pattern III's, it is usually highly effective in building a creative relationship.

Pattern III's need to be alert to those times when they are tempted to back off, depreciate themselves, and remain quiet when they should speak up. When they become aware this is a problem, they need to take the initiative in getting both their own feelings and the feelings of the Pattern II's out on the table. Pattern III's do this by moving into their Flex-pattern VI and becoming more warmly assertive toward the Pattern II's. Sometimes one of the most constructive things Pattern III's can do is make it easier for Pattern II's to get their feelings out in the open by first doing it themselves. Finally, Pattern III's need to express their Flex-pattern IV and blend more self-sufficiency and independence into their behavior.

Sometimes, Patterns II and III find they are having a problem because of their tendencies to emphasize their opposite lead strengths in thinking (II's tend to naturally emphasize practicality, and III's tend to naturally emphasize theory). To solve this problem, both need to shift their thinking emphasis to their supporting thinking strength. II's need to express their Flex-pattern IV, and III's need to express their Flex-pattern I. One of the most positive results of shifting emphasis to their supporting thinking strength is that it shows appreciation for the lead strength of the other. II's show appreciation for the value of Pattern III's' theoretical strengths, and III's show appreciation for the value of Pattern II's' practicality.

Bi/Polar Pattern Relationship II-IV

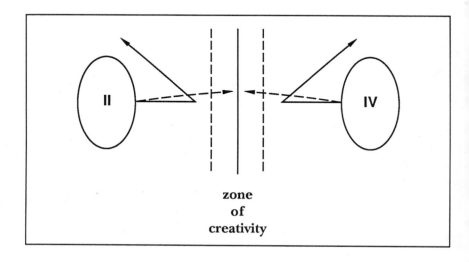

zone
of
creativity

Description

Patterns II and IV have similar patterns of polar strengths. Both are inclined toward thinking and independence. They are different in only one pair of Bi/Polar strengths — the thinking pair. The lead thinking strength of Pattern II's is practical thinking, and the lead thinking strength of Pattern IV's is theoretical thinking.

Patterns II and IV tend to be reserved in their relationships with each other. They like to follow the "live and let live" philosophy and usually don't interfere with each other nor do they want to be interfered with. They treat feelings gingerly and, in general, shy away from them. They both want space and distance in their relationship and prefer to deal with each other on an intellectual and rational basis rather than an emotional basis.

In a creative relationship, Pattern II's take the lead in identifying the problems, and IV's take the lead in finding the solutions. Together, they can be highly effective as creative problem-solvers. II's can develop clear perceptions of the problem itself, and IV's can develop a variety of possible solutions.

Typical Problems

A typical problem Patterns II and IV frequently experience in their relationship comes from their common interest in keeping feelings and emotions out of their relationship. A creative and satisfying relationship has emotional elements in it, and, if these feelings are not communicated in some way, the relationship tends to wither and die for lack of dynamic interaction. Sometimes Patterns II and IV find their most serious relationship problems come from a common refusal to express their feelings and let the others know what's going on inside.

Another problem Patterns II and IV sometimes experience arises out of their opposite orientation in thinking. It is natural for Pattern II's to emphasize facts and reality and, as a result, de-emphasize the importance of theories and ideas. Pattern IV's do the opposite —

they emphasize theories and ideas and, as a result, de-emphasize facts and reality. When this happens, both can feel "put down" and depreciated because the finest thing they have to offer is being depreciated by the other one in the relationship.

Strengthening the Relationship
Patterns II and IV can have a highly creative and productive relationship. Their common strengths and tendencies can provide a strong base of understanding between them. A clear understanding and appreciation of their differences can also contribute to the health of their relationship.

Being at opposite ends on the thinking scale provides an excellent basis for creative interaction between Patterns II and IV. By drawing on each other's thinking, they can cooperatively produce well-balanced and creative thinking. What makes it even stronger is that the different kind of thinking they contribute is, in each case, the greatest single strength of each.

In order to bring about a creative relationship, Pattern II's need to lead with their practical thinking, identify the problems, and then deliberately shift emphasis to their self-assertive strength by expressing their Flex-pattern VII. Specifically, they become assertive in asking the Pattern IV's for their help in coming up with possible solutions. Next, they shift to their Flex-pattern I, emphasize their dependent strength, and listen to what the Pattern IV's have to offer. In effect, this action gives Pattern II's practice in using their supporting strengths in assertiveness and dependence and gives Pattern IV's an opportunity to make their greatest contribution to the relationship (theoretical thinking).

Pattern IV's need to follow a similar process. They lead with their natural strengths in theoretical thinking and come up with an idea — then deliberately shift to their Flex-pattern VIII and assertively express their idea to the Pattern II's. Next, they emphasize their dependent strength by shifting to their Flex-pattern III and listen as

Pattern II's give a realistic evaluation of their ideas. This process gives Pattern IV's practice in using their supporting strengths in assertiveness and dependence and gives Pattern II's an opportunity to make their greatest contribution to the relationship (practical thinking).

If Patterns II and IV discover their problems are coming from their common tendency to hold their feelings within, they need to find a way to get these feelings expressed and out in the open. Either can take the initiative in starting the process, but both need to get involved before the relationship can improve. Pattern II's initiate the process by moving into their Flex-pattern VII and frankly telling the Pattern IV's how they feel about the relationship. Pattern IV's can also take the initiative by shifting to their Flex-pattern VIII and expressing their feelings. Once the interaction has been initiated by the expression of their assertive Flex-patterns, they need to shift into the proper Flex-pattern to emphasize their dependent strength — II's express their Flex-pattern I, and IV's express their Flex-pattern III. This expression of a creative blending of independence and dependence opens a communication bridge over which their opposite orientations in thinking can feed each other and produce highly creative thinking.

Bi/Polar Pattern Relationship II-V

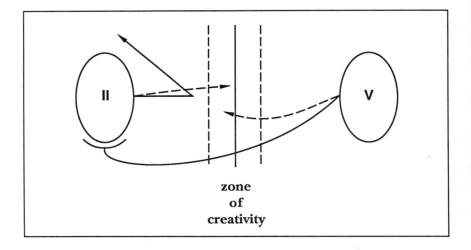

zone
of
creativity

Description

Pattern II's and Pattern V's are more different than they are alike. They are different in that they are at opposite ends on two pairs of polar strengths — the basic pair (thinking/risking) and the risking pair ((dependence/independence). Pattern II's lean toward thinking and independence; Pattern V's lean toward risking and dependence. They are alike in that they favor the same end of the thinking scale — both lean toward the practical, realistic side.

Pattern V's are warm, outgoing, and people-oriented. They move assertively toward other people and seek a close relationship. On the other hand, Pattern II's tend to be private, reserved people who like space and distance in their relationships. This is not to say that Pattern II's don't want relationships with other people. They need and want relationships just like anyone else, but they just want more distance and personal freedom in their relationships than do some other people.

In a relationship between Patterns V and II, the V's have a natural tendency to move assertively toward the II's and go across the line of creativity into the others' space. Pattern II's have a natural tendency to pull back and sometimes move away from Pattern V's.

It is natural for Pattern V's to be the initiators in establishing and deepening their relationship with Pattern II's. On the other hand, once the relationship is established, Pattern II's frequently take the "out-front" leadership role — particularly in situations that require an emphasis on thinking, objective analysis, and independent action.

Typical Problems

The most common problem Patterns II and V experience in a relationship with one another is related to their opposite tendency in relationships. Pattern II's tend to pull away from others and move back into their own self-sufficiency, whereas Pattern V's tend to center their attention on other people and move assertively toward them. If both follow their natural tendencies without some discipline, the relationship can become a very painful and frustrating experience for them. Pattern II's begin to feel smothered, caught, and fenced in by the attention being showered on them by the Pattern V's. On the other hand, Pattern V's begin to feel rejected, unloved, and unappreciated by Pattern II's.

Another problem sometimes arising in a relationship between Pattern II's and Pattern V's comes from a basic difference in their awareness. People are at the center of V's' awareness and interests. It is different with the Pattern II's. They are most aware of practical problems and the task to be accomplished. With V's, the task is on the periphery; with II's, people are on the periphery. As II's and V's are faithful to their own awareness, it tends to cause problems in their relationship. V's can begin to feel that Pattern II's are cold, uncaring, and no fun to be around. Conversely, Pattern II's can tend to view V's as lazy and irresponsible "do-gooders".

Strengthening the Relationship
The first requirement for a good relationship between Patterns II and V is for both to appreciate and express their natural strengths and tendencies. The second requirement is that they deal creatively with their tendencies when they become aware they are causing problems. One of the advantages of a relationship between Patterns II and V is that their tendencies cause problems quickly, thus presenting a growth challenge difficult to ignore.

Pattern V's need to watch for signals from Pattern II's that indicate they are being too assertive and trying to get too close. If V's get these signals, they need to call on their thinking strengths and back up some within themselves. They need to move into their Flex-pattern I and become more thoughtful and reserved in their relationship with Pattern II's.

Pattern II's need to watch for their tendency to move back into their own self-sufficiency and be too quiet and reserved. Rather than give in to their natural temptation to hold their feelings inside, II's need to tell the V's just how they are feeling and ask them to give them more room. II's do this by shifting into their Flex-pattern VII and becoming more assertive in their relationship with Pattern V's. Pattern V's usually appreciate II's expressing their feelings. If Pattern II's will only get their feelings out in the open, they usually find Pattern V's very skillful in dealing creatively with them.

The good thing about either one taking the actions suggested above is that once they are taken, it stimulates the other to respond in creative and appropriate ways. If Pattern V's deliberately become more reserved and thoughtful, Pattern II's develop more respect for them, feel less threatened, and are less inclined to move away. If Pattern II's deliberately express how they are feeling, Pattern V's have the interactions they are seeking and, as a result, tend to back off and give II's more room.

When the difference in their awareness (task versus people) is causing the problem, each has an appropriate response that can improve the relationship. Pattern II's need to first move into their Flex-pattern VII and be more assertive in their relationship with Pattern V's. In making this shift, they exercise their natural initiating strengths by asking Pattern V's to contribute their strengths in accomplishing the task at hand. Finally, Pattern II's need to move to their Flex-pattern I and emphasize their dependence upon V's. In this way, they show patience and warmth toward Pattern V's. V's need to emphasize a different set of strengths. They need to first go to their Flex-pattern I and emphasize their thinking strengths. While in their Flex-pattern I, they need to develop a better understanding of what is going on in the relationship and devise a plan of action to express more independence. After developing a plan of action, they need to express their Flex-pattern VII and assertively take an initiating role in accomplishing the task.

Bi/Polar Pattern Relationship II-VI

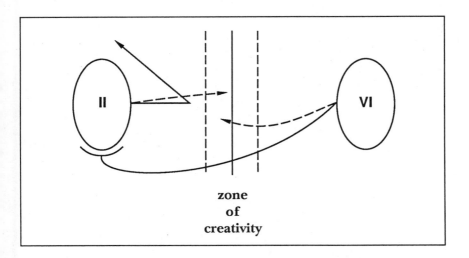

zone
of
creativity

Description

Patterns II and VI are polar opposites. First, Pattern II's favor practicality and prefer to operate from a sound factual base; Pattern VI's favor ideas and prefer living in a world of potential and possibility. Second, Pattern II's tend to feel self-sufficient and like distance and space in their relationships; Pattern VI's like deep emotional involvement with other people and prefer close, intimate relationships. Third, Pattern II's are thinking-oriented persons who prefer to base their actions on what "makes sense"; Pattern VI's come from an emotional base — "how they feel" is much more important to them than "what they think".

Since Patterns II and VI are very different — tending to come from opposite ends of all three of the polarities — it takes a good deal of understanding and self-discipline on both sides for them to create a productive and fulfilling relationship. Although it is difficult, the rewards far outweigh the effort, because each has what the other needs to become a mature and effective human being. In a creative relationship, they "rub off" on each other — II's become warmer and more expressive of their feelings, and VI's develop more self-confidence and rationality.

Pattern II's are natural initiators when the requirement is for a calm appraisal of the situation and a logical, well-thought-out plan to solve a practical problem. On the other hand, Pattern VI's are natural initiators when the need is for warm relationships. Pattern VI's are natural entertainers and, if given the opportunity to be themselves, can bring life, warmth, humor, and relaxation to a group of people.

Typical Problems

II and VI can experience a good deal of frustration and pain in their relationship. Since they have opposite strengths and tendencies, problems usually surface immediately. As Pattern VI's come on emotionally strong and obviously want a quick and close personal relationship, Pattern II's naturally back up and seek cover from what they experience as a smothering kind of aggressive act invading their space. Pattern II's tend to feel threatened by this perceived aggression and usually bristle or withdraw. This reaction tends to cause Pattern VI's to feel rejected and unworthy.

Sometimes Pattern II's are frustrated with what they consider Pattern VI's' disregard for reason and logic. II's want to talk in terms of facts and what is the reasonable thing to do, and they tend to become upset by Pattern VI's desire to talk about feelings and what is going on emotionally in the relationship.

If they both refuse to deal creatively with their natural tendencies and polarize more and more deeply on their own lead strengths, the relationship can become destructive. In a polarized relationship, Pattern VI's tend to see Pattern II's as cold, unresponsive, devoid of human compassion, uncaring, and just no fun to be around. On the other hand, Pattern II's tend to see Pattern VI's as flighty, highly emotional (thinking of emotion in a negative way), devoid of logic and rationality, living in a dream-world, and unable to compete in a practical world of reality.

Strengthening the Relationship
Patterns II and VI have much to gain if they can create a relationship in which both are affirmed and encouraged to contribute their natural strength. In order to do this, both need to affirm and express their own natural strengths until they become aware that this expression is causing a problem. When they become aware of a problem, one must take the initiative to deliberately and consciously express the needed polar strength. The relationship starts to improve and becomes more creative when the other makes an appropriate response.

When Pattern VI's become aware their assertive and relational tendency is causing problems in their relationship with Pattern II's, they need to find a creative way to rely more on themselves and give

Pattern II's more room. To do this, they need to first emphasize their thinking strengths by moving into their Flex-pattern III. This immediately brings more reserve and rationality into the relationship from their side. Their next step is to plan a course of action that will express more independence and personal responsibility in their relationship with Pattern II's. Finally, they need to shift to their Flex-pattern VIII and consciously emphasize their independent strengths. This brings more balance and creativeness to Pattern VI's' assertiveness and makes it easier for the Pattern II's to be assertive in the relationship.

Another way Pattern VI's can usually improve their relationship with Pattern II's is to approach them through their perception of reality. If VI's ask the II's to talk about the facts of a situation and suggest a practical plan of action, it tends to open up communications and strengthens their relationship. Not only does this tend to improve their relationship, but it can also contribute heavily to the personal growth of the Pattern VI's. It gives them an opportunity to grow in the area where they usually feel a great need — practical thinking.

When Pattern II's become aware their reserved and independent tendencies are causing problems in their relationship with Pattern VI's, they need to find effective ways to express their feelings and depend more heavily on the strengths of the Pattern VI's. The most natural way for II's to do this is to first move into their Flex-pattern VII and assertively express their feelings about the relationship. Once they have their feelings out on the table, they can then shift into their Flex-pattern I and express more dependence in their relationship with the Pattern VI's. These deliberate expressions of independence and dependence tend to create an open communication between them and provide the bridge over which Pattern II's can make their greatest contribution to the relationship — their clear perceptions of reality.

Sometimes, Pattern II's can improve their relationship with Pattern VI's by paying more attention to the positive values in warm relational strengths. If II's will deliberately think about the value of these relational strengths and encourage Pattern VI's to express them at appropriate times, it can be a very positive factor in building their relationship. The other great value for the Pattern II's is the stimulation of their own strength in dependence and encourages their own growth in the area in which they usually have their greatest need — the ability to trust and depend upon other people.

Bi/Polar Pattern Relationship II-VII

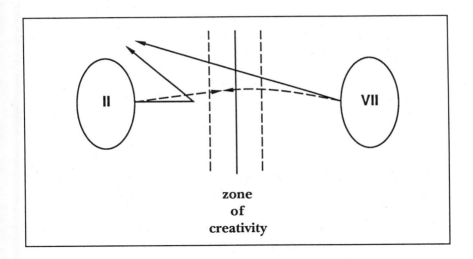

zone
of
creativity

Description
Patterns II and VII are quite similar in that they have the same lead strength in two of the Bi/Polar pairs and are at opposite ends on only one pair. Both tend toward practicality and independence but are different in that Pattern II's lean toward thinking while Pattern VII's lean toward risking.

The clear difference between Pattern VII's and Pattern II's is that Pattern VII's are initiators of action — riskers — and naturally assertive personalities. On the other hand, Pattern II's are thinkers and planners and tend to be more reserved in their relationships. If both the Pattern II's and the Pattern VII's can recognize and affirm these differences and appreciate the opposite strength of the other, their relationship can be highly creative. They can be much more effective as a team than they could be by themselves.

Those situations requiring strong self-assertion, dynamic give-and-take with other people, and initiation of action are best handled with the Pattern VII's as the leaders. Those situations requiring a thorough analysis of a situation, realistic judgment of the risk involved, and stable, consistent leadership are handled best with the Pattern II's as the leaders.

Typical Problems

The major problems faced by Patterns II and VII in their relationships with one another are usually related to the different emphasis that each puts on thinking and risking. In their personal relationship, the tendency of Pattern II's to be reserved and the opposite tendency of Pattern VII's to be assertive sets the stage for a problem. When Pattern VII's move assertively across the line of creativity and invade the space of Pattern II's, Pattern II's tend to feel resentment, hostility, and anger. When Pattern II's follow their natural tendency to pull back within their own self-sufficiency and refuse to respond, Pattern VII's feel frustrated and defeated because the interaction they are seeking is not there — they want a response but get nothing but a stone wall.

Sometimes the opposite emphasis they place on thought and action surfaces as a problem when they are on the same team trying to accomplish a common objective. Pattern II's want to carefully think things through before making a decision; Pattern VII's want to get into action and deal with the problems as they arise. Frequently each frustrates the other. Pattern II's see the VII's as brash and taking unnecessary risks, and Pattern VII's see the II's as procrastinating and not getting things done.

Sometimes Patterns II and VII have a problem because of their common tendency toward independence. Usually both are ambitious and have a strong desire to win. If they find themselves competing with each other, there is the possibility that they will start using their strengths in ways that are destructive to each other. In other words, the relationship can deteriorate into a fight rather than a healthy competition.

Strengthening the Relationship
Pattern II's and Pattern VII's can have a very creative and productive relationship with each other. Their two common lead strengths — practicality and independence — can provide a strong base of mutual respect, and their complementing strengths in thought and action can give balance and effectiveness to the things they do together.

When Pattern VII's become aware they have assertively crossed the line of creativity and invaded the space of the II's, it is time for them to stop talking and pushing and deliberately shift to their thinking strength. In short, they need to express their Flex-pattern II. This immediately brings more thoughtfulness and reserve to their behavior and helps them to move back out of the others' space in a natural and appropriate way. While in their Flex-pattern II, they need to plan a course of action that expresses dependence on the Pattern II's. Finally, Pattern VII's need to deliberately shift into their Flex-pattern V and assertively express more dependence in their relationship with the Pattern II's. To do this, they center their attention on the Pattern II's, ask them questions, and patiently listen to their response.

When Pattern II's become aware they are causing a problem by holding their real feelings within, it is time for them to get these feelings out in the open. II's reveal their feelings in a natural way by moving to their Flex-pattern VII and engaging the VII's in face-to-face confrontations. After getting their feelings out in the open, II's need to emphasize their dependent risking strength by shifting into their Flex-pattern I and showing respect for the Pattern VII's as individuals. These expressions of independence and dependence help to form an open relationship in which there is a good deal more communication between the Pattern II's and the Pattern VII's.

A relationship between Patterns II and VII usually becomes highly creative and satisfying when they appreciate their complementary strengths. Pattern II's recognize the value in the assertive, independent action of Pattern VII's, and Pattern VII's recognize the value of the analytical, evaluative thinking strength of Pattern II's. This attitude not only makes for a more satisfying personal relationship, but it contributes to their effectiveness in accomplishing a team project.

Bi/Polar Pattern Relationship II-VIII

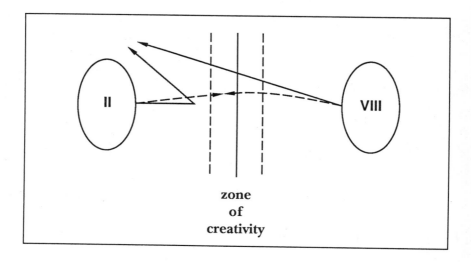

zone
of
creativity

Description

Patterns II and VIII are more different than they are alike. They are at opposite ends on two pairs of Bi/Polar strengths and at the same end on only one pair. They are at opposite ends on the thinking scale — Pattern II's being practical and fact-oriented, and Pattern VIII's being more imaginative and idea-oriented.

They are also at opposite ends on the thinking/risking scale. Pattern II's are oriented toward thinking, evaluating, and judging, whereas Pattern VIII's lean toward action, movement, and dynamism. Pattern VIII's tend to come on assertively and with flair. On the other hand, Pattern II's are initiators of stability. They tend to be reserved and prefer to remain in the background. When II's and VIII's relate to each other, Pattern VIII's have a tendency to come across the line of creativity and invade the space of Pattern II's. Sometimes Pattern II's appear to invite this kind of invasion; however, in reality, they usually resent it. II's are highly sensitive to invasions of their territory and quickly develop a good deal of hostility toward anyone who seeks to unduly influence them or restrict their authority to make their own decisions.

Patterns II and VIII are alike in that they both lean toward independence. This means they both tend to feel self-confident and are more aware of themselves than they are of each other. Neither has a natural tendency to be dependent on the other.

Typical Problems

Usually Patterns II and VIII face quite a challenge in their relationship. It is not uncommon for both of them to experience a good deal of pain and frustration as they relate to one another. As Pattern VIII's come on in their natural way — assertively promoting a grandiose scheme — Pattern II's feel hostility and resentment because of the perceived brashness of the VIII's. In addition, the VIII's strong dynamism threatens the Pattern II's authority and stability. On the other hand, Pattern VIII's tend to experience a good bit of frustration when Pattern II's withdraw into their own self-sufficiency and refuse to interact with them.

Since both Pattern VIII's and Pattern II's tend to have strong egos, sometimes their relationship ends rather abruptly, and they go their own ways. Both seem to sense they are coming from very different places and sometimes feel the task of finding a common meeting ground is not worth the effort.

Strengthening the Relationship

If Patterns II and VIII are in a situation in which they must relate to one another or decide the values in the possible relationship are worth the effort, they are faced with the challenge of having to understand each other.

They need to understand that they actually think differently. Pattern II's are logical and linear in their thinking; that is, they go from Point A to Point B in a very orderly, logical way — building fact on fact. Pattern VIII's think differently. They are intuitive thinkers who have "leaps of insight". Contrasted with how Pattern II's think, Pattern VIII's have difficulty documenting how they arrive at Point B from Point A, in spite of the fact that frequently their insight is very accurate. Pattern II's need to recognize that this kind of thinking can create visions of possibilities which can generate enthusiasm and motivation for productivity and accomplishment. Pattern VIII's, on the other hand, need to recognize the value of the linear, sequential kind of thinking and be willing to adjust their leaps of insight to the test of logical, fact-based analysis.

Patterns II and VIII also need to understand they naturally emphasize opposite ends of the thinking/risking scale. II's naturally emphasize thought, organization, and planning; VIII's naturally emphasize action, decision, and the actual doing part of a project. The recognition that both thought and action are needed in any creative and worthwhile accomplishment not only helps them to appreciate their own contributions, but also helps them to appreciate the contributions made by the other one in the relationship.

When Pattern II's find the assertiveness of Pattern VIII's is giving them a problem, their first conscious adjustment is to become more self-assertive — they need to move into their Flex-pattern VII and express their real feelings in a direct confrontation. Rather than follow their natural tendency to withdraw and pull away, they need to get their feelings out on the table and express themselves. The next step II's must take is to shift to their Flex-pattern I and emphasize their dependent strengths. They do this by putting themselves in the others' shoes — showing them respect, listening to what they are saying, and trying to understand where they are coming from. Through these expressions of independence and dependence, Pattern II's engage Pattern VIII's in a give-and-take interaction and creatively push Pattern VIII's back out of their territory. In turn, Pattern VIII's tend to appreciate the active response and enjoy the dynamic of the interaction.

When Pattern VIII's become aware Pattern II's are reacting negatively to their efforts to influence them, it is time for them to consciously alter their behavior. Their first step is to emphasize their thinking by moving into their Flex-pattern IV. They pull back within themselves and try to understand what is going on in the relationship. This immediately takes the pressure off the Pattern II's and brings more rationality and calm to the relationship. The next step for the Pattern VIII's is to formulate a plan of action to draw on the greatest natural strength of the Pattern II's — their practicality. Finally, VIII's need to put this plan to work by shifting into their Flex-pattern VI and actually drawing on the practicality of the Pattern II's. In practice, the best way for Pattern VIII's to do this is to center their attention on the Pattern II's, stop trying to influence them, stop talking, ask questions, listen, and consciously draw on the practical thinking strengths of the Pattern II's.

Bi/Polar Pattern Relationship III-III

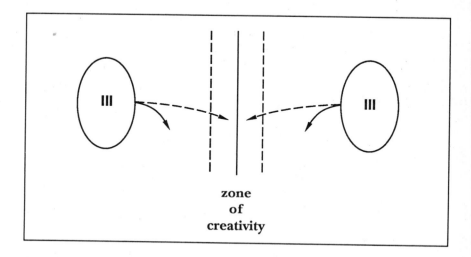

Description

Two Pattern III's usually find a common interest in theoretical discussions. Their relationship tends to be warm, accepting, discreet, and proper. Their common behavior toward one another is well-mannered, sensitive, appreciative, and respectful.

They tend to stay back from the line of creativity and wait for the other one to take the initiative. They approach each other gingerly and are careful not to offend one another. Their relationship tends to place an emphasis on intellectual matters and usually shows a general lack of dynamic qualities — particularly self-assertiveness.

Typical Problems

Although two Pattern III's can derive a good deal of enjoyment from their intellectual discussions, it is normal for them to eventually experience a need for more emotional stimulation and dynamic interaction. They can get "fed up" with theories and begin to experience a need for more emotional involvement and excitement in their relationship. When this happens, they may look to one another to bring more dynamism into their relationship. Since neither of them has a natural tendency to take the initiative and be self-assertive, the stage is set for problems to develop. Sometimes they just drift apart because the relationship becomes dull and boring. If they stay related, their relationship is likely to get progressively worse until they find some way to bring more dynamism into it.

Sometimes two Pattern III's stimulate each other's tendency to overemphasize theory and ideas. This can cause them to polarize even more deeply on their theoretical side. If they do polarize, they block out even more of their practical thinking strength. The final result could be that they end up being less creative together than they would be apart.

Strengthening the Relationship

It is natural for Pattern III's to be reserved and feel a need for more self-confidence. When two Pattern III's are feeling a need for more interaction and aliveness in their relationship, there are at least three ways in which they may make their relationship more dynamic.

First, they can, without outside help, make their relationship more exciting and creative on their own. This approach requires them to take the initiative to deal creatively with their natural reserved and relational tendency. This means they deliberately become more assertive. One of the best ways for them to become more assertive is to consciously emphasize their assertive strength by moving into their Flex-pattern VI. They share their feelings and let one another know what is going on inside. It works best if they become assertive in their natural way — leading with their dependent strengths and then showing stronger expressions of independence as the interactions progress. If one takes the initiative to become more assertive, it tends to stimulate the other to become more assertive also. If both get involved in the process, it can "spark" a give-and-take interaction that infuses new life into their relationship and makes it more exciting and fulfilling for both of them.

Second, two Pattern III's can express their assertive Flex-pattern VI by actively seeking a more dynamic individual and inviting that person into the relationship. Patterns VII or VIII fit this role the best because they naturally have most of what the relationship needs — more dynamism. This does not mean, however, that some of the other patterns would not work also — especially V and VI.

Third, they can join a dynamic group. If the group is dedicated to objectives in harmony with the interests and values of the two Pattern III's, it can be a very satisfying and fulfilling experience for them. Not only is their relationship with the group likely to be enjoyable for them individually, but it frequently brings new excitement to their own relationship with each other.

If two Pattern III's find their relationship is stimulating them to polarize on their theoretical strength, they need to find an effective way to bring more practical thinking into the relationship. They can do this by deliberately emphasizing their own practical strengths (shifting to their Flex-pattern I), or they can bring these practical strengths in from the outside. In practice, it seems to work best if they reach to the outside and bring in a person who naturally leads in practical thinking (Patterns I, II, V, or VII).

Bi/Polar Pattern Relationship III-IV

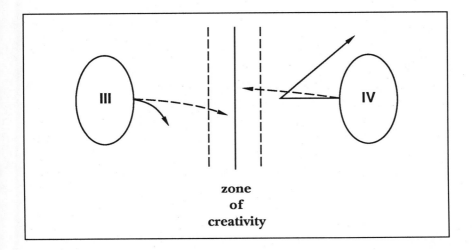

zone
of
creativity

Description

Patterns III and IV have very similar lead strengths. They both lead in thinking — tending to be reserved in their relationships and in theoretical thinking — tending more toward ideas than practical reality.

They are different in that they are on opposite ends of the risking polarity. Pattern III's lean toward dependence — valuing warm relationships with others, whereas Pattern IV's lean toward independence — valuing their personal freedom and autonomy.

Both III's and IV's have a tendency to be reserved in their relationships — neither is naturally assertive or outgoing. They are reserved for different reasons, however. Pattern III's are reserved out of their awareness of the strength of others and their respect for them. On the other hand, IV's are reserved and tend to stay uninvolved out of their desire for personal freedom and independence Pattern III's are more inclined to want the relationships but tend to stay back of the line of creativity and wait for the IV's to take the initiative. Pattern IV's are more inclined to want personal freedom and move away from the relationship when they begin to feel encumbered by it.

Typical Problems

A frequent problem in a relationship between Patterns III and IV comes about due to their common reserved tendency. Although they are reserved for different reasons, the result is the same — neither moves assertively toward the other, resulting in a generally low level of dynamic interaction. The relationship can become dull and boring for both if they don't consciously discipline themselves to be more assertive. They can lose the relationship through disuse.

Another problem they sometimes experience is related to their common leaning toward theoretical thinking. Since they both enjoy dealing with ideas and concepts, they tend to stimulate each other's imagination, making it easier to polarize on the theoretical side. Since polarization on theoretical thinking creates a blockage of practical thinking, it makes them even less effective in dealing with practical problems.

Other problems in a relationship between Patterns III and IV can arise because they are polar opposites on the risking scale — III's leaning toward dependence and IV's leaning toward independence. Out of their lead strength in dependent risking, Pattern III's feel most comfortable and are most effective when dealing with well-established, proven, and accepted ideas and theories. On the other hand, Pattern IV's have a major strength in independence which orients them to new and innovative ideas they think up on their own. Pattern III's can be threatened by these new (sometimes radical) ideas because it shakes the solid intellectual base on which they have placed a good deal of their security. The Pattern IV's tend to feel depreciated because Pattern III's do not immediately appreciate the value of their new insights.

When Pattern III's polarize on proven theories and ideas, they tend to reject and depreciate the new insights Pattern IV's have to offer. This depreciates the very thing IV's are most dependent upon and value most highly — it strikes hard at their egos. When this happens, IV's tend to view III's as unappreciative, devoid of insight, rigid, closed-minded, complacent, and text-bookish.

When Pattern IV's polarize on their own innovative ideas and leaps of personal insight, they tend to reject and depreciate the value of other people's ideas — particularly established ways of thinking. This threatens what III's are most dependent upon — proven and established theories and ideas. As a result, Pattern III's tend to view IV's as egotistical, conceited, radical, and going off on a tangent.

Strengthening the Relationship
When III's and IV's have a relationship, it is helpful for them to realize both of them are naturally reserved. If they want to build a more creative relationship, they must make a conscious effort to be more assertive than is their natural inclination. Specifically, Pattern III's need to express their Flex-pattern VI and be more assertive in their relationship with Pattern IV's. In doing this, they consciously express more dependence and independence and get a creative interaction going. Pattern IV's can initiate the interaction by moving to their Flex-pattern VIII and expressing a stronger blend of independence and dependence in their relationship with Pattern III's. Either can initiate the process and, when one becomes more assertive with a creative blend of independence and dependence, it stimulates the other to become more assertive also. A highly creative, productive, and deeply satisfying relationship can be developed if both apply themselves in this process.

If they find they are polarizing on theoretical thinking in the relationship, one must take the initiative (usually the one who is most mature) and consciously shift emphasis to their practical thinking — Pattern III's express their Flex-pattern I and Pattern IV's express their Flex-pattern II. If one takes the initiative in emphasizing practical thinking, it usually stimulates the other to do more practical thinking — this initiates a feeding process between them that improves the relationship and produces more creative thinking.

Another avenue open to Patterns III and IV when they are seeking to improve their relationship is bringing other people into their relationship. For example, they can deliberately bring a naturally self-assertive and practical person (say a Pattern VII) into the relationship and invite that person to be a contributing member. Not only can this create a highly effective team, but it also tends to strengthen the relationship between the Pattern III and the Pattern IV. A mature person with any basic pattern of strengths could be helpful in bringing balancing strengths to the relationship, but Pattern VII or Pattern II usually fit most naturally.

Bi/Polar Pattern Relationship III-V

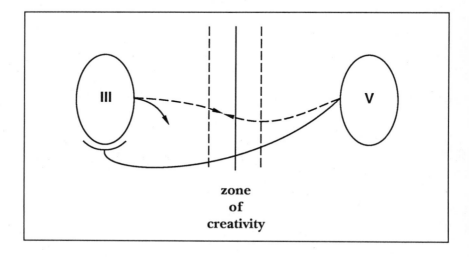

zone
of
creativity

Description

Both Patterns III and V lean toward dependence in their relationships. Assertive dependence is the natural inclination of Pattern V's, and reserved dependence is the natural inclination for Pattern III's. Since both patterns have natural relational tendencies, they tend to form relationships rather easily. Characteristically, Pattern V's are the initiators in the relationship, and Pattern III's provide long-term stability. There is usually a good deal of warmth in the relationship — with Pattern V's being more expressive in showing this warmth and Pattern III's being more reserved.

Patterns III and V are at opposite ends on the other two pairs of polar strengths. They complement each other on the thinking pair (practical/theoretical) — theoretical thinking is the lead strength of Pattern III's, whereas practical thinking is the lead strength in Pattern V's. They also complement each other in the basic pair (thinking/risking). Pattern III's are more thought-oriented, and Pattern V's are more action-oriented.

Typical Problems

Their differences are usually the source of the problems they experience in their relationship. The difference in the way they think can cause frustration on both sides. Pattern III's are sometimes frustrated by Pattern V's' seeming lack of interest and concern for theories and abstract concepts. Pattern V's sometimes experience III's as too abstract and theoretical and not really dealing with things that make a "real" difference in the world. If both polarize deeply on their own natural ways of thinking, they can develop some negative attitudes toward each other. Pattern III's can view V's as superficial, shallow, unreliable, unstable, and just not sensitive to the deeper values of life. Pattern V's can view III's as withdrawn, obtuse, dry, uninteresting, dull, and just "not with it".

Another problem III's and V's can experience in their relationship is related to their opposite leanings in the basic pair of strengths — thought and action. Pattern III's like relationships, but Pattern V's can come on too assertively and want to get too close. If this happens, Pattern III's can feel smothered and over-whelmed. On the other side, Pattern V's can become frustrated by Pattern III's' lack of response. If the Pattern III's "just sit there", it can cause the Pattern V's to come on even more strongly and try even harder to get a response. Sometimes this drives the Pattern III's farther away and makes matters worse.

Strengthening the Relationship
One of the best ways for Pattern V's to improve their relationship with Pattern III's is to approach them through their greatest strength — theoretical thinking. Pattern V's do this by first moving into their Flex-pattern I and emphasizing their own thought processes. This brings more rationality and reserve into the relationship from their side. Their next step is to shift to their Flex-pattern VI and reach out assertively to the Pattern III's for their strength in theoretical thinking. Pattern III's frequently have a vast reservoir of knowledge and information that can contribute a great deal to Pattern V's. With this kind of attitude and behavior toward Pattern III's, V's can gain stability, achieve deeper understanding of theoretical ideas, and participate more fully in the values well-ordered thought can give to their lives.

Pattern III's need to watch for those times when they are polarizing on thinking and forgetting about the values of feelings and dynamic interaction. When III's recognize they are overemphasizing thinking, they need to deliberately become more assertive in their relationship with the Pattern V's — they need to consciously express their Flex-pattern VI. This usually involves a frank and open expression of their feelings. Pattern V's can handle an open expression of feelings much better than they can a quiet and reserved response. If Pattern III's deliberately become more assertive in their relationship with Pattern V's, they usually find that, in the process, they themselves become more outgoing, more dynamic, more expressive. They also tend to develop more self-confidence.

Bi/Polar Pattern Relationship III-VI

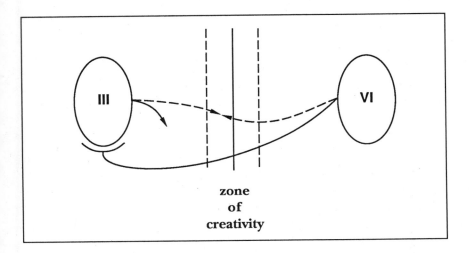

zone
of
creativity

Description

Patterns III and VI have a close kinship — they risk dependence naturally, and both lean toward theoretical thinking. Their patterns of strength differ only in the basic pair (thinking/risking). Pattern III's tend to be more thoughtful and reserved; Pattern VI's tend to be more action-oriented and assertive.

Both III's and VI's like and enjoy people. They have a ready willingness to relate, and they tend to be warmly supportive of one another. Pattern VI's are naturally more assertive and usually initiate the relationship. They also tend to be most assertive in seeking to make it a closer relationship. On the other hand, Pattern III's tend to wait for VI's to make the first move and then respond in a quiet, warm, and accepting way.

Typical Problems

A relationship between Patterns III and VI is likely to suffer because of a need for more independence. Pattern VI's can overwhelm

Pattern III's with their loving concern — sometimes to the point the Pattern III's feel "smothered" and "taken over" by kindness. Conversely, Pattern III's can frustrate Pattern VI's by too much "quietness" and lack of response. Frequently Pattern VI's appear irresponsible and too emotionally involved to Pattern III's. On the other hand, III's appear too academic and organized to Pattern VI's.

Another problem Patterns III and VI sometimes experience in their relationship with one another is related to the fact that they both have theoretical thinking as a major strength. They tend to naturally stimulate each other's imagination and make polarization on theoretical thinking more likely. If polarization develops, it blocks much of their practical thinking strength. This compounds their problem because practical thinking is a supporting strength for both of them.

Strengthening the Relationship
The major challenge Patterns III and VI face in strengthening their relationship is in their natural tendency to emphasize their two common lead strengths — dependent risking and theoretical thinking. When they become aware they are polarizing on dependence, they need to find a way to bring more independence into the relationship. They can do this by deliberately shifting emphasis to an expression of their own independence or they can invite a naturally independent person into the relationship (or any person who is aware of the need and has the maturity to emphasize the strength of independence). If Patterns III and VI find they are polarized on theoretical thinking, they can follow a similar procedure — deliberately exercise and express their own strengths in practicality or bring an outside person into the relationship for the purpose of shifting emphasis to the practical side.

Patterns III's can do some specific things to improve their relationship with Pattern VI's. Probably the most effective thing to do is to watch for those times when they are avoiding confrontation by not expressing their real thoughts and true feelings. When Pattern III's become aware that holding their feelings inside is causing a problem, they need to deliberately become more assertive and get their feelings out in the open. They do this by moving into their Flex-pattern VI and expressing a stronger blend of dependence and independence. This creates a communication bridge with the Pattern VI's. This process relieves Pattern III's of some painful pent-up feelings and allows Pattern VI's to exercise their natural lead strengths in dealing creatively with feelings. As the process continues, it becomes easier for Pattern III's to be more assertive and express more independence, not only in this relationship, but also in their relationships with other people.

Pattern VI's can also do some specific things to improve their relationship with Pattern III's. VI's need to watch for their tendency to come on too strong and push for a relationship that is "too close for comfort" for the Pattern III's. This is not to say that VI's should stop being assertively warm and dependent (that is a strength), but it is saying that, when it becomes a problem, they must deal creatively with it. When Pattern VI's become aware their warm assertiveness has created a problem for the Pattern III's, it is time for them to move to their Flex-pattern III and emphasize their thinking strengths. By emphasizing their thinking, they become more thoughtful and reserved in their relationship with Pattern III's. This takes the pressure off Pattern III's and makes them feel more comfortable in the relationship. While emphasizing their thinking strength through their Flex-pattern III, Pattern VI's need to formulate a plan of action that will express more independence in their relationship with the Pattern III's. Finally, they need to shift to their Flex-pattern VIII and express more dynamic independence in their relationship with the Pattern III's.

Bi/Polar Pattern Relationship III-VII

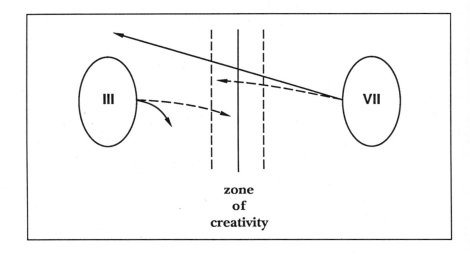

zone
of
creativity

Description

Patterns III and VII are direct opposites in all three pairs of Bi/Polar strengths. III's lean toward thinking, and VII's lean toward action. Pattern III's are theoretical and idea-oriented, whereas Pattern VII's are more practical and fact-oriented. Pattern III's tend to feel more comfortable in drawing on the strengths of others, whereas Pattern VII's tend to feel most comfortable in taking an independent stance and depending heavily on their own strengths. Since Patterns III and VII are at opposite ends on all three pairs of the polar strengths, they come from very different home bases and tend to experience themselves and the world around them in very different ways.

In relationships between Patterns III and VII, Pattern III's have a natural tendency to be quiet and wait for Pattern VII's to take the initiative. On the other hand, Pattern VII's are characteristically assertive and have a tendency to step out front and take over. Normally Pattern VII's take the leadership role in their relationships with Pattern III's.

Another clear difference between Patterns III and VII can be seen in their opposite orientation toward reason and emotion. Pattern III's are basically reasoning people, whereas Pattern VII's are basically action-oriented. Pattern III's are most confident when solidly based in their reasoning strength. On the contrary, Pattern VII's feel most confident when solidly based in their feelings of self— their own self-confidence and awareness of their personal goals.

Typical Problems
The major frustrations and deepest pains Pattern III's experience in their relationships with Pattern VII's are related to the assertiveness and self-confidence of the Pattern VII's and their own felt need for more self-confidence. It is natural for Pattern VII's to come on strong and invade the territory of Pattern III's — sometimes without being aware of the violation. Pattern III's are usually very much aware of this violation but tend to back up and not let the Pattern VII's know they have been violated and taken advantage of. They tend to freeze and take no initiative whatsoever— neither to respond nor to get out of the situation. Pattern III's wish Pattern VII's would have a greater sensitivity to them and stop themselves from making the violation rather than having to be pushed back.

The major frustrations Pattern VII's experience in their relationships with Pattern III's are associated with the nonassertive tendencies of Pattern III's. Pattern VII's want a reaction from Pattern III's and are extremely frustrated when they are quiet and unresponsive. Pattern VII's need a response from Pattern III's in order to know where they are coming from. If this response is not forthcoming, VII's feel as if they are punching a pillow or fighting the air and don't have any handles to get hold of. Pattern VII's frequently feel impatient with Pattern III's, particularly in regard to their tendency toward procrastination and delay.

Strengthening the Relationship

The relationship between Patterns III and VII has great potential for creativity and can be one of the most deeply satisfying and highly productive relationships either can have. However, it takes a good deal of effort and maturity on both sides to bring it off. The first requirement is that both of them must affirm their own pattern of strengths and feel good about who they are basically. Out of this kind of self-acceptance can come a healthy expression of their natural strengths, and each can make contributions to the other in the areas where each has the greatest need. The second requirement is that each affirm the positive value of the dominant strengths of the other. Out of this attitude can come an appreciation for the strengths of the other person. A third requirement is that both must recognize their personal tendencies and deal creatively with them.

Pattern III's need to be alert to those times when they are becoming polarized on thinking. When they become aware this is happening, they need to run the risk of becoming assertive and expressing their real feelings and thoughts. They need to express their Flex-pattern VI. By doing this, they move assertively towards the Pattern VII and make the response the Pattern VII's have been waiting for. Immediately, Pattern VII's develop a grater respect for Pattern III's, and this makes it easier for the Pattern III's to emphasize their independent strength. Finally, Pattern III's need to shift to their Flex-pattern IV and express their independence through a show of self-sufficiency.

Pattern III's also need to be alert to those times when they are polarizing on theoretical thinking. When they become aware they are polarizing on their theoretical side, they need to emphasize their practical thinking by moving into their Flex-pattern I and drawing on the practical thinking of the Pattern VII's.

Pattern VII's need to be alert to those times when they are polarizing on assertive independence. Pattern VII's need to realize it takes a good deal of courage for Pattern III's to stop them in their assertion. Realizing this, VII's can be part of creating a good relationship by learning to stop themselves before they have to be stopped by the Pattern III's. Pattern VII's can effectively stop themselves by moving into their Flex-pattern II and emphasizing their thinking. This makes them more reserved and thoughtful — tending to bring them back out of the others' territory. Their next step is to shift into their Flex-pattern V and center their attention on the Pattern III's as individuals. While in their Flex-pattern V, they encourage Pattern III's to talk by asking them questions, putting themselves in the others' shoes, and listening to what they have to say.

Another tendency Pattern VII's need to watch out for is overemphasizing practical thinking to the detriment of ideas and abstract thought. In dealing with this tendency, VII's need to consciously express their Flex-pattern II and emphasize their thinking. Next, they need to emphasize their dependent strength by shifting into their Flex-pattern V and drawing on the theoretical thinking strengths of the Pattern III's. By finally shifting to their Flex-pattern VIII, the VII's can participate fully in a theoretical give-and-take discussion with the III's.

Bi/Polar Pattern Relationship III-VIII

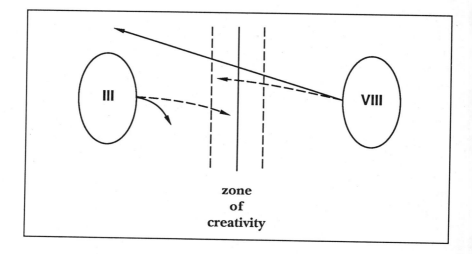

zone
of
creativity

Description

In relationships, Patterns III and VIII are quite different. They are at opposite ends on two pairs of polar strengths and at the same end on the third pair. In the thinking/risking pair, III's are oriented toward thinking, and VIII's are oriented toward risking. On the dependent/independent scale, III's lean toward dependence, and VIII's lean toward independence. They are at the same end on the practical/theoretical pair — both lean toward the theoretical side.

In a relationship between III's and VIII's, Pattern VIII's are normally the initiators and dynamic leaders. VIII's naturally move assertively across the line of creativity and into the space of the Pattern III's. Usually Pattern III's allow this assertion, remain quiet and unassertive, and adopt the "follower" role. In a normal relationship between Patterns III and VIII, the Pattern III's are reserved, soft-spoken, gentle, and introspective; the Pattern VIII's are assertive, self-confident, dynamic, colorful, and risk-taking.

Typical Problems

The most common problem in a relationship between Patterns III and VIII comes from their natural tendencies — Pattern VIII's move assertively into the territory of III's, and Pattern III's allow it to go on by being quiet and unassertive. If Pattern VIII's don't pull back on their own initiative or Pattern III's don't push them back, each tends to develop a negative attitude toward the other. Pattern III's begin to view the Pattern VIII's as abrasive, egotistical, selfish, prima donnas, obnoxious, "con artists", and untrustworthy. Pattern VIII's begin to see the Pattern III's as withdrawn, weak, pliable, easily manipulated, and not worth much attention — they tend to ignore them and "write them off".

Another problem Patterns III and VIII sometimes experience in their relationships with each other is related to their opposite tendency in decision-making. III's characteristically want to gather all the information before making the decision. This frequently results in delay and procrastination. Contrary to that, VIII's characteristically want to get into action. This frequently causes the VIII's to make decisions quickly. If III's and VIII's are making decisions affecting both, these opposing tendencies can create a great deal of frustration and anxiety in the relationships. Pattern III's feel exposed and anxious because of the snap decisions being made by Pattern VIII's, and Pattern VIII's are frustrated by the lack of action and movement being caused by Pattern III's' procrastination.

Strengthening the Relationship

Patterns III and VIII can have a highly creative and very satisfying relationship with each other. It takes understanding and expressions of courage on both sides to bring it about, but the rewards that each can receive in the relationship far outweigh the efforts expended.

Pattern III's need to push back when Pattern VIII's come into their territory. They need to express their real thoughts and feelings directly to the Pattern VIII's. This is not easy for Pattern III's, but they have the courage required if they will just call on it. Almost invariably an assertive, emotional expression by the Pattern III's improves the relationship. Pattern III's become assertive by expressing their Flex-pattern VI. This assertiveness on the part of Pattern III's gets the attention of Pattern VIII's and makes it easier for Pattern III's to express their independence. If Pattern III's follow this process, it not only tends to improve the relationship, but it also tends to help them develop more self-confidence.

Pattern VIII's need to pull back when they realize they have violated the territory of the Pattern III's. They pull back most naturally by deliberately moving into their Flex-pattern IV and emphasizing their thinking. While in their Flex-pattern IV, they need to formulate a plan of actin in which they express more dependence on the Pattern III's. Finally, they deliberately shift into their Flex-pattern VI and actually express this dependence upon the Pattern III's. In actual practice, Pattern VIII's center their attention on Pattern III's, ask them questions, listen to what they have to say, and try to understand them as individuals. If Pattern VIII's consciously think about the strengths of Pattern III's, it immediately becomes a positive force in the relationship. It can be even more positive if the Pattern VIII's become assertive in encouraging Pattern III's to express these strengths.

One of the best benefits coming out of a creative relationship between Patterns III and VIII has to do with their decision-making. The mutual confidence that develops in a good relationship between III's and VIII's brings a more creative blend of strengths to their shared decision-making. The thinking of the Pattern III's slows down the snap decisions of the VIII's, and the courage of the VIII's reduces the procrastination and delay of the Pattern III's, thus creating a more effective decision-making process.

Bi/Polar Pattern Relationship IV-IV

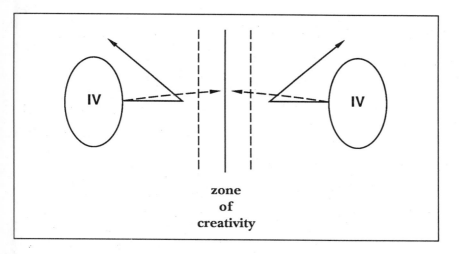

zone
of
creativity

Description

The relationship between two Pattern IV's tends to be based upon their common interest in ideas and concepts. A search for intellectual insight and conceptual understanding is usually the central driving force in their relationship. The excitement of the relationship comes primarily from intellectual stimulation — not so much from a dynamic interplay of independence and dependence. The relationship is characterized by reserve and a respect for the rights of others rather than a display of emotional warmth. When warmth is expressed, it is usually shown in a quiet and reserved way. When two Pattern IV's relate, the major objective is usually outside the relationship — not the relationship itself.

The relationship between two Pattern IV's tends to be tenuous and fragile. Their common interest in ideas is usually not sufficient to keep them together in a close personal relationship. Once contact has been made between two IV's, the interactions are usually infrequent unless there are some compelling outside forces keeping them together. Their common tendency is to move away from each other, do their own thing, and accomplish on their own. This is not to say that Pattern IV's don't want relationships — they want and need them the same as anyone else. The difference is that they tend to emphasize the values of distance, independence, and personal freedom within their relationships.

Typical Problems

The major problems in a relationship between two Pattern IV's comes from the fact that they have the same lead strengths — they don't provide complementary lead strengths for each other to draw on. For instance, they can easily stimulate one another in their strongest area — theoretical thinking. As a result, they overemphasize theory and begin to have problems in their relationship because of a need for more practicality. As they become aware of the need for more practical thinking, sometimes they turn to one another for the needed strength. Since neither has practicality as a natural lead strength, it takes a good bit of self-discipline and conscious effort for them to bring fact-oriented thinking into their relationship. It can be frustrating if they look to one another to provide a strength neither has in natural dominance.

They can also experience a problem because both tend to be reserved and unassertive. They are reluctant to express their feelings and, as a result, sometimes fail to make emotional contact and establish a bridge for communication. In failing to share their thoughts and feelings, the relationship can wither and die for lack of interaction.

Another problem two Pattern IV's can experience in their relationship is related to their common tendency toward independence and self-sufficiency. This tendency to withdraw into their own self-sufficiency can cause them to actively avoid one another and miss out on the creativeness that their interactions could produce. That is the problem — the potential creativeness that could come from their relationship is lost.

Strengthening the Relationship

Two Pattern IV's can have a creative and productive relationship, but it requires an awareness of their common tendencies and a mutual willingness to deal with them creatively.

In building and maintaining a creative relationship, the first step, always, is for both of them to be themselves and express their natural Pattern IV strengths. It is essential they both feel good about who they are and have an opportunity to lead with their major strengths.

The second step is equally important. They need to be alert to those times when they need to shift emphasis to their supporting strengths and bring practical, assertive, and warm dependent strengths into the relationship. When they find they are building too many dream castles, they must shift to their Flex-pattern II and emphasize practicality for awhile. When they find they are being too reserved, quiet, and unassertive, they must move into their Flex-pattern VIII and be more assertive and dynamic in their relationship with each other. They need to express their feelings and be more assertive by expressing a stronger blending of independence and dependence. Finally, when they discover they are getting wrapped up in their own self-sufficiency and their mutual independence is moving them too far apart, it is time for them to shift to their Flex-pattern III and express more dependence on one another.

Bi/Polar Pattern Relationship IV-V

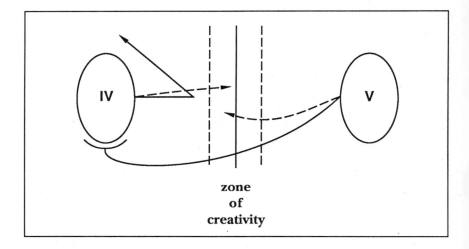

zone
of
creativity

Description

Patterns IV and V are at opposite ends of the scale on all three pairs of Bi/Polar strengths. Pattern IV's lead with thinking, theoretical thinking, and independent risking — the natural supporting strengths of V's. Pattern V's lead with risking, practical thinking, and dependent risking — the natural supporting strengths of IV's. Pattern IV's are idea-centered, and Pattern V's are people-centered. These differences cause them to think and behave very differently in their relationships.

In a relationship between Pattern V's and Pattern IV's, V's tend to come on strong and want to have a close, personal relationship, whereas IV's tend to back up and want more distance and privacy in their relationships.

Typical Problems

One of the keenest frustrations that Pattern IV's experience with Pattern V's is that the Pattern V's constantly need and demand recognition. Pattern IV's tend to feel that V's should know how they feel about them, and they shouldn't have to repeat it every day. Conversely, V's want to be told how much they are appreciated, every day! If this appreciation is not expressed regularly, V's begin to feel they are not appreciated.

Another problem Pattern IV's sometimes have in their relationships with V's has to do with Pattern IV's' orientation toward ideas and concepts and V's' orientation toward practicality. It can be personally depreciating and sometimes frustrating to IV's when Pattern V's fail to appreciate the significance of ideas — particularly if they are the Pattern IV's' original ideas.

Pattern V's can also experience much pain and frustration in their relationships with Pattern IV's. If Pattern IV's fail to give them adequate recognition and refuse to express their real feelings to them, it causes Pattern V's a great deal of pain. Pattern V's become very anxious and disturbed if they are living with tight-lipped IV's who are stingy in their expressions of praise and appreciation.

Pattern V's are frequently frustrated by the Pattern IV's' emphasis on ideas and concepts. In Pattern V's' world, the "real" value of ideas comes in the practical application of those ideas, not in the ideas themselves. If Pattern IV's dwell too long on just the idea, it can become very boring to Pattern V's.

Pattern V's can also develop very negative feelings about what they perceive as rejection when Pattern IV's withdraw into their own self-sufficiency and communicate "I don't need you". Frequently, Pattern IV's appear cold and unemotional to Pattern V's, and this can be very upsetting to Pattern V's, because warm relationships mean so much to them.

Strengthening the Relationship

Pattern IV's need to be alert to those times when they are hiding their feelings and not "leveling" with Pattern V's. When they become aware that holding their feelings within is causing a problem, they need to move into their Flex-pattern VIII and become more assertive in expressing their thoughts and feelings — particularly feelings. Pattern IV's need to keep in mind that they are appealing to Pattern V's' greatest strengths by expressing their feelings. V's can handle expressed feelings a lot better than they can ideas and concepts. Pattern IV's' next step is to deliberately emphasize their dependent strength by shifting into their Flex-pattern III. While in their Flex-pattern III, they bring the Pattern V's into the center of their attention, ask them to share their own feelings about the relationship, listen to what they say, and try to understand where the V's are coming from. These actions on the part of Pattern IV's establish emotional contact with Pattern V's and create a communication bridge between them.

Pattern IV's also need to watch for those times when they are caught up in theory and forgetting about the facts of reality. When they become aware they are neglecting the practical in their relationship with Pattern V's, the appropriate thing for them to do is to move into their Flex-pattern III and ask the Pattern V's to make practical suggestions. Sometimes it is very effective if they just ask the Pattern V's to evaluate a situation on a realistic basis. After listening to the Pattern V's, they can shift to their Flex-pattern II and make their own evaluation of the facts.

Pattern V's need to be particularly sensitive to those times when they are being assertive in trying to get close to Pattern IV's. When they discover they are crowding Pattern IV's, they need to deliberately emphasize their thinking by expressing their Flex-pattern I. This is the best way for Pattern V's to back off and show more reserve in the relationship. Not only does this introduce more intellectual understanding into the relationship, but it also tends to take the pressure off Pattern IV's and engender more respect from them. While Pattern V's emphasize thinking and move into their Flex-pattern I, they need to plan a change of behavior that expresses a stronger blend of independence in their relationship with Pattern

IV's. Their final step is to shift into their Flex-pattern VII and assertively express this new blend of independence. Frequently, this independence is expressed most creatively by Pattern V's' taking charge of their own lives and becoming more personally responsible. In other words, they emphasize their independence by directing their energies toward the accomplishment of their own personal goals and ambitions.

Pattern V's also need to be on the lookout for those times when they are overemphasizing practicality and depreciating the value of theoretical thinking. When V's become aware they are polarizing on the practical side in their relationship with Pattern IV's, they need to deliberately shift to their Flex-pattern VI and emphasize their dependence on the Pattern IV's' strength in theoretical thinking. In doing this, Pattern V's not only avail themselves to the greatest interest of Pattern IV's (theoretical thinking) but they do the most effective thing they can do to build communications with them.

Bi/Polar Pattern Relationship IV-VI

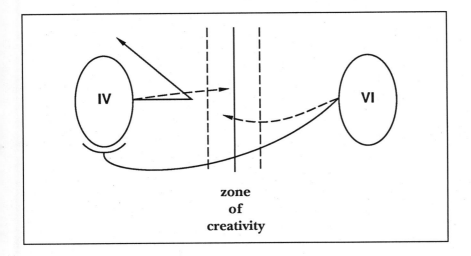

IV

VI

zone
of
creativity

Description

Patterns IV and VI are more different than they are alike. They are at opposite ends on two of the Bi/Polar pairs and at the same end on the third. They are at opposite ends on the basic pair (thinking/risking) and the risking pair (dependent/independent). IV's lead with thinking and reserved independence, whereas VI's lead with action and assertive dependence. They tend in the same direction on the thinking pair (practical/theoretical) — both lean toward the theoretical side. The most natural bridge for their relationship is their common interest in ideas. This bridge can be even stronger if these ideas deal with human relationships and potential for human growth.

In relationships between Patterns IV and VI, VI's tend to be assertive and come across the line into the space of the Pattern IV's. They tend to center their attention on the IV's and approach them with full positive feelings, wanting to have a close and accepting relationship. IV's tend to experience this warm assertiveness as an invasion of their space and a threat to their personal freedom and independence. Sometimes Pattern IV's feel that, if they would give in to the assertive closeness pursued by Pattern VI's, they would just be smothered to death.

Pattern IV's are reason-oriented and Pattern VI's are emotion-oriented. IV's like to deal with ideas and concepts and experiment with them in reality. VI's prefer to deal with feelings and experience themselves and other people in relationships. IV's usually communicate in written words. VI's communicate best by talking. Another interesting difference between IV's and VI's is that IV's tend to think things through, then talk, whereas VI's tend to think while talking. If both patterns can recognize and affirm these differences, it usually contributes to strengthening their relationship.

Typical Problems

The pains that Patterns IV and VI tend to experience in their relationships are related mainly to their differences. Normally

Pattern VI's feel a good deal of frustration because of their need for a close, warm relationship and the opposite tendency of the Pattern IV's to shy away from that much warmth. On the other hand, IV's feel that their freedom and independence are threatened when Pattern VI's invade their space and push for a close and warm relationship.

Another frustration IV's and VI's generally experience results from the difference in the relative emphasis they put on reason and emotion. Pattern IV's prefer to live in a world of structured thought processes and experience some difficulty in handling expressed emotions — both their own and those of other people. On the other hand, Pattern VI's prefer to live in a world of emotion and feel comfortable and effective there. VI's tend to feel somewhat less comfortable in the world of logic and reason.

One of the biggest hurdles Patterns IV and VI need to overcome is their difference in just how much closeness they want in their relationship. Pattern IV's feel more comfortable in a relationship that has distance, and Pattern VI's feel more comfortable when the relationship is warm and close. This is the fundamental problem, and the extent to which it is solved usually determines the quality of their relationship. If Pattern VI's polarize on warm relationships and fail to give due value to independence and self-autonomy, they can literally chase after the Pattern IV's and eventually suffer rejection from them. If Pattern IV's polarize on distance and fail to acknowledge the values of concern and human warmth, they can eventually lose the concern, warmth, and support of Pattern VI's. IV's want and need the warmth and support of Pattern VI's — they just want it to come to them in a more reserved and respectful way.

Strengthening the Relationship

Pattern IV's need to watch for their tendency to withdraw into their own self-sufficiency and pull back from interactions with Pattern VI's. When this tendency causes a problem, IV's need to first express their Flex-pattern VIII and become more assertive toward the Pattern VI's.

This establishes emotional contact and gets the interactions going. Pattern IV's' next step is to move into their Flex-pattern III and emphasize their dependence on the Pattern VI's — they center their attention on Pattern VI's, ask them how they feel about the relationship, listen to their response, and try to understand where the Pattern VI's are coming from.

Pattern VI's need to be alert to those times when they are causing a problem in their relationship with Pattern IV's by pushing too hard for an intimate relationship. When they become aware of a problem here, the first thing they need to do is to emphasize their thinking strengths. They do this by shifting into their Flex-pattern III. This automatically makes them more thoughtful and reserved and tends to pull them back out of Pattern IV's' territory. In turn, Pattern IV's feel less threatened and more willing to interact with Pattern VI's. While Pattern VI's are in their Flex-pattern III and emphasizing their thinking, they need to develop a plan to express more independence. Their next step is to shift into their Flex-pattern VIII and deliberately express a stronger blend of independence in their relationship with the Pattern IV's. Their basic strength of warm dependence is still there, but now their interactions become more creative because of a stronger emphasis of independence.

Since both IV's and VI's lean toward the theoretical side, their relationship can sometimes become more creative and satisfying if they consciously emphasize the practical side. They can do this by shifting emphasis to their own strengths in practical thinking. (IV's express their Flex-pattern II, and VI's express their Flex-pattern V.) Another way is for them to bring practical people into the relationship. Either way can work; however, it is frequently more effective for them to interact with other people outside the relationship — people who are naturally fact-oriented.

Bi/Polar Pattern Relationship IV-VII

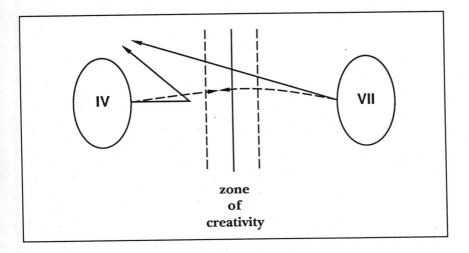

zone
of
creativity

Description

IV and VII are more different than they are alike. They are at opposite ends on two pairs of Bi/Polar strengths and at the same end on the third pair. They are at opposite ends on the basic pair (thinking/risking) and the thinking pair (practical/theoretical). Pattern IV's lean toward thought and ideas; Pattern VII's lean toward action and practicality. On the third pair (dependence/independence), they both favor independence.

In spite of the fact that Patterns IV and VII are very different in terms of their Bi/Polar strengths, they frequently appear quite similar. One of the reasons may be that they both are intuitive — in a different way, however. Pattern IV's are intuitive thinkers in the sense that they have intuitive insights they leap to an insight without going through a logical, step-by-step process. They "know" it is right "intuitively". On the other hand, Pattern VII's are intuitive in the sense of having a "feel" for a situation — it's more of an emphasis on a "seat-of-the-pants" feel rather than intellectual cognition. So, in a sense, one could say both patterns are intuitive, but they are intuitive in a different way — coming from a different sense.

In spite of the fact that their intuition has a different source, it is expressed in their behavior in very similar ways. An intuitive insight of the Pattern IV's initiates quick, strong, confident, independent action, and the intuitive insight of the Pattern VII's elicits the same kind of behavior. This common intuitive characteristic, coupled with a common leaning toward independence, may be the basis for many of the similarities observed in the behavior of Patterns IV and VII.

In a relationship between Patterns IV and VII, VII's are assertive and usually self-confident in their relationships. Conversely, IV's tend to be reserved and self-contained. Pattern VII's are usually the initiators in their relationships, and IV's tend to stay back in a reserved and independent way.

Pattern IV's are natural leaders when the need is for (1) new ideas, (2) understanding of basic concepts, and (3) planning in an organized, comprehensive way. Pattern VII's are natural leaders when the need is for (1) dynamic leadership of other people, (2) initiation of practical projects, and (3) practical communication of new ideas.

Typical Problems

The typical problems that arise in a relationship between IV's and VII's are related primarily to their differences. IV's sometimes feel frustrated or even "put down" by Pattern VII's' lack of appreciation for their original ideas. IV's are sometimes pained by the assertiveness of Pattern VII's — particularly when the VII's invade their space and push hard for their own advantage. Another frustration IV's frequently experience in their relationships with VII's comes from VII's' tendency to talk and not listen — Pattern IV's want to be listened to.

Probably the greatest frustration VII's experience in their relationships with Pattern IV's comes from the tendency of Pattern IV's to withdraw into their own self-sufficiency and refuse to interact with them. Another problem VII's sometimes experience with IV's is related to the IV's' tendency to speculate too much and change things without due regard for practical considerations.

Strengthening the Relationship

Pattern IV's need to recognize their tendency to withdraw and deal with this tendency when it causes a problem. The most effective way is to deliberately express their Flex-pattern VIII become more assertive in their relationships with Pattern VII's. This results in a strong expression of their thoughts and feelings — just what the Pattern VII's want and can deal with most easily. IV's need to keep in mind that VII's don't expect a "perfected" response — they just want a response. Learning to be more assertive in appropriate ways is probably the most important contribution Pattern IV's can make to their relationship with Pattern VII's.

IV's also need to watch out for those times when they are tending to polarize on ideas and "what could be". When they become aware they are going overboard on the possibilities, they need to shift to their Flex-pattern II and ask the Pattern VII for a realistic evaluation of the situation. Not only does this improve the relationship, but it also tends to make IV's and VII's more creative and effective as a team.

Pattern VII's need to watch out for those times when they are polarizing on their own desires and concerns and talking too much. When VII's become aware they are talking too much and polarizing on their own self-interests, they need to become more thoughtful by emphasizing their thinking strengths. They do this by shifting into their Flex-pattern II. While in their Flex-pattern II, Pattern VII's need to develop a plan to express more dependence on the Pattern IV's. Their next step is to implement their plan by moving into their Flex-pattern V and deliberately expressing a stronger blend of dependence. They do this by centering their attention on the Pattern IV's, asking them questions, and listening to what they have to say. If Pattern VII's ask questions that draw heavily on the imaginative thinking of Pattern IV's, they draw on the finest thing IV's have to offer and show their greatest appreciation for them.

Patterns IV and VII have much to give each other, and with an appreciation for each other's strengths, they can develop a highly rewarding and creative relationship. IV's can contribute new ideas and visions of possibilities, along with a structured plan to accomplish them. Pattern VII's have the confidence and skill with people to "put legs" on these ideas and make them practical and functional in the real world. Together they can form a cooperative effort that is much stronger, well-balanced, and effective than either could do by themselves.

Bi/Polar Pattern Relationship IV-VIII

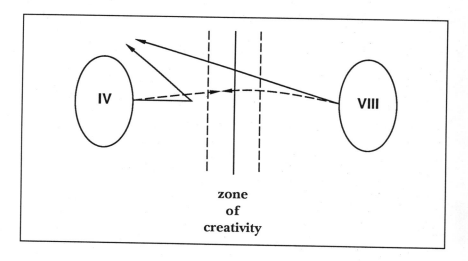

Description

Patterns IV and VIII have similar patterns of strengths. They are at the same end on two pairs of Bi/Polar strengths and at opposite ends on the third. Both patterns lead with theoretical thinking and independence. They are different in that Pattern IV's lean toward thought, and Pattern VIII's lean toward action.

In a relationship between Patterns IV and VIII, the IV's tend to be quiet, reserved, and thoughtful, and the VIII's tend to be assertive, dynamic, and action-oriented. VIII's tend to come on strong in a self-assertive way and invade the space of Pattern IV's. IV's tend to keep within themselves and, if possible, try to avoid the assertiveness of Pattern VIII's.

Typical Problems

The most common problem in a relationship between Patterns IV and VIII comes from their opposite tendencies — the Pattern VIII's' tendency to come on strong and go across the line of creativity into IV's' space, and the Pattern IV's' tendency to stay back from the line of creativity, avoid contact, and refuse to interact with the Pattern VIII's. Pattern IV's can develop a great deal of unexpressed anger and hostility toward Pattern VIII's who continue to invade their space and show them disrespect. Pattern VIII's can experience a good deal of frustration when Pattern IV's withdraw and refuse to interact with them.

Sometimes their common leaning toward independence can create a problem. If they are on opposite sides and start competing with each other, their egos are likely to get involved, and each becomes a threat to the other. This can get them into a fight where they are trying to destroy each other.

Still another problem Patterns IV and VIII can have in their relationships stems from their common tendency to emphasize imaginative thinking. They can stimulate one another's imagination so much they end up on "cloud nine", and their relationship begins to suffer because there is not enough practical thinking. They have a vivid picture of the possibilities and potential, but are ineffectual in practical accomplishment because many factual realities are overlooked.

Strengthening the Relationship
Patterns IV and VIII have a strong natural base for building creative relationships — both are idea-oriented and independent. Their complementary strengths in thought and action create a potential for productive and rewarding relationships. Pattern IV's can conceive new ideas, and Pattern VIII's can promote the ideas the IV's think up.

Pattern IV's need to watch for those times when they are withdrawing into their own self-sufficiency. When they become aware their withdrawal is causing a problem, they need to become more assertive in their relationships with Pattern VIII's. They need to express their own Flex-pattern VIII and get their feelings out in the open. They do this most effectively by facing the Pattern VIII's straight across and telling them what they are thinking and how they are feeling about the relationship. This action tends to defuse the negative feelings the Pattern IV's have been holding within and gets the attention of the Pattern VIII's. Pattern VIII's tend to develop a new respect for Pattern IV's and almost automatically begin to back up — out of Pattern IV's' territory. An additional good result is that it gets an interaction going between them.

If Pattern IV's find they have polarized on their independence and are in a destructive fight with Pattern VIII's, it is time for them to take the initiative to deliberately shift emphasis to an appropriate expression of dependence. IV's do this in a natural way by expressing their Flex-pattern III. They are still reserved, but they shift their attention to the Pattern VIII's, use their thinking to put themselves in the Pattern VIII's' shoes, and try to understand how they are thinking and feeling.

Pattern VIII's need to watch for those times when they are assertively going across the creative line and showing disrespect to the Pattern IV's by invading their territory. When they become aware they are violating the Pattern IV's' territory, the first thing they need to do is deliberately express their own Flex-pattern IV. They need to emphasize thought and understanding. With this emphasis on thinking, Pattern VIII's become more reserved and thoughtful in their relationships with Pattern IV's, thus tending to pull back within themselves and out of Pattern IV's' territory. This takes the emotional pressure off Pattern IV's, reduces their defensive feelings, and makes them more willing to interact with the Pattern VIII's.

If Pattern VIII's discover their relationship with Pattern IV's has deteriorated into a fight, it is time for them to deliberately shift to their dependent strength. They do this by shifting into their Flex-pattern VI and consciously putting the Pattern IV's in the center of their attention. They become assertive in showing an active interest in and concern for the welfare of the Pattern IV's.

Sometimes when Patterns IV and VIII are in a relationship, they find that together they are polarizing on their theoretical thinking (a common lead strength) and they need a strong dose of practicality. They can deal with this problem by deliberately emphasizing their own natural strengths in practicality. Pattern IV's express their Flex-pattern II, and Pattern VIII's express their Flex-pattern VII. Frequently it is much more creative and better for the relationship if they call on people outside the relationship who are naturally oriented toward the practical side. Patterns II and VII are excellent patterns for them to bring into the relationship when they discover they have a need for practicality.

Bi/Polar Pattern Relationship V-V

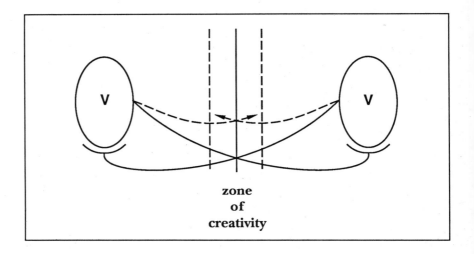

zone
of
creativity

Description

Usually there is considerable movement and interaction in a relationship between two Pattern V's. Each is assertive in moving toward the other — they naturally move to a close and intimate relationship in a hurry. Their relationship is characterized by an open show of mutual affection, a good deal of excited talking, and quite a lot of touching — hugging is a favorite activity. There is an obvious display of genuine enjoyment of each other and excitement over the relationship. At least initially, they like what is going on between them.

Typical Problems

In a relationship between two V's, both have a tendency to go past the line of creativity and into the territory of the other. This is still invasion of the others' "space" even if the intent is to be helpful. The problem is that it gets to be too helpful and in the process becomes destructive to their individuality — their separate, independent selves. They run the danger of losing themselves in the relationship.

The other real problems that tend to arise in their relationship come from the fact that they have the same pattern of relative strengths and tend to experience the same tendencies. This is a problem, because they stimulate each other in their common area of major strengths, and this increases the likelihood of polarization — particularly on dependent risking, their greatest strength.

Strengthening the Relationship

The initial stages of a relationship between two Pattern V's is likely to be very rewarding and enjoyable for both of them. But after the honeymoon is over, pains and frustrations begin to appear. Frequently the problem comes from an overemphasis on the emotional side — uncontrolled feelings tend to dominate the relationship. If this is happening, the relationship needs to "cool off" with the expression of more reserve and rationality. To bring this about, both need to emphasize their thinking strengths by expressing their Flex-pattern I. This tends to slow the interaction down and gives them time to think about what is going on in the relationship and develop a plan to deal with their problems. Usually the strongest and most mature one will take the lead in initiating this process.

If two Pattern V's have a good practical understanding of how they are expressing too much assertive dependence on one another, their next challenge is to imagine ways they could change their behavior in order to bring stronger expressions of independence into their interactions. This calls for emphasis on their theoretical thinking and a shift into their Flex-pattern VI. The final step in the process is to actually express their independence by expressing their Flex-pattern VII. This process doesn't require that they lose the relationship or even like each other less. They need to keep their natural warmth and concern for each other, but the introduction of more independence allows them to grow as individuals and makes it a more creative and rewarding relationship in the long run. Frequently a Pattern VII can be an effective facilitator of this process.

One of the most effective ways Pattern V's can improve their relationship is to redirect their assertive relational strengths away from each other and toward other people outside the relationship. This diversion has the effect of taking the "heat" off their relationship and "cooling" it off a bit. This is particularly fruitful if they relate to people who have natural patterns of strengths different from their own. In reaching out to people who have opposite lead strengths, they are stimulated to grow in their supporting strengths, which tends to make their relationship better balanced, more creative, and more satisfying for both.

Bi/Polar Pattern Relationship V-VI

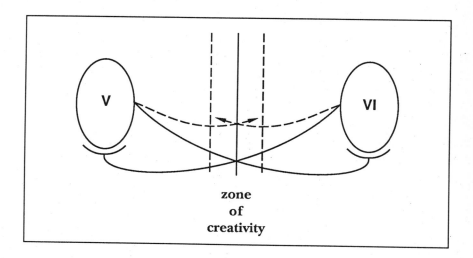

zone
of
creativity

Description

Patterns V and VI are very similar — particularly in their relationships. They have the same lead strengths in two of the three pairs of Bi/Polar strengths — both lean toward the emotional feeling side in the basic pair (thinking/risking) and toward dependence in the risking pair (dependent/independent). The only place they differ is in the way they think — V's lean toward practicality, and VI's lean toward ideas and imagination.

In a relationship between Patterns V and VI, both move assertively toward each other. They tend to make immediate contact and interact with "gusto" at the outset. There is usually a good deal of talking, laughter, and excited interchange between these two patterns — particularly when they first meet. Their relationship over the long term is characterized by interdependence and mutual sharing of feelings. Both are warmly accepting and supportive of each other. They enjoy basking in each other's warmth.

Typical Problems
Usually, there are few problems in the initial stages of a relationship between Patterns V and VI — their real problems come later on. A healthy human being can get too much of anything — even warmth and concern from another human being. Caring, warmth, and closeness can polarize on themselves and become destructive to individuality and self-identify. When this happens, a person feels smothered and "taken over". Probably the most frequent problem experienced by V's and VI's in a relationship with each other is a loss of independence and self-identify.

The other problems Patterns V and VI tend to experience in their relationships stem from their common tendency to emphasize feelings and de-emphasize rationality. When they relate together, they naturally stimulate one another in their greatest strength — emotional dependence — and tend to polarize even more deeply on feelings. The result is even more blockage of their own rationality.

Strengthening the Relationship
The major challenge Patterns V and VI face in their relationship with each other is finding creative and effective ways of bringing more

thought and independence into their relationship. Since they naturally stimulate each other in their lead strengths (emotion and dependence), being in a relationship compounds their natural tendency to emphasize these strengths. This makes it even more difficult and important for them to gain skill in consciously bringing more thinking and independence into their relationship. Broadly speaking, there are two ways in which they can bring these strengths into their relationship: (1) from within — where they deliberately shift emphasis to their own supporting strengths in thought and independence, and consciously use these strengths to improve the relationship; and (2) from outside — where they seek to bring the needed strengths into the relationship from others.

The first step in maintaining any creative relationship is for both to be themselves — to express their natural strengths. The second step is to deal creatively with the problems created by following their natural tendencies. Those principles are no less true for Patterns V and VI. First, they need to be themselves — go ahead and be assertive and relational with one another until some kind of problem develops. Now, with awareness of the problem, they can either use their own strengths to solve the problem or draw on people outside the relationship. If they rely on their own strengths, their first step is to shift emphasis to their rational thinking strengths (Pattern V's express their Flex-pattern I, and Pattern VI's express their Flex-pattern III). This shift to thinking "cools off" the emotional interactions and gives them an opportunity to develop a plan to express more independence in their relationship. Finally, both of them must emphasize their independent strengths (V's express their Flex-pattern VII, and VI's express their Flex-pattern VIII). The initial expression of independence is the hardest — they are likely to feel they are threatening the relationship and may lose it. Understanding that the only way they can save the relationship and make it even stronger is by expressing this independence can encourage them to do it in spite of the risk involved.

Frequently, the most creative and effective way for Patterns V and VI to bring more thought and independence into their relationship is to draw on the strengths of people outside the relationship. After all, this is their greatest strength — the ability to relate and draw strength from others. Although a mature person with any Bi/Polar pattern can be helpful, those people who have the needed strengths in natural dominance — Patterns II, IV, VII, and VIII — would normally fit best, depending upon the particular need at the time. And bringing in another person serves to increase their span of relationships.

Bi/Polar Pattern Relationship V-VII

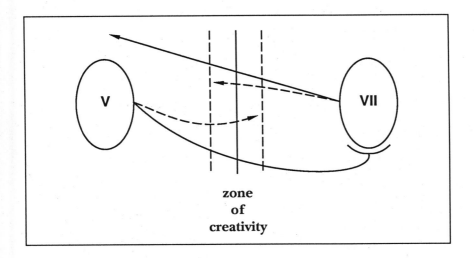

Description
Patterns V and VII are more alike than they are different. They are alike in that both tend toward the risking end of the thinking/risking scale and toward the practical end of the practical/theoretical scale.

They are different in that Pattern V's lean toward dependent risking, and Pattern VII's lean toward independent risking. They are similar in that both are assertive, talkative, practical, and action-oriented. They differ in that Pattern V's are warm and other-people-oriented, and Pattern VII's are independent and self-oriented.

Since both V's and VII's tend to be assertive, they usually establish a relationship rather quickly and generally enjoy quite a lot of interaction with one another. Both tend to go across the line of creativity in their relationship; however, they come from a different home base in doing so. The assertion of Pattern V's comes from their strong relationship strength and ready willingness to depend upon and draw strength from Pattern VII's. The assertiveness of Pattern VII's comes from a different source the independent strength that tends to say "you need me!". VII's express the kind of assertiveness that tends to establish dominance, directing and sometimes protecting the other person.

Typical Problems

The most common problem in a relationship between Pattern V's and Pattern VII's arises from their polar differences on the risking scale. V's naturally risk dependence on other people and have to consciously discipline themselves to risk on their own. On the other hand, VII's naturally risk in an independent way and have to consciously discipline themselves to risk dependence on other people.

When Pattern V's follow their natural tendency and depend too heavily on Pattern VII's, they create a situation in which Pattern VII's, in following their natural tendencies, tend to take advantage of them and use them for their own purposes. When this happens, not only do Pattern V's suffer from being taken advantage of, but they also tend to experience a painful loss of self-respect and self-confidence. Sometimes they develop a good deal of resentment and hostility toward Pattern VII's and begin to see them as impatient, egotistical, selfish, and domineering. If something is not done to improve the relationship, Pattern V's eventually withdraw their loyalty and support from the Pattern VII's.

When Pattern VII's follow their natural tendency to "take over" the relationship and use it to accomplish their personal ambitions, they create a situation in which Pattern V's, following their own natural tendencies, tend to express more and more dependence. As this process deepens, Pattern V's show less independence and personal responsibility — they wait for the Pattern VII's to tell them what to do rather than take initiative on their own. When this happens, Pattern VII's see Pattern V's as unproductive, burdensome, undependable, and not able to follow through on their own. This can cause Pattern VII's to lose confidence in Pattern V's and, as a result, depend even less on them.

Although their common leaning toward action and practicality provides a good basis for a relationship between V's and VII's, it can also be a source of difficulty for them. They can stimulate one another to move into action too fast, resulting in mistakes that could be avoided if they would take more time to think and plan.

Strengthening the Relationship

Patterns V and VII need to be alert to those times when their natural tendencies cause problems in their relationship. Specifically, Pattern V's need to watch out for their tendency to become too dependent on Pattern VII's, and Pattern VII's need to keep alert to their tendency to get caught up in their own self-interests and concerns and forget about the Pattern V's as individuals.

When Pattern V's discover they have gone overboard in depending upon Pattern VII's, it is time for them to consciously move into their Flex-pattern I and develop a plan of action to express more independence in their relationship with the Pattern VII's. After they have developed a plan, they need to shift into their Flex-pattern VII and assertively express this independence. Usually this means a direct confrontation with the Pattern VII's. An expression of independence gets the attention and respect of Pattern VII's and usually has the effect of pushing them back toward the line of creativity.

When Pattern VII's become aware they are polarizing on their own self-interests and disregarding the interests of Pattern V's, it is time for them to express their Flex-pattern II and develop a plan of action to express more dependence on the Pattern V's.

To do this most effectively, Pattern VII's need to deliberately shift their attention to Pattern V's and think about them as people. They need to think of them in terms of their strengths and look for practical ways these strengths may be used. After developing a plan of action, Pattern VII's need to move to their Flex-pattern V and actively express their dependence on the Pattern V's in face-to-face interaction.

If Patterns V and VII find that all they can see are the problems, it is time for them to consciously shift to their own theoretical thinking abilities (Pattern V's shift to their Flex-pattern VI, and Pattern VII's shift to their Flex-pattern VIII). Sometimes they find it easier and more effective to relate to a person outside the relationship who is naturally idea-oriented and ask that person to contribute ideas about how their problems may be solved.

If they are polarizing on action and feeling a need for more thinking and planning, they need to consciously shift emphasis to their thinking strengths — Pattern V's move into their Flex-pattern I, and Pattern VII's move into their Flex-pattern II. Frequently, it is more effective for them to bring a natural "thinker" into the relationship and ask that person to contribute his or her thinking strengths.

Bi/Polar Pattern Relationship V-VIII

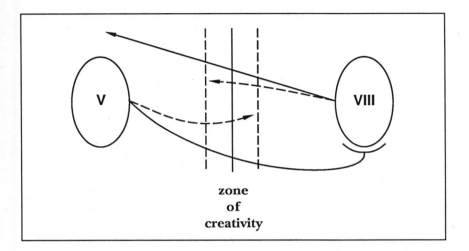

zone
of
creativity

Description

Patterns V and VIII are at opposite ends on two pairs of polar strengths and at the same end on the third. They are different in that Pattern V's lean toward practical thinking and warm relationships, whereas Pattern VIII's lean toward imaginative thinking and independence. They come from the same place in the third pair of polar strengths — both are riskers, tending toward the emotional side.

Their common leanings toward the dynamic, action-oriented strengths gives them common ground on which to establish and maintain a creative relationship. Both are assertive in making contact and getting interactions going. Although both express assertive behavior in their relationships with one another, they are assertive for different reasons. The underlying motivation for the Pattern V's is to gain support and approval. On the other hand, the motivation for the Pattern VIII's is to establish dominance and leadership so they may engage the strengths of the Pattern V's to help accomplish their own goals and ambitions.

Typical Problems

The typical problems in a relationship between Patterns V and VIII come primarily from their differences. The opposite emphasis they place on the dependent/independent scale seems to give the most problems. As Pattern V's naturally emphasize warmth and dependence in their relationship with Pattern VIII's, they tend to overexpose themselves and inadvertently tempt Pattern VIII's to take advantage of them. Sometimes the Pattern VIII's give in to this temptation, and the Pattern V's are hurt. As Pattern VIII's naturally emphasize their independence and self-interest strengths, they move assertively into Pattern V's territory and use them for their own personal advantage. This violation tends to depreciate Pattern V's and causes them to suffer a loss of self-esteem. In turn, V's tend to develop feelings of resentment and hostility toward the Pattern VIII's. They begin to view VIII's as egotistical, vain, and self-centered. Pattern VIII's can also suffer in this process. When V's develop resentment and hostility toward Pattern VIII's, they naturally withdraw their loyalty and support. This loss is especially painful for Pattern VIII's.

Patterns V and VIII can also have problems based upon their difference on the practical/theoretical scale. As Pattern V's emphasize practicality, they can sometimes inadvertently throw cold water on the dreams of Pattern VIII's and threaten the Pattern VIII's' self-esteem. Conversely, Pattern VIII's can threaten Pattern V's by pushing too hard for "change" and disregarding the values of established ways of doing things.

Still another problem Patterns V and VIII can have in their relationship is related to their common tendency to emphasize action and de-emphasize thought. By stimulating each other on the action side, they can become polarized on action and make mistakes that could have been avoided with more forethought.

Strengthening the Relationship

Patterns V and VIII can have a creative and satisfying relationship by expressing their natural blend of strengths and dealing creatively with their tendencies when they are causing problems in their relationship.

Pattern V's need to lead with their natural dependent strength in their relationship with Pattern VIII's, but keep alert to those times when they have gone too far and become too dependent. When this realization comes, they need to deliberately shift into their Flex-pattern I by emphasizing their thinking strength. While in their Flex-pattern I, they need to develop a plan of action to express more independence and take a more assertive, independent stance with the Pattern VIII's. Finally, they need to shift into their Flex-pattern VII and actually confront the Pattern VIII's with behavior that expresses more independence. Not only is this likely to improve the relationship, but it usually results in giving the Pattern V's more self-confidence.

Pattern VIII's need to follow their natural assertive and independent tendencies and assume a leadership role in their relationship with Pattern V's. However, they need to watch for those times when their assertiveness turns into aggression and they are depreciating Pattern V's by getting into their territory. When they become aware they are hurting the relationship with their aggressive invasion, they need to consciously move into their Flex-pattern IV and figure out an approach to the problem. While in their Flex-pattern IV, they need to develop a plan to express more dependence on the Pattern V's. Finally, they need to actually express this dependence by shifting into their Flex-pattern VI. They do this most effectively by centering their attention on the Pattern V's, looking straight across, asking them how they feel about the relationship — and then listening to what they say.

If Pattern V and VIII are having problems because of their opposite orientation in thinking, both need to shift emphasis to their supporting thinking strength. Pattern V's need to make a shift to their Flex-pattern VI and speculate a bit more about the possibilities. Pattern VIII's need to make a shift to their Flex-pattern VII and look hard at the practical realities. When both make this kind of shift, it is very likely that their thinking, both individually and as a team, will become much more creative.

If Patterns V and VIII discover they have a problem because they are stimulating one another to make snap decisions without enough forethought, they can solve the problem in two ways. First, they can deliberately emphasize their own thinking strengths — Pattern V's shift to their Flex-pattern I, and Pattern VIII's shift to their Flex-pattern IV. Second, they can reach out to other people and bring the thinking strength in from the outside. Usually the second approach is easier and works most effectively, especially if they draw on the strengths of a person who naturally leans toward the thinking side.

Bi/Polar Pattern Relationship VI-VI

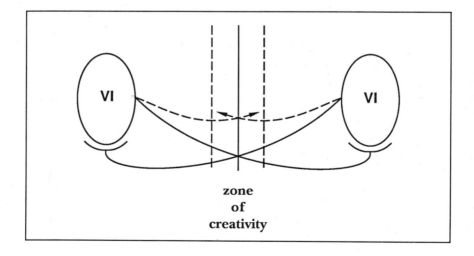

zone
of
creativity

Description

Typically, there is a great deal of interaction between two Pattern VI's. They move assertively toward each other and tend to develop a warm and close relationship quickly. There is an open show of positive feelings and obvious enjoyment of each other's company. There is usually a good deal of laughter, talking, and touching (lots of hugging) going on in the relationship.

Typical Problems

Although the initial stage of a relationship between two Pattern VI's is usually very exciting and enjoyable for both, their common tendency to push closer and closer eventually causes one or both to start feeling smothered. Rather than enjoying the warmth of the relationship, they begin to experience it as oppressive, restrictive, and destructive to their distinctiveness as individuals. They can get so involved in each other that they start losing their own individuality and sense of self.

Another problem two Pattern VI's usually experience in a long-term relationship stems from their common leaning toward idealism. In their interactions, they tend to stimulate each other's idealistic tendency and, as a result, spend less time on the practical side. Initially, this polarization on the idealistic side causes more problems in their relationship with the outside world than it does within the relationship itself. Because of a lack of emphasis on facts and reality, their practical accomplishments in the real world can be very limited. These failures dramatically emphasize their common need for more practical thinking and the necessity to bring more practicality into their relationship.

Strengthening the Relationship

Two Pattern VI's can have a creative, productive, and satisfying relationship by following their natural relational tendency and dealing creatively with it when its expression begins to cause problems. When they become aware their relationship is deteriorating because of a lack of independence, they need to deliberately express their Flex-pattern III and bring more thinking and reserve into the relationship. This "cools off" the relationship a bit and gives them time to formulate a plan of action to change their behavior toward each other. While in their Flex-pattern III, they need to develop a plan to blend more independence into their behavior. The final step requires that they shift into their Flex-pattern VIII and assertively express their independence — probably in a direct confrontation with one another. The stronger and more mature one usually takes the lead in initiating this process. Once it is started, the other one is stimulated to respond in a like manner and, in doing so, contributes to the creative development of the relationship. There is no guarantee that the other one will respond in a positive way, but the odds favor it.

If two Pattern VI's find their relationship is suffering because of a need for more practical thinking, they need to move into their Flex-pattern III and begin to think of ways they could bring more practicality into their awareness. Frequently they discover the most effective and natural way is to use their strength of dependence and draw upon an outside person who is naturally oriented toward the practical.

Usually the easiest and most effective way for two Pattern VI's to improve their relationship is to draw on the balancing strengths of other people. This works best if they first identify the strength their relationship needs, then seek out a person having that strength in natural dominance. Their interaction with a third party stimulates them to express more of their own strength in the area of need and to grow personally. Frequently the third party is only a catalyst that stimulates the expression of the needed strength within the two Pattern VI's which, once started, continues to be expressed under its own power.

Bi/Polar Pattern Relationship VI-VII

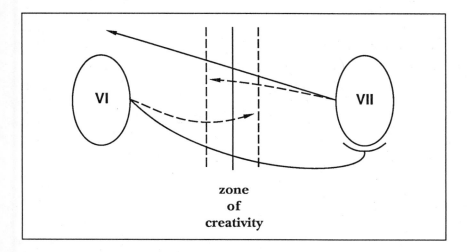

zone
of
creativity

Description

VI and VII are at opposite ends on two of the Bi/Polar pairs of strengths and on the same end on only one. They are on opposite ends of both the thinking pair (practical/theoretical) and the risking pair (dependent/independent) — Pattern VI's lean toward idealism and dependence, and Pattern VII's lean toward practicality and independence. They lean in the same direction on the basic pair (thinking/risking) — both tend toward the dynamic risking side.

Relationships with other people are the center of Pattern VI's world. They assertively seek out relationships with other people and derive a good deal from them. Pattern VII's are also assertive in seeking relationships with others; however, their purpose in doing so is much different that that of Pattern VI's. Where Pattern VI's have an interest in drawing strengths from other people, Pattern VII's have a great interest in establishing dominance and using the strengths of other people to help them accomplish their own personal goals. Since Pattern VI's and Pattern VII's have this common characteristic of assertiveness, they frequently establish contact and have, at least, a trial run at establishing a relationship.

Pattern VII's tend to be emotional leaders in their relationship with Pattern VI's. This is fitting because of their natural patterns of strengths — with VII's having their greatest strength in independence and self-assertion, and VI's having their greatest strength in dependence and warm relationships.

Typical Problems
Most problems Patterns VI and VII experience in their relationship are based upon their differences — in the way they think and feel about themselves and other people.

Probably the most common problem Pattern VI's experience in their relationship with Pattern VII's comes from the tendency of VII's to be strongly assertive and dominate the relationship. Sometimes this seems to squelch Pattern VI's and tends to make them feel inferior and weak.

One of Pattern VII's most frequent frustration in their relationship with Pattern VI's is associated with what they sometimes refer to as the "soft emotionality" of Pattern VI's. VII's can experience a great deal of impatience with Pattern VI's high interest and concern for people's feelings and their relatively low interest in accomplishing a task — getting the practical job done. Pattern VII's want to "get with it" and accomplish a goal; Pattern VI's want to have good relationships. Of course, both patterns want to do both — the emphasis makes the difference.

If they polarize on their differences, their relationship can get into a spiral of decay and become more and more strained and uncomfortable for both of them. In this decay spiral, VII's emphasize independence and depreciate the warm relationship strengths of the Pattern VI's. They also emphasize practicality and depreciate the idealism of the Pattern VI's. On the other hand, Pattern VI's emphasize potential and possibilities. When VI's are polarized on the potential, they tend to reject reality as an inferior kind of value — practicality being a base kind of interest that is not nearly as valuable as the ideal they see so clearly. When Pattern VI's are polarized on their dependent risking, they view the independence of VII's as a selfish, destructive force that interferes with close and warm relationships. As the relationship worsens, each views the other in very negative ways — Pattern VI's describe Pattern VII's as overbearing, egotistical, harsh, selfish, unsympathetic, ambitious to a fault, and will run over people to accomplish their own personal goals. On the other hand, Pattern VII's view Pattern VI's as weak, too idealistic, ineffectual in really doing anything practical, overly concerned with feelings, flighty, not tough enough, and emotionally unstable.

Strengthening the Relationship
If Patterns VI and VII find their relationship in a spiral of decay similar to that described above, they both need to consciously deal with their own tendencies or the relationship will continue to get worse. Either can make the first move, but both need to work at it if any real progress is to be made.

Pattern VI's can make the first move. Their creative move is to recognize that they are overemphasizing their own lead strengths and are a part of the problem. They need to make a deliberate shift to stronger expressions of practicality and independence. Pattern VI's do this most effectively if they first move into their Flex-pattern III and devise a plan of action to express more independence in the relationship. Next, they need to shift into their Flex-pattern VIII and assertively confront the Pattern VII's with a stronger blend of independence. An expression of independence on the part of VI's almost invariably produces positive and creative results — it gets the attention and respect of VII's and tends to give Pattern VI's more self-confidence in the relationship.

It is just as creative for Pattern VII's to make the first move. When VII's realize they have gone too far in asserting their own self-interests, they need to consciously shift their interest and concern to the Pattern VI's as individuals and express dependence on them. They do this most naturally by moving to their Flex-pattern II and formulating a practical plan to change their behavior so they express more dependence on the Pattern VI's. Next, they need to shift into their Flex-pattern V and actually express this stronger blend of dependence in their relationship with the Pattern VI's. They do this by centering their attention on the Pattern VI's, looking straight across at them, asking them how they are feeling about the relationship — and then listening patiently. This assertive expression of dependence on the part of Pattern VII's can effectively turn the relationship around to a creative interaction that solves the problem and builds the relationship.

In a creative relationship between Patterns VI and VII, both are expressing their patterns of natural strengths and affirming their differences as stimulating to their own personal growth. They see each other as giving more balance and effectiveness to the things they do together, and they regard each other as sources of strength in those areas where they usually feel their greatest need.

Bi/Polar Pattern Relationship VI-VIII

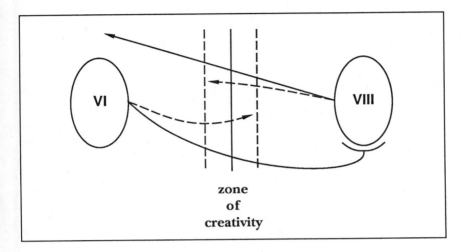

Description

Patterns VI and VIII are very similar. Both are action-oriented and lean toward imaginative thinking. They are at opposite ends on only one pair of Bi/Polar strengths — the risking pair. Pattern VI's lean toward warm, dependent relationships; Pattern VIII's lean toward independence and self-sufficiency.

Both are naturally assertive in their relationships. Pattern VI's are assertive in seeking relationships for their own sake. The approval, support, and recognition they receive in their relationships with Pattern VIII's are prime values for them. Pattern VIII's, on the other hand, assertively seek relationships to get assistance and support in accomplishing their own personal goals and ambitions. In their relationships with one another, VIII's are natural leaders and VI's are natural followers.

Patterns VI and VIII tend to form a relationship rather quickly. They interact a good deal and usually find the relationship enjoyable.

Since both tend to be spontaneous and impulsive, they usually have a dynamic relationship characterized by frequent violations of each other's territory.

Typical Problems
The initial phases of a relationship between Pattern VI's and Pattern VIII's are usually exciting and enjoyable for both. However, a number of problems can crop up in a long-term relationship. One of the most common problems is related to their natural tendency to overemphasize their own greatest strengths — Pattern VI's tend to overemphasize their dependent strength, and Pattern VIII's tend to overemphasize their independent strength.

When Pattern VI's overemphasize their dependent strength, they allow Pattern VIII's to come into their territory unchallenged. Pattern VIII's keep coming on — taking over more and more. This can cause Pattern VI's to experience a good deal of pain. As the violations intensify, VI's tend to lose self-confidence, develop feelings of inferiority, and experience hostility and resentment toward the Pattern VIII's.

When Pattern VIII's overemphasize their independent strength, they encourage the VI's to become excessively dependent upon them. Pattern VI's keep depending more and more until they are making little independent response. When this happens, VIII's are frustrated by the VI's' lack of independent response and begin to feel "weighted down" with an unproductive relationship.

Patterns VI and VIII can also have problems in their relationship because of their common strengths and tendencies. Both lean naturally toward the dynamic action side and have the tendency to "jump at a decision". In a relationship together, their tendency to move into action too fast is aggravated, and they may jump even quicker, making even more serious mistakes.

A similar problem can develop because they both tend to favor theoretical thinking. They naturally stimulate each other's imagination and, as a result, run an even greater risk of polarizing on the theoretical side. To the extent they do polarize on their theoretical thinking, they block their natural abilities on the practical side. This can become a critical loss, because practical thinking is very important to their ultimate success.

Strengthening the Relationship
When Pattern VI's begin to develop negative feelings (usually a loss of self-confidence and feelings of resentment toward the Pattern VIII's), it is a signal that they have gone too far in using their strength of dependence. When they become aware they are overusing their dependent strength, it is time for them to shift emphasis to their independent strength. The most effective and natural way for VI's to express more independence is to first emphasize their thinking strength by moving to their Flex-pattern III. When they gain an understanding of the problem, they can then plan a course of action to express more independence in their relationship with the Pattern VIII's. (They may do this thinking and planning alone or with the help of another person.) The final thing they must do is to actually confront the Pattern VIII's with behavior that has a greater blend of independence within it. They do this by moving to their Flex-pattern VIII and consciously expressing stronger independence in their relationship with the Pattern VIII's. They still show their VI qualities but deliberately emphasize their independent strength.

Pattern VIII's need to keep alert to those times in the relationship when they are polarizing on their own independence and not depending enough on the Pattern VI's. Frequently, the cue is a feeling of being "weighted down" by the dependence of the Pattern VI's or an expression of sudden hostility and resentment coming from the VI's. When Pattern VIII's become aware their independence is causing a problem in the relationship, it is time for them to blend more dependence into their behavior. They do this most effectively by following this sequence. First, they move into their Flex-pattern

IV and develop a plan for expressing more dependence on the Pattern VI's. Second, they shift to their Flex-pattern VI and actually express more dependence in a face-to-face interaction with the Pattern VI's.

If Patterns VI and VIII find that together they are polarizing on action and thereby making mistakes that could be avoided with more forethought, they need to find some way to bring thinking into their relationship. They can do this by deliberately emphasizing their own thinking strengths; however, it is usually more effective if they bring another person into the relationship — preferably one who has a natural leaning toward thinking. They may use the same process if they discover they are polarizing on the theoretical side. Usually the best solution is to find a mature person who naturally leads in practical thinking and invite that person to contribute practicality to the relationship.

Bi/Polar Pattern Relationship VII-VII

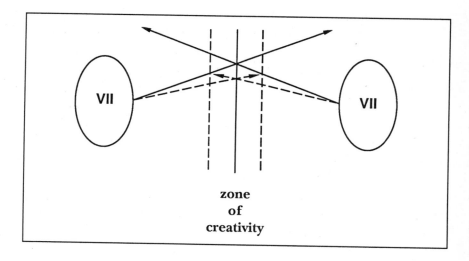

zone
of
creativity

Description

Usually there is a good deal of assertiveness and dynamic interaction in a relationship between two Pattern VII's — both seek to establish dominance, to be the leader, and to gain control of the relationship. They have the common tendency to move assertively across the line of creativity into the territory of the other. This makes them very much aware of each other and creates an immediate potential for a rewarding relationship as they discover the line of creativity between them in a give-and-take interaction. But it also creates a potential for the development of a destructive relationship in which each seeks to destroy the other. In any case, if the two Pattern VII's stay together, their relationship is likely to be very active, dynamic, and competitive.

Competitiveness is usually a dominant element in a relationship between two Pattern VII's. Both are stimulated by a competitive challenge and enjoy a give-and-take interaction with another assertive person. They both like action and feel best in the "heat of the battle".

The dynamics of the relationship between two VII's are affected greatly by the objectives they are trying to accomplish. If they have a common objective and view each other as team members, their relationship can be very cooperative and supportive. If, on the other hand, they have conflicting objectives, their relationship is likely to be highly competitive. The overriding and controlling factor is their intense desire to win. If they can win by cooperating, they will cooperate. If they can win by competing, they will compete. In any case, neither can stand the thought of losing.

Typical Problems

The early stages of a relationship between two Pattern VII's can be stimulating, exciting, challenging, and enjoyable to both parties. However, if their assertive and independent tendencies are given free rein, serious problems can result. For example, if both continue to assertively invade the territory of each other and neither backs up, the relationship can deteriorate into an open conflict. They begin fighting and hurting one another. As fear and hostility intensify on both sides, they become openly aggressive and inflict more pain on one another. The relationship becomes progressively more destructive until something triggers an expression of dependence from one or both of them — or they simply give up on the relationship altogether.

Other problems two Pattern VII's can experience in their relationship come from their having the same patterns of strengths. If two VII's have joined forces in a team effort to accomplish a common objective, they will tend to stimulate each other in their common areas of major strengths — action, practicality, and self-confidence. Accomplishment of any creative and worthwhile goal eventually requires an emphasis on the other three polar strengths — thinking, imagination, and dependence. That is the problem. The stimulation both are receiving in their lead strengths makes it doubly hard for them to consciously shift emphasis to an expression of any of their supporting strengths.

Strengthening the Relationship

Two Pattern VII's can have a very creative, rewarding, and satisfying relationship. In order to accomplish this, however, both must express their natural lead strengths (risking, practical thinking, and independence) and deal creatively with their natural tendencies — especially their assertive independent tendency.

If two Pattern VII's are engaged in a destructive conflict, the only way the relationship can be improved is for both to consciously shift emphasis to an expression of dependence. In actual practice, one takes the initiative in expressing more dependence, and the other reciprocates by also expressing more dependence. The Pattern VII's who take the initiative usually find it natural to follow this procedure. First, they move into their Flex-pattern II and try to understand what is actually going on in the relationship. Second, they formulate a plan of action to express more dependence. Third, they shift into their Flex-pattern V and actually emphasize their dependent strength in a face-to-face interaction with the other Pattern VII's. Their actual behavior in this interaction follows these guidelines — they deliberately center their attention and concern on the other Pattern VII's, ask the other VII's to tell them what they see is going on between them, and then actively listen to what is said.

An expression of dependence from one tends to encourage the other to do likewise. If the other one actually does express more dependence, it becomes a healthy, give-and-take relationship that normally progresses toward interactions in a zone of creativity.

Although an initial expression of dependence has the effect of influencing the other person in the relationship to reciprocate and express dependence also, there is no guarantee it will happen — that is the risk. If the second person fails to reciprocate by expressing dependence and takes independent advantage of the situation, the relationship is worsened and it becomes a much more difficult task to turn it around in the future.

Sometimes a third party can be helpful when two VII's are suffering in a destructive relationship. If both VII's want to keep the relationship and their pain is sufficiently great, sometimes they are willing to express dependence on a third party. If this happens, the third party is in an excellent position to give wise counsel and lead them toward a more creative and rewarding relationship.

If two Pattern VII's are trying to accomplish a common objective as team members and find there is a need for emphasis on thinking, imagination, or dependence (their supporting strengths), they can deliberately shift emphasis to these strengths within themselves, or they can look to the outside for a person or persons who have the needed strength in natural dominance. In practice, bringing the needed strengths in from the outside seems to work the best. Not only is the strength usually stronger when it comes from a person who has it as a natural lead strength, but bringing the strength in from the outside allows Pattern VII's to continue to make their best contributions with their own lead strengths.

Bi/Polar Pattern Relationship VII-VIII

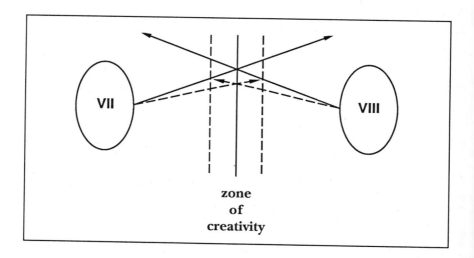

zone
of
creativity

Description

Patterns VII and VIII have common lead strengths in two of the Bi/Polar pairs and are at opposite ends on only one pair. They are similar in that both have lead strengths in risking and independence. They are different in that Pattern VII's lead in practical thinking and Pattern VIII's lead in theoretical thinking. Both are dynamic, independent riskers. But they risk in different ways — Pattern VII's tend to take calculated risks; Pattern VIII's tend to risk on the basis of vision and possibilities.

Both tend to move assertively into the others' territory. They like dynamic interaction with people and have a strong tendency to take over and be the leaders. They have a common problem of tending to talk too much and not listen enough.

When Patterns VII and VIII relate to each other, there is considerably more talking on both sides than listening. If one is being quiet while the other is talking, usually the quiet one is not really listening, but rather thinking about what he or she intends to say next. Both want control and hesitate to put themselves in a dependent position. Since they are both more feeling-oriented than reason-oriented, the strongest forces in their relationship are emotional in nature.

In a healthy, creative relationship between Patterns VII and VIII, there is a good deal of dynamic interaction — lots of give and take. They know where the line of creativity is between them, and both discipline themselves to come back into their own territory when they become aware they have gone too far.

Typical Problems

In a relationship between Patterns VII and VIII, their most common problem comes from their natural assertive independence, competitiveness, and desire to establish dominance and control. If they become polarized on their self-interest and out of that polarization block their natural capacities to be concerned for and aware of the other person, the relationship becomes nonproductive, painful, and frustrating for both. If they become polarized on their feelings and refuse to let reason and rationality bring stability to their relationship, the relationship becomes very volatile and frequently destructive.

Another problem they sometimes experience comes from their different orientation in thinking. Pattern VIII's tend to naturally emphasize the potential and possibilities in a situation; Pattern VII's naturally emphasize the hard realities. If they both polarize on their natural orientation, it can become a sore spot in their relationship. A VII can begin to see the Pattern VIII as a "visionary" who has lost contact with reality; an VIII begins to see the Pattern VII as a "shortsighted realist" who can't see any farther than the nose on his face.

The relationship between Pattern VII's and Pattern VIII's can deteriorate and become progressively more destructive to both if they get in a "dog-fight" — each grabbing for the ball and trying to establish dominance over the other. If they stay together and polarization deepens on both sides, things get worse negative feelings and attitudes become more intense — more fear, more hostility, more jealousy, and more threats. Both look more and more to their own advantage and are less and less concerned for the welfare of each other. In this kind of destructive relationship, Pattern VII's tend to see VIII's as "wild-eyed promoters" who can't be trusted, and Pattern VIII's see VII's as aggressive "sharp-shooters" who take every advantage.

Strengthening the Relationship

In a relationship between Pattern VII's and Pattern VIII's, both need to keep alert to their personal tendencies to be assertive and get in the others' territory when they shouldn't be there. When they sense they have a problem brought on by their natural assertiveness, it is time for them to consciously express more dependent risking in their behavior. They need to start putting themselves in the others' shoes and really listening to each other. If the relationship has deteriorated to a marked degree, sometimes it is best to sever the relationship and have a cooling-off period before they come back together and risk an expression of dependence on each other.

Pattern VII's naturally build a greater expression of dependence in their behavior by first moving into their Flex-pattern II and thinking through what is going on in the relationship. Next, they shift into their Flex-pattern VIII and identify the benefits they can derive from improving their relationship with the Pattern VIII's. Next, they construct a practical plan of action that will require them to express more dependence. Finally, they shift into their Flex-pattern V and actually express this stronger dependence in face-to-face interaction with the Pattern VIII's.

Pattern VIII's follow a similar process: First, they need to bring more rationality into the relationship by moving into their Flex-pattern IV and formulating a plan of action to express more dependence on the Pattern VII's. Finally, they need to shift into their Flex-pattern VI and actually express this stronger dependence in face-to-face interaction with the Pattern VII's.

If the relationship is being injured by their different orientations in thinking, just the simple recognition that they have different contributions to make to the relationship can be helpful. With this attitude, Pattern VII's can ask Pattern VIII's to contribute their ideas and visions of potential, and Pattern VIII's can invite Pattern VII's to contribute practicality and realism when appropriate. In this way, both can make their greatest contribution to their cooperative effort and participate in the creativeness of their interactions.

Sometimes their relationship can be strengthened by bringing in a third party. If the trust level between the VII's and the VIII's is low and neither is willing to make the first move in expressing dependence, the introduction of a third party into the relationship can sometimes be the most effective way to get the relationship on a creative track. If they can start listening to a third party, sometimes it becomes easier for them to start listening to each other.

Bi/Polar Pattern Relationship VIII-VIII

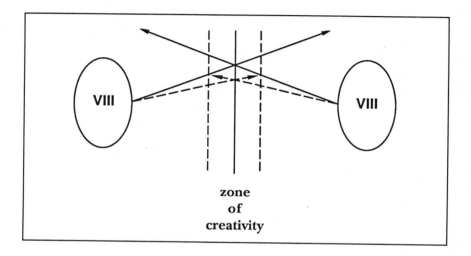

Description

Pattern VIII's are usually assertive, persuasive, and competitive in their relationships with each other. As two Pattern VIII's relate to one another, each tends to go across the line and invade the territory of the other. This assertiveness tends to create a very exciting relationship characterized by conflict and competitiveness. Frequently two Pattern VIII's just decide not to have a relationship with each other. When they do this, they carefully avoid one another and give each other a wide berth.

Typical Problems

When two Pattern VIII's form a relationship, they are likely to experience problems related to their common assertiveness toward each other. If each responds to the violation of the other by becoming even more assertive, they set up a process in which the intensity of the conflict increases and the associated feelings of hostility, anger, and fear become stronger and stronger. If this process continues, they suffer more and more pain and can reach a point where they are actually destroying each other.

The other problems two Pattern VIII's experience in their relationship come from their having the same pattern of strengths. They tend to stimulate one another in their common lead strengths (risking, independence, and theoretical thinking), causing them to experience even greater temptations to polarize on these strengths. This compounds their normal challenge in dealing creatively with their tendencies and can result in their being less creative together than they would be apart.

Strengthening the Relationship

When two Pattern VIII's find they are destroying one another in a competitive battle, there are at least three avenues they may take to stop this destructive process. One avenue is to separate and no longer have a relationship. This sometimes happens when both realize they are hurting each other. Neither is willing to bring the strengths of reason and dependence into the relationship, and they see that the best way to stop the pain and frustration is to simply get out of the situation. Sometimes this can be a good solution, because it does effectively stop the process in which both are being hurt. However, it is not a "growth" solution, because they haven't learned the skill of more effectively blending their reasoning and dependent strengths into their behavior. They are likely to simply repeat the destructive relationship as they relate to other independent, assertive people in the future. Getting out of the relationship can solve a specific problem and will sometimes be desirable on the basis that it gives them an opportunity to develop skills in relationships under less intense pressure. In other words, they can leave the highly-charged situation with the recognition that they are not equipped to handle it. Later, through practice in more conducive learning situations, they can acquire the skills they need to deal effectively with this kind of conflict in the future.

A second avenue for improving a relationship between two Pattern VIII's engaged in a destructive "battle of wills" is for them to face the problem and change their behavior toward one another. Although one of them generally makes the first move, both must alter their behavior before the relationship can become better. The first step is to move into their Flex-pattern IV and bring more reason and rationality to bear on the problem — they must understand the destructive process they are engaged in. Their next step is to shift to Flex-pattern VII and formulate a practical plan of action that will enable them to blend more dependent risking into their behavior. Finally, they need to move into their Flex-pattern VI and actually express a stronger blend of dependent risking in a face-to-face interaction with one another. They express this stronger blend of dependent risking by consciously centering their attention and concern on the other Pattern VIII, putting themselves in their shoes, asking them what they see is going on in the relationship, then actively listening to what the other VIII has to say.

If one of the Pattern VIII's takes the initiative to follow the steps outlined above, it encourages the other to respond in a similar way. This is not to say that it automatically forces the other to change his or her behavior and express more dependence. In fact, the other one may respond by continuing to express strong independence and taking advantage of the situation. If this happens, the relationship gets back on its destructive course and becomes even harder to improve. On the other hand, if the second person responds in a positive way by expressing dependent risking on his own, the relationship is turned toward creativity and is on the way to becoming a highly rewarding and meaningful relationship for both of them.

A third avenue Pattern VIII's may take when they recognize that they have a deteriorating and destructive relationship is to ask an outside person to help them bring more reason and cooperation to their relationship. Frequently, a mature person whom they both respect can be highly effective in helping them to think creatively about their relationship and express more of their natural ability to depend on each other. If a third party can be effective in helping to turn the situation around and get it on a creative course, frequently two Pattern VIII's can take it from there and build a creative relationship on their own.

Conclusion

What should you expect to gain from Bi/Polar? There are two distinct kinds of benefits that you should get. You should have experienced some benefits already. However, as time goes along and you use Bi/Polar in your daily life, you will find the benefits growing and growing.

First, there are direct benefits. The direct benefits are the ones that apply to you personally in all areas of your life. These have to do with understanding yourself, gaining a greater acceptance of yourself and other people, strengthening your relationships with family, friends, and co-workers, and understanding how to participate in the growth process of which we are all a part.

Second, there are indirect benefits. These indirect benefits point toward your ability now to gain more from other training, development, and educational activities that you attend. (You can even look backward now and take a fresh look at experiences that you have had in the past.) You will be able to understand how to personally experience and incorporate other learning experiences through the unique combination of strengths that you possess. And because you understand the growth process, you know how to actually make changes in your attitude and behavior to truly utilize knowledge you gain in the future.

We hope most of all that you have found in your Bi/Polar experience something that speaks to the depths of who you are. Maybe it was in understanding yourself — or your boss — or how to manage more effectively. Everyone gets something a little bit different from the experience. But to really put Bi/Polar to work for you, you must make your own personal choice to use it — in constructive ways to better yourself, your relationships, and your productive contributions in your work. We wish you the best.

For More Information

For additional information about how Bi/Polar can be used in an organization to increase personal productivity and organizational profitability, please contact:

The Institute of Foundational Training and Development
P.O. Box 160220
Austin, Texas 78716-0220

Telephone: 1-800/899-5115 or 512/327-2656

About the Authors

J. W. (Jay) Thomas is a management psychologist with over 35 years of experience consulting with management people in business and education. He is the originator of the Bi/Polar Concept and has been working on its development since 1961.

This is the fifth book he has written on Bi/Polar since 1971. He is the primary developer of the *Bi/Polar Analysis of Core Strengths* (the original psychological instrument used to identify an individual's lead and supporting strengths). He is also the primary developer of the *Bi/Polar: Foundations of Productivity* seminar used in organizations to put the Bi/Polar Concept to practical use.

Dr. Thomas attended Stanford University and Southern Methodist University before earning his Bachelor's Degree in mathematics and philosophy at Oklahoma State University. He earned his Master's and Doctor's Degrees in psychology and education at Oklahoma State University.

Dr. Thomas maintains a consulting relationship with several clients and is Chairman of the Board of The Institute of Foundational Training and Development. He is a Licensed Psychologist in the State of Texas.

About the Authors

T. J. (Tommy) Thomas is an educational psychologist with over 10 years of experience leading seminars on Bi/Polar, training the trainers who conduct the seminars for their own organizations, coordinating research on Bi/Polar, and consulting with client organizations.

He conducted extensive research on the *Bi/Polar Analysis of Core Strengths* in his 1982 dissertation. He has contributed to the development of seminars and other publications on Bi/Polar since the early 1980's.

Dr. Thomas attended The University of Texas at Austin. He received his Bachelor's degree in Plan II (an honor liberal arts program) in 1973 and his Doctor of Philosophy degree in educational psychology in 1982.

Dr. Thomas conducts seminars for clients and is President of The Institute of Foundational Training and Development. He is a Licensed Psychologist in the State of Texas.

Index

Pattern relationships
   locator chart, 203
Patton, George, 63
Perfect relationship, 156
Perkins School of Theology, 53
Personal choice
   influence on personality, 92-93
   limitation of, 93-94
   nature of, 91-92
Personality
   Bi/Polar theory of, 21-30
   definition of, 23
   forces, 23-30
Polarization
   process of, 117-118
   results of, 118-119
Practical thinking, 39-41
Primordial creative force, 26, 32

Relating to patterns
   chart of how to, 200
Relationship characteristics
   of patterns, 173-189
Relationship dynamics, 155-158
Relationship tendencies
   assertive and independent, 170-171
   assertive and relational, 168-170
   reserved and independent, 166-168
   reserved and relational, 164-166
   dealing with, 193-196
Risking, 33-39
Roosevelt, Franklin D., 63
Roosevelt, "Teddy", 63
Rogers, Will, 63

Sacrificing our fruits, 133-134
Saint Paul, 63

Skinner, Dr. B.F., 1
SMU, 53-54

Tendencies
   common, 112
   dealing with, 134-150
   definition, 109
   natural vs. learned, 109-110
   relationship, 163-171
Theoretical thinking, 39-41
Thinking, 33-39
Thoreau, Henry David, 63
Tillich, Paul, 35, 41
Truman, Harry, 62
Twain, Mark, 63

Wilson, Woodrow, 63

Zone of creativity, 161-162